ID0848927

Theology, Hermeneutics, and Imagination

Theology, Hermeneutics, and Imagination

The Crisis of Interpretation at the End of Modernity

GARRETT GREEN

CAMBRIDGE
UNIVERSITY PRESS

PUBLISHED BY THE PRESS SYNDICATE OF THE UNIVERSITY OF CAMBRIDGE
The Pitt Building, Trumpington Street, Cambridge, United Kingdom

CAMBRIDGE UNIVERSITY PRESS
The Edinburgh Building, Cambridge, CB2 2RU, UK
http://www.cup.cam.ac.uk
40 West 20th Street, New York, NY 10011-4211, USA
http://www.cup.org
10 Stamford Road, Oakleigh, Melbourne 3166, Australia

© Garrett Green 2000

This book is in copyright. Subject to statutory exception and to the provisions
of relevant collective licensing agreements, no reproduction of any part may
take place without the written permission of Cambridge University Press.

First published 2000

Printed in the United Kingdom at the University Press, Cambridge

Typeset in Janson 11/13 pt [wv]

A catalogue record for this book is available from the British Library

Library of Congress Cataloguing in Publication data

Green, Garrett.
    Theology, hermeneutics, and imagination: the crisis of interpretation at the
end of modernity / Garrett Green.
    p.   cm.
A revised and expanded version of the Edward Cadbury lectures delivered at
the University of Birmingham in February and March 1998, under the title:
'The faithful imagination'.
Includes bibliographical references and index.
ISBN 0 521 65048 8 (hardback)
1. Bible – Hermeneutics. I. Title.
BS476.G72 2000
220.6'01 – dc21   98-33303 CIP

ISBN 0 521 65048 8 hardback

For Priscilla
sine qua non

Contents

Preface

This book is a revised and expanded version of the Edward Cadbury Lectures, delivered at the University of Birmingham in February and March 1998, under the title "The Faithful Imagination: Theological Hermeneutics in an Age of Suspicion." The present text includes additional material, for which time did not suffice during the lectures, as well as a few revisions undertaken in response to the insightful comments of several members of the audience. Professor Denys Turner was a gracious and articulate host on behalf of the Department of Theology from beginning to end, setting the tone of respectful though not uncritical attention that characterized my reception in Birmingham. Other members of the department whose hospitality I recall with appreciation include Martin Stringer, Isabel Wollaston, and J. K. Parratt. To Gareth Jones, though no longer a member of the Birmingham department, I owe a special debt of gratitude; for without his initiative and imagination the lectures would never have taken place. He also left behind him a coterie of eager postgraduate students, whose presence – right in the center of the audience at every lecture – helped to keep me focused.

Some of the materials comprising this book have appeared in earlier versions in previous publications, whose editors have kindly granted permission to reprint. Portions of several chapters had their origin in 1995, when I was invited to deliver four lectures at the annual conference of the Netherlands School for Advanced Studies in Theology and Religion. The interchange with Professor Hendrik M. Vroom and his colleagues from the various Dutch theological faculties, which took place over four days in a lovely setting near Amersfoort, gave an early impulse to ideas that have now taken final shape in this book.

An earlier version of chapter 2 was first presented to the Nineteenth Century Theology Working Group of the American Academy of Religion and later appeared in *Pro Ecclesia* 4 (Summer 1995): 301–17.

Chapter 3 contains a revision of material that was previously published in the volume *What Is Enlightenment? Eighteenth-Century Answers and Twentieth-Century Questions*, edited by James Schmidt (Berkeley and Los Angeles: University of California Press, 1996), pp. 291–305. My translation of Hamann's letter to Christian Jacob Kraus also first appeared in that volume (pp. 145–53) and is included in the appendix of this book by permission of the publisher. I am grateful to Professor Schmidt and my fellow members of his NEH Summer Seminar at Boston University for their support and encouragement during this phase of my research.

Much of the material in chapter 4 was originally presented as a paper in the Nineteenth Century Theology Working Group of the American Academy of Religion and was subsequently revised and published in *Christian Faith Seeking Historical Understanding: Essays in Honor of H. Jack Forstman*, edited by James O. Duke and Anthony L. Dunnavant (Macon, GA: Mercer University Press, 1997), pp. 45–65.

The research on which chapter 5 is based was carried out during my residence at the Center of Theological Inquiry in Princeton in 1993. I am especially appreciative of the support offered by its staff and then director, Professor Daniel Hardy.

Chapter 6 grew out of my participation in the 1996

Calvin College Faculty Summer Seminar in Christian Scholarship on "Postmodern Philosophy and Christian Thought," funded by The Pew Charitable Trusts. Portions were presented in a preliminary version at the 1997 Faculty Spring Conference in Christian Scholarship in Grand Rapids and a longer version will be included in the volume *Postmodern Philosophy and Christian Thought*, edited by Merold Westphal and published by Indiana University Press. The support and friendship of my colleagues in the seminar and its director, Merold Westphal, as well as the Summer Seminar staff at Calvin College, have been invaluable.

The final phase of preparation for the Cadbury Lectures, together with the conversion of the lectures into this book, was carried out during a splendid sabbatical year as a Visiting Fellow of Clare Hall at the University of Cambridge. I would like to thank the fellows and staff of Clare Hall and its President, Dame Gillian Beer, for providing a working environment that successfully combines the traditional setting of the ancient university with the innovative and democratic spirit of one of its newer colleges. Most of all, I wish to thank Professor David F. Ford, who assisted in the arrangements for a year in Cambridge, welcomed us to the community and the Faculty of Divinity, and was a valued conversation partner as I struggled to work out the ideas that became this book.

Various members of the Connecticut College community have provided support and encouragement along the way, including Robert E. Proctor, who served as Provost and Dean of the Faculty during most of the time I was working on this book. I am especially grateful for sabbatical leave and for contributions towards my research and travel. For computer support (even from across the Atlantic!) I am grateful to Connie Dowell, Chris Penniman, Gerard D. Poirier, and other members of the Information Services staff. I want also to acknowledge my colleagues in the Religious Studies Department, as well as the secretarial services of Diane Monte. Colleagues in other departments, especially Kristin Pfefferkorn and the late John S. King, helped me with German language materials – most heroically in the struggle to render Hamann's arcane German into English.

Other friends and colleagues have contributed to this volume in ways that I, and perhaps they, may no longer remember, through conversations and the exchange of ideas in papers and professional meetings. Some of those whose contributions I do recall include Donald H. Juel, Richard B. Hays, and Daniel Breazeale.

Finally I want to acknowledge the one to whom this book is dedicated: traveling companion (in both the geographical and metaphorical senses), skilled editor of academic prose, teacher extraordinaire, mother of our children (now too old to be dragged along on sabbaticals) – in short, no mere "partner" but my wife, Priscilla Green.

1

Theological hermeneutics in the twilight of modernity

> When philosophy paints its gray on gray, a form of life has grown old, and with gray on gray it cannot be rejuvenated but merely recognized. The Owl of Minerva begins her flight only at the coming of twilight.
>
> Hegel

> ... there are no facts, only *interpretations*.
>
> Nietzsche

Theological hermeneutics began in the Garden of Eden, as any careful observer of the serpent, that subtle hermeneut of suspicion, will at once recognize. In the earliest recorded misinterpretation of a religious text, he asks the woman, "Did God say, 'You shall not eat of any tree of the garden'?" We do not need to have read Foucault in order to discern the power ploy underlying the serpent's exegesis. And even without a Freudian or a feminist to decode the real meaning of snakes who offer their interpretive services to young women, we may suspect that gender (not to mention sex) plays a role in the interchange. Now, whether or not the issues we call hermeneutical have really been

The first epigraph is from Georg Wilhelm Friedrich Hegel, *Vorlesungen über Rechtsphilosophie 1818–1831*, ed. Karl-Heinz Ilting (Stuttgart/Bad Cannstatt: Friedrich Frommann Verlag (Günther Holzboog), 1974), vol. II, p. 74; the second is from Friedrich Nietzsche, *The Will To Power*, § 481 (my translation).

around since creation, they have surely been with us for a very long time indeed – as long as human beings have appealed to oral or written texts for orientation and meaning in their lives.

Even though issues of textual interpretation have ancient roots, however, there is something inescapably *modern* about the seemingly intractable hermeneutical questions that we encounter so frequently in theology and religious studies today; and it is the modern discussion on which I plan to focus our attention in the following chapters. If we could discover why it is that virtually every important religious issue from the late seventeenth century onward leads ineluctably to hermeneutical questions, I think we would have the key to modernity itself. Now I am not so rash as to suggest that I can deliver that key. But I think I know the direction in which theologians should be looking for it: namely, in the interpretation of the Bible, together with all the attendant issues of authority, canon, and meaning. Moreover, the problem of scriptural interpretation is an important clue to the obsession with hermeneutics that afflicts not only Christian theology but virtually every humanistic discipline today. Even though theological hermeneutics therefore has implications for various fields, I intend to concentrate on these issues as they impinge specifically on Christian theology. But that does not mean my remarks are intended only for the ears of Christians, or of academic theologians. I cannot share in the theological separatism that has recently become fashionable in some theological circles, because I do not believe that the church exists as a distinct linguistic community separated from the secular society that surrounds it. The line that separates religious language from secular, that distinguishes Christian discourse from the many other forms of modern and postmodern speech, runs not around the perimeter of the Christian community but right through the middle of the church itself. Speaking for myself, I can say that the line runs through me, through my own experience and therefore through my attempts to think about what it means to live as a follower of Jesus Christ in the present age. Thinking Christianly about the interpretation of scripture is therefore not something Christians can do by withdrawing from the secular world into a realm of allegedly pure biblical or ecclesiastical discourse. Likewise, and for similar reasons, secular humanists, those who deny the Christian vision and reject its hope, cannot ignore two thousand years of theological tradition, for it has helped to shape them and remains in important ways a part of themselves. So I invite you, whether you see yourself as a Christian insider struggling with the meaning of the Bible in the modern world, or as an outsider to the Christian faith, to join me in thinking through some fascinating and baffling challenges to the claim that the Bible should continue to be the source and norm for human life today, in the twilight of modernity, just as it has been for generations of Christians before us.

Hermeneutics demystified
Those uninitiated into the mysteries of academic theology, philosophy, or literary criticism may be excused for paling upon seeing a phrase like "theological hermeneutics." Let me hasten to assure such readers that even those of us accustomed to chatting away in the argot of our disciplines are not necessarily any clearer about interpretation, or able to read texts any better, than many a lay member of the church or reader of books from the public library. Indeed, I believe that in some cases hermeneutical theory has actually obscured interpretive practices that good nonspecialist readers know implicitly. But that, of course, is the rub: scholars want to make explicit what lay people know implicitly. And when lay people become confused about practices they once took for granted – as in the case of the Bible over the past two or three centuries – scholars attempt to shine a theoretic light into the cultural murk in the hope that it may aid us in finding our way back to the path. Theories of this kind generally go under the name

hermeneutics. Hans Frei, who did so much to clarify the issues surrounding the modern interpretation of the Bible, once noted that "Hermeneutics, by and large, is a word that is forever chasing a meaning."[1] He also liked to point out that it used to mean something far more straightforward in premodern times than it has come to mean in the past couple of centuries. And unlike most theologians today, he also preferred to use the word in its older, more straightforward sense.

Put most simply, hermeneutics is the "theory of interpretation."[2] Even that definition may be too formal, since hermeneutics originated, not among philosophers or theologians in search of a theory, but among biblical interpreters, who compiled lists of rules one should follow in order rightly to interpret scripture. Out of this originally practical need for guidelines in reading the Bible, there eventually emerged the theoretical enterprise of hermeneutics. One reason for the widespread perception that hermeneutics is an especially dense and arcane field of inquiry is the direction taken by modern hermeneutical theory in its dominant line of development since the early nineteenth century. Friedrich Schleiermacher (1768–1834), who is widely acknowledged to be a major figure in modern Christian theology, has also been called "the father of modern hermeneutics" because he is the one responsible for developing it into a philosophical theory of understanding.[3] Schleiermacher's approach was developed by later thinkers, the most important of whom are Wilhelm Dilthey, Martin Heidegger, and Hans Georg Gadamer. For recent theology and religious studies, this tradition is represented by such thinkers as Paul Ricoeur and David Tracy. In this tradition – which is frequently simply identified with the

[1] Hans W. Frei, *Types of Christian Theology*, ed. George Hunsinger and William C. Placher (New Haven, CT and London: Yale University Press, 1992), p. 16.
[2] Ibid., p. 16; Werner G. Jeanrond, *Theological Hermeneutics: Development and Significance* (London: Macmillan, 1991), p. 1.
[3] See, for example, Jeanrond, ibid., pp. 44ff.

enterprise called hermeneutics – the focus of attention shifts from the interpretation of texts to the nature of human understanding. From its beginnings in Schleiermacher right up to the present day, hermeneutics as understood in this way has been concerned with (in Frei's words) "the notion of a unitary and systematic theory of understanding" rather than "the older view of hermeneutics as a set of technical and *ad hoc* rules for reading."[4] Frei offers compelling reasons, which I shall not repeat here, for rejecting this modern sort of hermeneutical theory in favor of an approach more like the older *ad hoc* variety.[5]

There is a still more substantial reason – a specifically theological one – for eschewing the approach of modern hermeneutical theory. One of the hallmarks of modern theology (for which Schleiermacher is once again a paradigmatic figure) has been its tendency to preface the work of theology proper – what has been traditionally called dogmatics – with methodological prolegomena, whose purpose is to locate theology on the map of the academic disciplines, to describe its warrants and proper method of inquiry, and to justify it to the wider academic community – before one actually begins to do theology. The first 125 pages of Schleiermacher's chief work of systematic theology, *The Christian Faith* (or *Glaubenslehre*), is the classic example, in which he "borrows" theses from other disciplines in order to describe and justify theology in terms of extratheological criteria.[6] One can find countless examples of similarly nontheological introductions in the works of theology produced since Schleiermacher's day. Indeed, in the twentieth

---

[4] Hans W. Frei, *Theology and Narrative: Selected Essays*, ed. George Hunsinger and William C. Placher (Oxford: Oxford University Press, 1993), p. 124.

[5] For Frei's argument, see his essay "The 'Literal Reading' of Biblical Narrative in the Christian Tradition: Does It Stretch or Will It Break?," in *Theology and Narrative*, pp. 117–52, and George Hunsinger's summary of his case against Ricoeur and Tracy in the volume introduction, pp. 15–18.

[6] Friedrich Schleiermacher, *The Christian Faith*, ed. H. R. Mackintosh and J. S. Stewart (Edinburgh: T. & T. Clark, 1928). This work is commonly referred to as the *Glaubenslehre* ("Doctrine of Faith").

century many works of academic theology amount to little
more than extended prolegomena to theology. (In other
words, theologians are forever telling us what it is they
would be doing should they ever actually *do* any theology!)
As theology has been progressively marginalized in modern
society and academia, one could say, its quest for identity
and justification as a discipline has threatened to become
its primary subject matter. Karl Barth, more than any other
modern theologian, exposed the self-contradictory and self-
defeating character of doing theology in this way, and
taught us instead to see that theological definition and
methodology are properly theological enterprises – part of
the subject matter of theology, not a preliminary activity in
which one engages before starting to do theology. To see
the practical effects of this point of view, one need only
compare the table of contents of his *Church Dogmatics* with
that of Schleiermacher's *Glaubenslehre*. Barth's first volume
does indeed contain a discussion of the nature of the discipline of theology and its proper method, but he calls it not
"Prolegomena" or "Introduction" but "The Doctrine of
the Word of God."[7] As such it does not precede his dogmatics but rather comprises its opening chapter. Barth also
has much to say about the issues of theological hermeneutics, yet he produced no work with such a title (nor one
that might appropriately be given that title) because these
reflections form an integral part of his dogmatics.

The theological character of theological hermeneutics is
an instance of what is frequently called the "hermeneutical
circle." I am tempted to say "the much overrated hermeneutical circle," for I am convinced that it is neither as
troublesome nor as interesting as most writers on hermeneutics seem to assume; but that case cannot be made until
a little later, when we get to the question of postmodernity

---

[7] Karl Barth, *Die kirchliche Dogmatik* (Zurich: TVZ, 1932–67), vol. I, part 1; *Church Dogmatics*, ed. G. W. Bromiley and T. F. Torrance (Edinburgh: T. & T. Clark, 1956–69),
vol. I, part 1, 2nd edn. (1975).

and the paradigmatic imagination. Werner Jeanrond identifies two "dimensions" of the hermeneutical circle.[8] The
first is produced by the fact that "we need some form of
prior understanding in order to begin our engagement with
a text or work of art," a situation that can be described in
a way that sounds paradoxical or worse: we cannot understand something unless we already have a preliminary
understanding of it; but if we already understand it, even
preliminarily, our understanding will be biased or "subjective." The circularity of the situation is troublesome to the
extent that one assumes there to be a neutral vantage point
for understanding, from which one can gain an "objective"
view of things. But that is an assumption that fewer and
fewer people are prepared to make (more on this later,
when we venture into postmodernism). Jeanrond's other
form of the hermeneutical circle "consists in the fact that
we can never understand a whole without understanding all
of its parts; nor can we adequately understand the parts
without seeing them functioning in the overall composition
to which they contribute." In other words, understanding
the whole presupposes an understanding of the parts; but
understanding the parts presupposes that one has understood the whole. This form of the hermeneutical circle is
more interesting, for it turns out to be an indicator of the
holistic nature of human perception and understanding,
and thus a basic clue to the paradigmatic imagination.[9]
Again, it is troublesome only to the extent that one remains
committed to epistemological neutrality. At any rate, it is
undeniable that interpretation has an inherently circular
logic, and Barth's insistence on defining theology theologically indicates his acknowledgment of that hermeneutical
circularity.
    I propose accordingly to discuss the issues raised by the

---

[8] See Jeanrond, *Theological Hermeneutics*, pp. 5–6. The surprising brevity of Jeanrond's
    account is, I think, a sign of the inflated character of the "hermeneutical circle."
[9] See Garrett Green, *Imagining God: Theology and the Religious Imagination* (Grand Rapids,
    MI: William B. Eerdmans Publishing Co., 1998), especially chapters 3 and 4.

hermeneutics of suspicion, not as a prolegomenon or propaedeutic *to* Christian theology, but as an exercise *in* Christian theology. This volume, in other words, might appropriately be classified under "theological hermeneutics" only if this phrase is preceded by no definite or indefinite article, expressed or implied: what you are about to read, then, is not *a* theological hermeneutics (much less, heaven forbid, *Die theologische Hermeneutik!*) but rather an *ad hoc* theological exploration of some pressing hermeneutical issues confronting us today. And because we do not live in hermetically sealed linguistic universes, as I indicated earlier, I am hopeful that this piece of theologizing might also be of interest, and perhaps even of use, to those who are neither Christians nor theologians.

Modern or postmodern?

I have already found it impossible to avoid another exasperating, if trendy, term: "postmodern." (Professor Frei once confessed that "in the next life, if I have any choice, there will be two terms that I shall eschew, one is 'hermeneutics,' the other is 'narrative'!"[10] I should like to add "postmodern" to the list. But just as Frei, in this life, found it necessary to speak frequently of both hermeneutics and narrative, I seem to be stuck with postmodern.) So I would like to introduce a distinction, for the sake of clarity and simplicity, between two senses of "postmodern." The first, which may be called *descriptive postmodernism*, is simply a way of referring to the "nonfoundationalist" situation that increasingly characterizes our cultural world. If modernity is defined by the Enlightenment appeal to universal norms to which in principle we have access through the right use of reason, postmodernity can be defined in negative terms as the rejection of that possibility. Modernist thinkers seek to ground our knowledge and experience of the world in certain incorrigible foundational truths or experiences. If

[10] Frei, *Theology and Narrative*, p. 155.

we define the modern in this way, the postmodern begins wherever foundationalist certainty ends. The descriptive use of the term "postmodern" neither celebrates nor vilifies; it simply points to the cultural-historical fact that we seem to have lost the foundationalist certainty in universal criteria that transcend traditions, cultures, and languages. In this sense, to describe our situation as postmodern is simply to take note of the fact that fewer people today are willing to accept the "modernist" axiom that there are universal norms of truth and morals, transcultural and transhistorical, to which we have access through reason. But there is also a *doctrinaire* or *normative postmodernism*, flourishing especially among continental philosophers and their disciples, which denies that texts have any determinate meaning of the kind that modernist interpreters presuppose. This latter kind of postmodernism is a philosophical doctrine – one of several that respond to the postmodern situation in the descriptive sense. My distinction between descriptive and normative postmodernism, I should point out, is not the same as John Milbank's attempt to distinguish "benign" from "malign" forms of postmodernism. The former, he says, remains "optimistic about the possibility of admitting irreducible difference, and the historical situatedness of all truth-claims, without lapsing into a perspectivism which denies absolute truth and value altogether."[11] This benign postmodernism, which Milbank finds exemplified in Alasdair MacIntyre, represents a sympathetic if not finally satisfactory attempt to recover classical and Christian tradition in a postmodern age. The other, "malign" variety of postmodernism is Milbank's primary target, the avowed enemy of Christianity, which he also calls "Nietzschean postmodernism" or (more often) simply "nihilism." Both of Milbank's types fall under what I am calling normative postmodernism, because both are

---

[11] John Milbank, *Theology and Social Theory: Beyond Secular Reason* (Oxford: Blackwell, 1990), p. 61.

philosophical responses to the situation depicted by descriptive postmodernism. I will be exploring the roots of normative postmodernism in Nietzsche in chapter 5, and examining a contemporary version in the thought of Jacques Derrida in chapter 6. In the meantime, I will be using the word in its descriptive sense, without implying any predilection for the doctrinaire kind of postmodernism. As will become evident, however, I am not nearly as convinced as Milbank that this kind of postmodern thought can simply be dismissed as "malign."

Remaining for the time being, then, at the level of description, ought we to describe our cultural present as postmodern? There can be little doubt that modernist axioms have come increasingly under criticism, and a number of contemporary intellectuals are proclaiming the arrival of the postmodern age. Even some of the leading postmodernist philosophers, however, hesitate simply to declare the end of modernity. Jean-François Lyotard, for one, prefers to see the postmodern as a continuing possibility arising out of the modern. Calling postmodernism "the condition of knowledge in the most highly developed societies," he prefers to describe it as "undoubtedly a part of the modern" rather than an age following upon and supplanting the modern.[12] So, rather than simply describing the contemporary cultural situation as postmodern, I will adopt a more modest discourse, employing the metaphor of twilight – an image that echoes Hegel's Owl of Minerva as well as the language of Nietzsche's madman – suggesting that modernity is not simply past and gone but rather survives in a state of profound crisis and self-doubt. As Hegel's owl knew, twilight is a particularly favorable vantage point from which to look back over the course we have traveled in order better to understand our present situation and the

---

[12] Jean-François Lyotard, *The Postmodern Condition: A Report on Knowledge*, trans. Geoff Bennington and Brian Massumi in *Theory and History of Literature*, vol. X (Manchester: Manchester University Press, 1984), pp. xxiii, 79.

demands and choices it forces upon us. What some now refer to as the "project of Enlightenment"[13] (usually in the past tense) continues to exert a powerful cultural force, though it can no longer simply be taken for granted. For theology to side too quickly with the enemies of Enlightenment would, I believe, be a grave error (a claim I will try to substantiate in later chapters). For the time being, I will assume that we inhabit a liminal world, in which the confident universalism of the Enlightenment is giving way to something new, the precise shape of which is not yet evident. Whether Christians should welcome it or not remains an open question, but they can ignore it only at their peril.

The hermeneutics of suspicion

Paul Ricoeur, who is both a Christian in the Reformed tradition and a major figure in contemporary hermeneutical theory, has contributed an important historical thesis about the origins of the modern crisis of interpretation. His name for this development, the "hermeneutics of suspicion," has become a familiar watchword employed in theology and religious studies, and not only by those who are persuaded by his constructive hermeneutical theory. His historical analysis of the problem has proved even more influential than his own philosophical attempts to respond to it. I propose to take Ricoeur's historical insight (though not his constructive hermeneutics) as a point of departure, a provisional posing of the modern and postmodern problem of interpretation for which we urgently need to discover an adequate theological response.

According to Ricoeur's historical analysis, a major break occurred in the nineteenth century that has fundamentally altered the way people today read the authoritative texts of their traditions, especially the Bible. This hermeneutical revolution, which he believes to be irreversible, is epitomized by the thinkers he calls "the three masters of

---

[13] For example, Milbank, *Theology and Social Theory*, p. 260.

suspicion – Marx, Nietzsche, and Freud."[14] Though each taken alone has serious flaws, together they constitute a powerful critique of culture, focusing especially on religion – a critique that can be summarized in Marx's term *false consciousness*. This critique is of an unprecedented kind, "completely different from the critique of religion that is rooted in the tradition of British empiricism and French positivism." According to the analyses of these masters of suspicion, Ricoeur writes, "Religion has a meaning that remains unknown to the believer by virtue of a specific act of dissimulation which conceals its true origin from the investigation of consciousness."[15] In Marx the concealed meaning of religion lies in its relation to class struggle and economic interests, in Nietzsche to motives of resentment and the vengeance of the weak against the strong, and in Freud to repressed desires of aggression and especially sexuality. But Ricoeur is more interested in what they have in common, namely a *suspicion* of religious faith rooted in a new kind of doubt that "is totally . . . different from Cartesian doubt."[16] This new doubt is not so much epistemological as moral; it undermines the credibility of religion by attacking not its objects of belief (at least not directly) but rather its motives. "After the doubt about things," Ricoeur states aphoristically, "we have started to doubt consciousness."[17] Merold Westphal characterizes the common hermeneutic of suspicion in Marx, Nietzsche, and Freud as follows: "the deliberate attempt to expose the self-deceptions involved in hiding our actual operative motives from ourselves, individually or collectively, in order not to notice how and how much our behavior and our beliefs are

---

[14] Paul Ricoeur, "The Critique of Religion," *Union Seminary Quarterly Review* 28 (1973): 205.

[15] Paul Ricoeur, "Religion, Atheism, and Faith," in *The Conflict of Interpretations: Essays in Hermeneutics*, ed. Don Ihde (Evanston, IL: Northwestern University Press, 1974), p. 442.

[16] Ricoeur, "The Critique of Religion," p. 206.

[17] Paul Ricoeur, *Freud and Philosophy: An Essay on Interpretation* (New Haven, CT and London: Yale University Press, 1970), p. 33.

shaped by values we profess to disown."[18] As I shall argue in chapter 5, the situation is rather more complex in the case of Nietzsche, who is both an example of the modern hermeneutic of suspicion and the precursor of a distinctly postmodern suspicion. Before we get to that point, however, there is one more major term to be introduced into the discussion: imagination.

Interpretation and the paradigmatic imagination

Ricoeur makes a persuasive case for the seminal importance of the three great "masters of suspicion"; the tremendous cultural impact of the ideas of Marx, Nietzsche, and Freud would be hard to overestimate. In order fully to grasp the significance of their new kind of suspicious hermeneutics, however, it is necessary to take a step back and to look at the philosopher who deserves to be called the father of the suspicious critique of religion – the *Urmeister* of suspicion, we might say – Ludwig Feuerbach. With the help of a new interpretation of Feuerbach's critique of religion by Van A. Harvey,[19] I will argue in chapter 4 that the basic moves later articulated by Ricoeur's triumvirate have their origin in Feuerbach – in both the famous (or infamous) argument of *The Essence of Christianity* (1841) and his lesser-known later theory of religion, which Harvey thinks is not only different but superior. I will argue, furthermore, that even Harvey overlooks the significance of the *object* of Feuerbach's critique, the religious imagination. The later hermeneutics of suspicion developed by Marx, Nietzsche, and Freud are unquestionably more sophisticated and (with all due respect to Professor Harvey) more persuasive than Feuerbach's often heavy-handed projectionism and naturalism. But Feuerbach in his unnuanced way enables us to see something highly significant about suspicious

---

[18] Merold Westphal, *Suspicion and Faith: The Religious Uses of Modern Atheism* (Grand Rapids, MI: William B. Eerdmans Publishing Co., 1993), p. 13; Westphal's italics.

[19] Van A. Harvey, *Feuerbach and the Interpretation of Religion* (Cambridge: Cambridge University Press, 1995).

hermeneutics – namely, the object of suspicion. By rather ingenuously combining the descriptive claim that imagination is the engine of religion with the tendentious judgment that religious consciousness is therefore false consciousness, Feuerbach gives us the clue to the mainspring of modernist suspicion about religion.

Here the shift from a modern to a postmodern context becomes hermeneutically significant. For the modernist – and Feuerbach is a virtually pure example of the species – imagination, unless it remains securely subject to critical reason, has the potential to become the source of speculation, fantasy, and illusion. As such, "imagination" is the diametric opposite of "reality"; it is the organ of fiction and error. At the root of the modernist hermeneutic of suspicion is the following assumption: religion is the product of imagination; *therefore* religious claims are untrue. In Feuerbach this reasoning appears on the surface; but it is there as well in Marx and Freud, though usually presented in more sophisticated language and often disguised in subtle ways. It is also evident in the "modernist Nietzsche," who rails against Jews' and Christians' hatred of "reality." As soon as one makes the postmodern turn, however, the first thing to go is the foundational confidence that we have reliable access to a "reality" against which imagination might be judged "illusory." Imagination now becomes the unavoidable means of apprehending "reality," though there is, of course, no guarantee that it will succeed.

The new place of imagination is nowhere more evident than in recent philosophy of science, which one might summarize by saying that the history of science is the history of the scientific imagination, the narrative of the successive paradigms that have held sway in communities of scientists for shorter or longer periods, enabling them to agree about the theory, methods, and results of their research. At the popular level there is no better indicator of the shift from modern to postmodern than the fate of interest in "science and religion." In the heyday of modernism a century ago, military metaphors prevailed: the "warfare between science and religion"; the "conflict between science and theology."[20] One of the strongest indicators that modernity survives in our world is the persistent popular assumption that science and religion are somehow fundamentally opposed. For those on the postmodern side of the divide, on the other hand, scientific discovery increasingly appears as an analog of religious conversion – and vice versa. Modern culture – virtually by definition, as I see it – has taken its authoritative paradigms from modern science. From Galileo and Newton to Einstein and Stephen Hawking, the reigning scientific models of the cosmos have provided the larger culture with powerful analogies and metaphors that shape its epistemology, its poetry, its politics, and its religion. Here the postmodern shows itself in continuity with modernity, for many of the leading postmodernist ideas borrow much of their imagery and not a little of their social prestige from scientific notions of relativity, uncertainty, and incommensurability. It is therefore prudent for theologians to ponder the relation of their work to the world of modern science.

As dangerous as it sounds to orthodox believers who still hear with "modern" ears, the thesis that religion – including the Christian religion – is a product of human imagination ought to be accepted, and even welcomed, by theologians today.[21] For, if we have truly left the security of foundationalist apologetics behind, what else *could* it be? To insist that our truth claims are not mediated by imagination is to claim unique exemption from the limits of

---

[20] These phrases come from the titles of two influential works, John William Draper's *History of the Conflict between Religion and Science* (1874) and Andrew Dickson White's *History of the Warfare of Science with Theology in Christendom*, 2 vols. (1896). See John Kent, "Religion & Science," in *Nineteenth Century Religious Thought in the West*, ed. Ninian Smart, John Clayton, Steven Katz and Patrick Sherry (Cambridge University Press, 1985), vol. III, pp. 1–36.

[21] My book *Imagining God* is an attempt to articulate and defend this thesis. The argument in this paragraph amounts to a summary of conclusions that are more fully presented and argued in that book.

bodily and historical existence to which our contemporaries are subject. It is also – as I shall try to show in the last two chapters – a sign of faithlessness toward the God whom we acknowledge to be the author and guarantor of those truths, a claim of ownership over goods that we have been granted in trust. To acknowledge, on the other hand, that we hold those truths as stewards rather than as masters, in the earthen vessels of imaginative paradigms, is a sign that we have indeed heard the gospel message contained in those very truths. The mark of the Christian in the twilight of modernity is therefore imaginative faithfulness, trust in the faithfulness of the God who alone guarantees the conformity of our images to reality, and who has given himself to us in forms that may only be grasped by imagination.

The emerging postmodern context, especially as it appears in the sciences, may thus be more hospitable to theological work than the modern world it is rapidly supplanting. The reason can be simply stated: an intellectual culture that thought it had achieved access to secure, secular foundations for human knowledge and behavior – and saw itself therefore as the legitimate successor to an antiquated religious enterprise – is giving way to a culture that acknowledges that all data are theory-laden, all theories based on paradigms, all knowing dependent on imagination. In short, the postmodern sensibility acknowledges that the use of reason not only does not oppose, but necessarily entails, some kind of faith. Nietzsche's claim that there are no facts but only interpretations is an emblem of that sensibility. Taken in one direction (the one usually associated with postmodernism), the point sounds either cynical or playful, depending on the mood of the postmodernist. If you are John Milbank, it sounds positively malign, the nihilistic opposite to the peaceable kingdom of Christian social theory. Since there are no facts, say the postmodernists, there is no "truth," and we are left with an endless spinning out of interpretations – which is either (in the cynical version) grounds for despair or (in the playful version) the occasion to delight in the creativity of the imagination. Neither of these options holds much promise for reading the Bible as scripture.

There is another way, however, to read the Nietzschean aphorism, and it runs like this: There are no facts – that is, there is no theory-neutral foundation against which to measure interpretations – because "facts" are themselves a function of interpretation. We can continue to appeal to the facts, to aim at a truth beyond our own subjectivity, as long as we remember that all theoretical concepts, even the concept of *facts*, are paradigm-dependent. In other words, right interpretation depends on right imagination; whether we get things right or not is a function not only of our intelligence and powers of observation but also of the lenses through which we observe. If this situation epitomizes the postmodern world, then theologians may hope once again to become serious participants in the cultural conversation. An Enlightenment that thought it had discovered the foundation of all knowledge marginalized theology as the domain of mere faith. A postmodernity that acknowledges the fiduciary element inherent in all human activity cannot reasonably exclude theology on the grounds that it appeals to faith. Modernists are quick to label as "fideist" any enterprise that does not play by their rules; postmodernists know that the Enlightenment is no longer the only game in town. In Judaism, because it has always been a minority religion, the relationship between religious commitment and the modern world has been clearer than it has been for Christians, who until fairly recently could identify their own norms with those of the wider community. The emergence of Jewish Orthodoxy, as Jacob Katz has pointed out, is not simply the perpetuation of earlier Jewish tradition into modernity but rather a self-conscious commitment to a tradition that can no longer simply be taken for granted. The experience of Jews in the modern world foreshadows the stance of faith for Christians in a postmodern age: "loyalty to tradition [is] the result of a conscious decision."[22] The properly biblical metaphor for minority existence for both Jews and Christians, as I shall develop in the final chapter, is exile. And exile is not as dire a situation as might be supposed, as long as we continue to hold in imagination's eye the vision that enlightens our present darkness – or twilight – and draws us forward into the future that our Lord has gone ahead to prepare for us.

Intimations of things to come
Finally, let me offer a brief overview of the arguments presented in the following chapters.

Debates about postmodernity have focused, for good reason, on the interpretation of texts – especially culturally authoritative texts, among which scriptures represent the most authoritative of all. The point at which the late modern crisis of interpretation touches theology most directly, therefore, is the authority and interpretation of the Bible. I plan accordingly first to take an owl's-eye look at a few of the major figures who have influenced the way we read the Bible in the twilight of modernity. The purpose of this exercise (like all historical theology) will be twofold: to better understand our situation by grasping how we got into it in the first place, and at the same time to reopen questions which have seemed to be closed for us during the reign of Enlightenment modernism. Nietzsche is surely right that something central to European culture and civilization has died, or is dying; whether it is a God or an idol, however, is not nearly so clear. (Even here, Nietzsche may have got it right despite himself: for he speaks not only of the death of God but also of the twilight of the idols.)

The first voice we will hear belongs to that supreme definer and advocate of Enlightenment himself, Immanuel

[22] Jacob Katz, "Orthodoxy in Historical Perspective," in *Studies in Contemporary Jewry II*, ed. Peter Y. Medding (Bloomington: Indiana University Press, 1986), p. 4.

18

Kant. A closer look with our twilight-sensitized eyes at what he says about religion, and about the Christian religion in particular, will bring into view the central theological issue of modernity: what in the eighteenth century was called "positive religion." Kant's attempt to "interpret away" the offensive positivity of the gospel thus comes to epitomize the modernist way in theology, becoming the model for what I call accommodationist theology. Our unique vantage point at the end of modernity also makes us able to hear clearly for perhaps the first time a uniquely Christian voice crying in the enlightened wilderness of eighteenth-century Königsberg: Johann Georg Hamann, the "Wise Man from the North." His uncannily prescient metacritique of Enlightenment criticism in its heyday offers us some useful hermeneutical hints now that the mainstream of European culture is catching up at last with his insights.

The next historical figure to whom we shall listen introduces the issue of suspicion, which Ricoeur takes as the hallmark of the great hermeneutical sea-change in modern culture. As I have already indicated, I will argue that the corrosive suspicion that Ricoeur has taught us to associate with the triumvirate of Marx, Nietzsche, and Freud in fact received its original impulse from Feuerbach, the forgotten father of the hermeneutics of suspicion. Attending to his voice with late modern ears will allow us to hear more clearly the source and target of his suspicion, the imagination. Imagination, according to Feuerbach, is both the engine of religion and the ground of its falsity. The suspicion of imagination (or perhaps we should say the suspicious imagination) in the nineteenth century achieves its most brilliant and extreme expression in the figure of Friedrich Nietzsche, who makes the Christian vision of the world into the Great Lie. At the same time, this foe of the gospel focuses attention on the crucial issues that theology must face, and does so with greater clarity than most of Christianity's "friends."

Before turning explicitly to the theology of suspicion and trust in our late modern present, we will need to consider the most recent variety of hermeneutical suspicion – one that takes Nietzsche as its inspiration and claims for itself the label "postmodern." Of the several voices we might usefully consider, I have chosen Jacques Derrida as representative of the most influential and hermeneutically interesting form of postmodernism. The perspective of deconstruction, by apparently undermining the claims of every text to stability, let alone self-sufficiency, appears to present the ultimate threat to any acknowledgment of biblical authority. Nevertheless, the striking if unexpected hermeneutical similarities between Derrida's philosophy of signs and Karl Barth's theology of signs show that deconstruction ought not to be viewed simply as a threat to theology but rather as the secular counterpart to some of its own deepest hermeneutical convictions.

The cumulative effect of the various forms that the hermeneutics of suspicion has taken over the past two centuries has been to call into question the very possibility of taking a set of written texts as the norm for life and thought – something that most, if not all, of the world's religions do in one form or another. Under the suspicious eye of (post)modern critique, every faith in scriptural authority appears as a form of false consciousness, every sacred text as a surreptitious rhetoric of power. The rise of suspicion in the nineteenth century is integrally related to a major shift in the way modern Christian culture has read the Bible: it is the other face of what Hans Frei has identified as the eclipse of biblical narrative. As Christians stopped imagining the world through the lens of scripture, they began trying to accommodate the Bible to secular visions of reality – thus reversing the direction of interpretation and preparing the way for the radically suspicious hermeneutical projects of Feuerbach and his spiritual children, and precipitating the hermeneutical crisis of modern and postmodern culture that we have been investigating. A

Christian hermeneutics suited to the twilight of modernity must begin by taking the *sensus literalis* of the biblical text with renewed seriousness – that is, by appropriating the scriptural paradigm of the world as the place where God makes himself available to human imagination. Imagining God and the world scripturally requires the hard work of never-completed interpretation, under the pressure of the hermeneutic imperative. As Hamann recognized in the eighteenth century, the world imagined Christianly is *deutungsbedürftig*, continually in need of interpretation. This task is not an onerous one imposed upon us, whether by sin or the critique of unbelief, but is the hermeneutical consequence of living in a divinely created world, the yearning of the human spirit for its source in God.

Christian theologians have responded to the hermeneutics of suspicion in various ways: by treating it as a useful tool that can be adapted to theological purposes (liberation and feminist theologies); by attempting to appropriate the suspicious perspective by redescribing it in Christian categories (Westphal); or by subjecting the hermeneutics of suspicion to a kind of metasuspicion that attempts to turn the tables on the critics by exposing their own presuppositions to doubt (Milbank). While each of these responses offers useful insights that can contribute to a Christian theology of suspicion and trust, none is finally adequate. A properly theological response cannot treat suspicion merely as a positive or a negative impulse from *outside* the source of theology. When theology attends to its proper task of describing the grammar of scriptural imagination, it discovers a source of suspicion potentially and actually more radical than that advocated by any of the secular "masters of suspicion." The final chapter will thus examine, first of all, the biblical grounds for that suspicion in what I call the "hermeneutics of the cross." But since every kind of suspicion depends, whether explicitly or implicitly, upon a trust of some kind, the real question raised by the hermeneutics of suspicion is the ground of its trust. For Christians that trust, which we call faith in the God of Jesus Christ, commits us to a form of suspicion more radical than the secular kinds because it is the hermeneutical expression of God's judgment. And since God's judgment is always the shadow of his grace, Christians are able to live their lives and do their thinking in the hopeful insecurity of the faithful imagination.

Part I
The modern roots of suspicion

2

The scandal of positivity: the Kantian paradigm in modern theology

I have found it necessary to deny *knowledge*, in order to make room for *faith*.

Kant

... Kant (in the end, an *underhanded* Christian) ...

Nietzsche

The opening chapter introduced the crisis of interpretation faced by theology in late modernity, first by demystifying the rather intimidating term *hermeneutics* and then by placing the problem of scriptural interpretation in cultural and historical perspective. I also invoked Paul Ricoeur's suggestive thesis about the "hermeneutics of suspicion": that sea-change in the way we read authoritative texts that Ricoeur associates with the "masters of suspicion," Marx, Nietzsche, and Freud. Starting in this chapter I want to step back in time to the eighteenth century, when the modern age was young, in order to explore the origins of the problems that confront us now, in the "twilight" of modernity. The protagonist (perhaps it would be more

The first epigraph is from *Immanuel Kant's Critique of Pure Reason*, trans. Norman Kemp Smith (New York: St. Martin's Press, 1965), p. 29 (B xxx). The Nietzsche passage is from *Twilight of the Idols*, "'Reason' in Philosophy," § 6; Kritische Studienausgabe (hereafter KSA), ed. Giorgio Colli and Mazzino Montinari (Berlin and New York: Walter de Gruyter, 1967–77), vol. VI, p. 79.

accurate to say the villain) will be that great philosopher of the modern age, Immanuel Kant; and the key term will be one unfamiliar to late twentieth-century ears, *positivity*.

The concept of positivity

When the 25-year-old Hegel wrote an essay in 1795 on "The Positivity of the Christian Religion," he appealed to a concept that had become one of the staples of philosophy of religion in the Enlightenment.[1] Though it continued to be employed from time to time in the nineteenth century, the term *positivity* had all but fallen out of use by the time Hegel's early writings on theology were belatedly published in 1907. The fact that the content of his essay is less interesting to us today than its title is due largely to the fact that Hegel was still under the influence of the Kantian critical philosophy and had not yet achieved the philosophical point of departure that would make him one of the next century's towering intellectual figures. Following Kant and the Enlightenment generally, the young Hegel rejects the core beliefs of Christian orthodoxy on the grounds that they are "positive" – that is, teachings grounded not on universal reason but rather on an arbitrary appeal to the authority of specific historical figures and occurrences. But the term *positivity* has a usefulness that goes beyond the young Hegel's rather cut-and-dried rationalism, for it allows us to isolate the logical characteristic of the Christian gospel that is most responsible for the tension between Christian belief and the assumptions of modern secular thought. The positivity of orthodox belief and practice became the primary focus of the modern suspicion that has been directed against religion since the eighteenth century. This feature of modern religious thought has generally been overlooked, at least in part because the

---

[1] Georg Wilhelm Friedrich Hegel, *Hegels theologische Jugendschriften, nach den Handschriften der Kgl. Bibliothek in Berlin,* reprint of 1907 edn. (Frankfurt am Main: Minerva, 1966); *On Christianity: Early Theological Writings,* trans. T. M. Knox and Richard Kroner (New York: Harper & Brothers, 1961).

concept of positive religion, though widely used in the eighteenth century, virtually disappeared from the vocabulary of theologians and philosophers after Hegel. It is worth recovering at the end of the twentieth century because it will help us to see that aspect of traditional Christian belief most responsible for tension and conflict with the new secular ideals that emerged from the European Enlightenment. I will argue that the positivity of the gospel cannot be reduced to a merely formal aspect of the faith distinguishable from its essential content, but rather that it constitutes an inescapable feature of the grammar of Christian faith, an essential part of the logic of belief in Jesus Christ as the revelation of God in human history. Because Christians, like other religious believers, apprehend divine truth through the use of imagination, what earlier philosophers called "positivity" is necessarily characteristic of faith.

The notion of "positive" religion – in contrast not to "negative" but to "natural" religion – was adapted by Enlightenment thinkers from the traditional legal distinction between *natural* laws (those based on the nature of things, and therefore accessible to reason) and *positive* laws (those whose validity is grounded in the authority of the lawgiver, whether human or divine). In reaction against the confessional violence that had devastated Europe in the years prior to 1648, the Enlightenment appealed to reason, understood as the universal and *natural* basis for knowledge, against divisive claims to heteronomous authority, whether of church or state. In philosophy of religion a fateful distinction came to be drawn between *natural religion*, allegedly common to all humanity and universally accessible through reason, and the *positive religions*, based on arbitrary and contradictory claims to the authority of particular historical persons, texts, or traditions. The latter, deemed to be the source of conflict and strife, ought inevitably to yield to the former. A great deal of religious thought from the eighteenth century to the present can be usefully understood as an ongoing attempt to "depositivize" the historic religious traditions of the West – meaning first of all Christianity. The fading of the term *positivity* did not at all signal the demise of the project with which it was associated. A few modern thinkers have always resisted the drive to purge Christian thought of its offensive particularity – one thinks especially of Søren Kierkegaard in the nineteenth century and Karl Barth in the twentieth – but by and large the friends of the Christian gospel have agreed with its enemies that religious positivity is harmful, and that consequently an important theological task is what we might call the "naturalization" of the gospel in the modern world.

Although the expressions *positivity* and *positive religion* seldom appear in twentieth-century writings, they have a long history in Western thought. Thinkers of the Enlightenment before Kant were accustomed to divide religion into *positive* and *natural* forms. This usage is dependent on two common distinctions in medieval thought. The use of *positive* and *natural* as coordinate terms rests on a long-standing distinction in the field of law. Deriving from the past participle *positus* of the Latin verb *ponere* (to put, place, lay down), *positive* laws are those laid down or "posited" by divine or human authority; they have their ultimate foundation in the will of the lawgiver. *Natural* laws, on the other hand, are grounded in eternal rational principles and are hence available to unaided reason. The adoption of the distinction between positive and natural into the philosophy of religion was especially convenient for Enlightenment rationalists, since their use of the term *religion* included what the Middle Ages had called *lex* or *jus*; that is, they generally assumed that religion was constituted essentially by laws or commands. Matthew Tindal, for example, argues in his *Christianity as Old as the Creation* (1730), a classic of English deism that was in Kant's library, that there is no difference between morality and religion, except that the one is "acting according to the Reason of Things consider'd in themselves; the other, acting according to the

same Reason of Things consider'd as the Will of God."[2]
This doctrine provides Kant with his basic definition of
religion.[3]

When modern rationalists applied the old legal distinction between *positive* and *natural* to religion, they also drew
on the related medieval distinction between *revealed* and
natural theology. St. Thomas Aquinas distinguished the
principles of natural reason from the principles of faith,
revealed in scripture and articulated by the fathers of the
church.[4] For the rationalists of the Enlightenment, the
phrase "the positive religions" became simply a brief desig-
nation for the actual religions of the world, all of which
were understood to derive their authority from some historical occurrence, usually an original teacher or founder.
Since this historical origin was thought regularly to involve
revelation (understood to be the supersensible receiving of
propositional religious truth), *revealed* religion was usually
synonymous with *positive* religion. The terminology of natural and revealed religion was the usual language of the
English rationalists and the Germans before Kant.

Because the rationalists of the seventeenth and eighteenth centuries contrasted these historically revealed religions with the natural religion of reason, *positive* took on
a pejorative connotation, which was generally maintained
whenever the term was used by the German Idealists and
their nineteenth-century successors. With the discrediting
of the Enlightenment version of "natural religion," positive

---

[2] Matthew Tindal, *Christianity as Old as the Creation*, ed. Günter Gawlick (London, 1730; facsimile reprint, Stuttgart/Bad Cannstatt: Friedrich Frommann Verlag [Günther Holzboog], 1967), p. 298.

[3] "Religion is (subjectively regarded) the cognition of all our duties *as* divine commands" (the emphasis is Kant's, even though the published English translation does not indicate it). Immanuel Kant, *Die Religion innerhalb der Grenzen der blossen Vernunft*, ed. Karl Vorländer, Philosophische Bibliothek, vol. XLV (Hamburg: Felix Meiner, 1956), p. 153; Immanuel Kant, *Religion within the Limits of Reason Alone*, trans. Theodore M. Greene and Hoyt H. Hudson (New York: Harper & Brothers, 1960), p. 142. Subsequent references to this work will be given parenthetically; the first number refers to the page in the German original, the second to the English translation.

[4] See, for example, *Summa theologiae* 1a. 1. 8.

religion (as its counterpart) likewise ceased to be employed as a familiar category by philosophers and theologians. The first edition of *Die Religion in Geschichte und Gegenwart*, published in 1913, included a definition of positivity that offers a summary of its earlier usage and provides a convenient preliminary definition for its use by Kant. The element of the positive, according to this definition, refers to "what is factually given in contrast to what is derived from general concepts or principles, to what is logically constructed; thus *positive religions* are the actual, historical religions appealing to divine revelation in contrast to 'natural religion.' "[5] The omission of this entry in the most recent edition of this reference work in 1959 indicates the progressive disappearance of the term in recent theological discussion.[6]

Kant's two projects in the *Religion*

Kant's *Religion within the Limits of Reason Alone* undertakes two interconnected projects not clearly distinguished by the author himself – one philosophical and descriptive, the other theological and normative. This seminal work, in other words, is not simply the critical philosophy of religion that it has usually been taken to be but is also a work of theological apologetics that makes bold claims on behalf of the Christian religion. Moreover, Kant's reinterpretation of Christianity became the prototype for the mediating Protestant theologies of the nineteenth century and their twentieth-century heirs, Roman Catholic as well as Protestant. The success or failure of Kant's apologetic project in the *Religion* is therefore a crucial question for historical theology, with important implications for systematic and

---

[5] "Positiv," *Die Religion in Geschichte und Gegenwart*, 1st edn., vol. IV, p. 1685.

[6] For further discussion of the concept of positivity at the end of the eighteenth century, see Garrett Green, "Positive Religion in the Early Philosophy of the German Idealists," Ph.D. dissertation, Yale University, 1971. Chapters 1 and 2 are devoted to an analysis of Kant's *Religion* at greater length than is possible here. Several passages from these chapters appear here in slightly revised form.

philosophical theology right up to the present. My theological thesis emerges out of these historical conclusions. Taking Nietzsche's attack on Kantian practical reason as a touchstone, I will argue that historic Christianity cannot survive Kant's attempted translation. The price of accommodating Christian doctrine and symbols in this way to the presuppositions of modernity is the sacrificing of the essential positivity of the gospel – a price that believers cannot afford to pay.

Interspersed in Kant's constructive argument on behalf of his version of natural religion are polemical thrusts against positive religion. He does not treat the polemical aspect of the *Religion* with the same architectonic organization that he devotes to his constructive case; but a number of factors, all of which Kant sees as threats to rational religion, reveal a generally consistent pattern. Taken together, these elements of positivity constitute a coherent structure of positive religion, a kind of antitheology with an inner logic of its own, opposed fundamentally to the Kantian theology of religion within the limits of reason alone. The difficulty of isolating Kant's own view of natural religion is due in part to the fact that it is mixed with this ongoing polemic against positive religion.

The critique of positivity also serves an apologetic function in the argument of the *Religion*: Kant intends to reinterpret historic Christian faith by purging it of its positivity. Although Kant was exceptionally well informed for an eighteenth-century European about other religions of the world (as is evident in a number of passages and notes in the *Religion*), it should be clear to any reader that a Christian context is assumed throughout. Kant generally avoids making explicit reference to Christian churches, creeds, theologians, and dogmas, but their presence is only thinly disguised. Since he knew that he was writing for the government censor as well as for his philosophical public, he may have had political motives for disguising the theological implications of his argument. Kant has other reasons, however – reasons internal to his argument – for avoiding explicit appeal to Christian doctrine. He is engaged, after all, in an apologetic reinterpretation of the Christian faith whose major thesis is that essential Christianity conforms to "pure rational faith" and depends to no significant degree on "positive" doctrines or practices. He must therefore demonstrate this rational content without appealing to church doctrine. Having made his case "philosophically" rather than "theologically," he can then claim that "of all the public religions which have ever existed, the Christian alone is moral" (51–2/47).

The term *positive* occurs explicitly in a few passages of the *Religion*. Kant speaks, for example, of "positive doctrines of revelation"[7] and again of a "positive law of revelation."[8] Finally, he speaks very generally about believing "what is positive" in religion.[9] More often, however, he refers to positive religion by means of various terms denoting its specific aspects or manifestations: "ecclesiastical faith," "historical faith," "statutory religion," "religion of divine worship," or "revealed religion." How these terms all relate to a general concept of positivity is never explicit in Kant, but it is implicit in his presentation and argument. One particularly compact sentence illustrates the close relation of these aspects of positivity: "There can be no doubt," Kant writes, "that the legislation of [God's] will ought to be solely *moral*; for statutory legislation (which presupposes a revelation) can be regarded merely as contingent and as something which never has applied or can apply to every man, hence as not binding upon all men universally" (104/95). The logic of positive religion as seen by Kant thus involves the interrelations of such elements as morality (the key term), statutory laws, revelation, contingency, and universality.

---

[7] "positiver Offenbarungslehren" (157/145).
[8] "positives ... Offenbarungsgesetz" (187/175).
[9] "Positives" (188/176).

Kant's Christian apologetic is most obvious in the last book of the *Religion*, where he belatedly defines *religion* and offers a rather bewildering typology of its different varieties. The project is implicit in the very definition of religion: "the cognition of all duties *as* divine commands" (153/142). The pivotal term *"as"* (whose emphasis by Kant is omitted by his English translators) stands as a kind of fulcrum between potentially equal quantities, which correspond to natural (rational or moral) religion and positive religion.[10] This definition sets up the conceptual apparatus for Kant's apologetic argument that in the case of Christianity, the two are in fact equivalent. Far from being mutually exclusive, positive and natural religion can coincide ("in this case," he writes, "the religion is *objectively* a natural one though *subjectively* a revealed one" [156/144]); and the heart of his apologetic is the claim that Christianity is the only historical example of such a happy coincidence of subject and object. Both have the same content; they differ only in form. The error, Kant claims, lies in trying to make what ought to be mere form – positivity – into the essential content, that is, the case of a "religion which, because of its inner constitution [*inneren Beschaffenheit*], can be regarded only as revealed" (156/144).

The more interesting and fruitful arena for observing Kant as Christian apologist, however, is not the confusing and formalistic apparatus in book IV but the actual examples of the apologetic at work at key points throughout *Religion within the Limits of Reason Alone*. I believe that the hermeneutical key to this work lies in the author's constant attempt to carry out his tandem projects at once: the construction of "pure rational faith" and the argument that Christianity – stripped of its positivity – can be interpreted as such a faith. The key *theological* point at stake is the con-

---

[10] For a discussion of the important logic of the connective "as" in modern religious thought, see Garrett Green, *Imagining God: Theology and the Religious Imagination* (Grand Rapids, MI: William B. Eerdmans Publishing Co., 1998), pp. 134–41.

comitant claim that the positivity of the Christian religion is merely formal and can thus be eliminated without loss to Christian truth.

The first occurrence of Kant's dual strategy at work is in book I, where he presents his philosophical argument that human nature is radically evil and reinterprets the Christian doctrine of original sin accordingly. No better evidence could be found against classifying Kant as a typical thinker of the Enlightenment. If a naive optimism about human nature is a characteristic feature of Enlightenment anthropology, Kant clearly violates its spirit at this point. He chooses to introduce his treatise on religion by investigating and describing the dynamics of what he himself calls "radical evil" in human nature. He delineates its logic with great precision, seeking on the one hand to refute the simple optimism of moralists "from *Seneca* to *Rousseau*" (20/16), but on the other hand to avoid making evil so essentially a part of human nature that the nerve of moral responsibility is severed. Concern with this delicate distinction, of course, has run throughout the history of Christian thought at least since the time of Augustine. Kant, though he struggles valiantly to reconcile moral autonomy with the idea that human beings are innately evil, emerges a Pelagian in the end.[11] Why does he arrive at a moralistic conclusion after seeing so clearly the superficiality of earlier moralists? Gordon Michalson calls radical evil "the most profound threat . . . the riderless horse in Kant's total vision" and the root of the "vicious circularity" that bedevils his entire philosophy, leading him in the end to an illegitimate appeal to divine grace.[12] While agreeing with Michalson's interpretation of Kant's argument, I would account for the Kantian religious dilemma rather

---

[11] Space does not allow for a presentation of the evidence for this conclusion, but it has been extensively documented elsewhere. See Green, "Positive Religion," esp. pp. 16–27. The same conclusion has been reached more recently by Gordon E. Michalson, Jr., in *Fallen Freedom: Kant on Radical Evil and Moral Regeneration* (Cambridge: Cambridge University Press, 1990). See especially pp. 7, 102, and 132, where he comments on Kant's "basically Pelagian instincts."

[12] Ibid., pp. 18, 26, 28.

differently. It is not as though he set out "to have human autonomy succeed God"[13] and then unaccountably adopted a doctrine of radical evil that could only be overcome by an illicit appeal to grace; rather, Kant is forced to confront *both* his nemeses – radical evil and divine grace – for the same reason: he does not wish to leave Christianity behind on the ash heap of history in favor of a secular ethical rationalism, but wants to *rescue* Christian doctrine from the paralysis of supernaturalist orthodoxy and show its compatibility, indeed virtual identity, with "pure rational faith." Radical evil and divine grace present him with such difficulties because they are the aspects of Christian teaching that stand in the greatest tension with Enlightened moral autonomy.

His dual strategy is evident in the way that Christian language and concepts – most notably original sin – emerge in the argument of book I. He does not begin in the fashion of the theological apologist with original sin and then seek to show its compatibility with Enlightened rationality. Instead, he begins as the critical philosopher, expounding a doctrine of radical evil "within the limits of reason alone," and then developing it in such a way that (lo and behold!) we discover we have arrived at the very insights contained in the positive teachings of biblical faith. After constructing his philosophical account of evil, he can announce that "the foregoing agrees well with the manner of presentation [*Vorstellungsart*] that Scripture employs, whereby the origin of evil is depicted as having a *beginning* in the human race" (41/36). The distinguishing feature of the biblical treatment of evil is its presentation "in a narrative," whereby the philosophical priority of evil is translated into *temporal* categories. Once we make allowances for this formal difference, we can see that both accounts are making the same point. In a highly significant footnote, Kant summarizes the key hermeneutical principle. "It is possible," he claims, "to explain how an historical account can be put

[13] Ibid., p. 140.

35

to moral use without deciding whether this is the author's meaning as well or merely our own interpretation [*oder wir ihn nur hineinlegen*] . . ." (47n./39n.). He urges that historical issues be bracketed since they have "no valid relation to everyone" – that is, because they lack universality. He assigns them to "the adiaphora," the class of theologically neutral matters about which individuals may freely differ.

The dual strategy of Kant's *Religion* reappears in book II, when he turns to the solution of the problem of radical evil. Here is the culmination of his intricate attempt to preserve the moral autonomy fundamental to rational religion while showing that Christianity, rightly interpreted, contains the same teachings. If any more evidence were needed to demonstrate Kant's apologetic interest, the presence of what amounts to a Christology in a book on the religion of reason should be the clincher. Space does not permit an analysis of Kant's complete doctrine of salvation and regeneration;[14] however, I will focus on a question at the very heart of the Kantian project: the issue of divine righteousness, which Kant himself calls the most difficult problem. Although he never mentions the fact explicitly, he is here dealing with the central issue of Reformation theology, as his choice of terms indicates: he refers to his own solution of the problem of divine righteousness as a "deduction of the idea of a *justification*" (76/70). His reason for *not* discussing the historical background is his desire to deal with religious problems *rationally* – "within the limits of [practical] reason alone." The entire enterprise deliberately abstracts from every particular experience and proceeds as a kind of project of thought. To put the discussion into historical perspective might compromise the universality of the project; Kant, at any rate, has little interest in the

---

[14] For a fuller account, see Green, "Positive Religion," chapter 1; and Michalson, *Fallen Freedom*, part II. On most points my account and Michalson's are in close agreement. Some of the differences are addressed below.

history of theology. He is, after all, trying to discover the one, true, rational meaning of religion in general.

The key problem is the following:

> Whatever a man may have done in the way of adopting a good disposition, and, indeed, however steadfastly he may have persevered in conduct conformable to such a disposition, *he nevertheless started from evil*, and this debt he can by no possibility wipe out.

> 72/66

It is impossible, he reasons, for anyone to earn a surplus of merit after adopting a good disposition, since it is always one's duty to do every possible good; neither is there any way for one person to pay off the debt of sin accrued by another. Kant here takes very seriously the state of radical evil that he described so carefully in book I. He draws the pessimistic conclusion that everyone apparently must look forward to endless punishment.

Kant's solution depends on two anthropological distinctions. First, man can be regarded both as a *physical* being ("according to his empirical character as sensible entity") and as a *moral* being ("as intelligible entity"). The other distinction is between a person before and after a "change of heart"; that is, between the "old man" in a state of radical evil (sin) and the "new man" with the perfectly good disposition. Using these two distinctions, Kant will seek to accomplish the following:

> Let us see then whether, by means of the concept of a changed moral attitude, we cannot discover in this very act of reformation such ills as the new man, whose disposition is now good, may regard as incurred by himself (in another state) and, therefore, as constituting *punishments* whereby satisfaction is rendered to divine justice.

> 73–4/67

37

Now when a person departs from the life of the old man and enters into a state of righteousness, this amounts to a sacrifice – a sacrificial death of the old man – as well as "an entrance upon a long series of the evils of life." At this point it is important to remember that the "Son of God" in Kant's religion is merely a name for the archetype of the morally perfect disposition. Thus, the new man undertakes this sacrifice and life of trials "in the disposition of the Son of God" (74/68). Using both of the distinctions described above, Kant is able to express the matter as follows:

> Although the man . . . is *physically* the selfsame guilty person as before and must be judged as such before a moral tribunal and hence by himself; yet, because of his new disposition, he is . . . *morally* another in the eyes of a divine judge for whom this disposition takes the place of action.

74/68

The sharp distinction between the old man and the new man allows Kant to offer real hope of salvation from radical evil without at the same time compromising his moral rigor. The distinction between physical man and moral man, on the other hand, serves to provide a genuine continuity between the old and new man. Kant is faced here with the difficult problem of trying simultaneously to affirm an absolute moral change while maintaining the personal identity of the old with the new. He is able to succeed only by relying on one of the most fundamental distinctions in his entire thought: the sensible and the intelligible. Morality (and hence religion) has to do only with the realm of the intelligible; thus, while sensibility provides the necessary substance for radical moral change, it is, strictly speaking, irrelevant to morality. This presupposition is of major importance in Kant's treatment of religious positivity.

It also has interesting immediate consequences for Kant's own theological treatment of justification. For, he says, "if we personify this idea," we can say that the Son of God himself vicariously bears the sacrifice for our sins, redeems us from the consequences of divine justice, and is the advocate for all men before the throne of divine justice. "In this mode of representation [*Vorstellungsart*]," however, "the suffering that the new man, in becoming dead to the *old*, must accept throughout life is represented [*vorgestellt*] as a death endured once for all by the representative of mankind" (74–5/69). Of course, if such a *Vorstellung* were to be taken literally, it would lead to morally destructive consequences as well as grave epistemological problems.[15]

This deduction of justification is the key to Kant's soteriology. For he has now succeeded in solving the problem of the divine righteousness by showing that a surplus of merit is after all possible.[16] The new man (alias the Son of God) sacrifices himself for the sins of the old man. Kant is able to conceive such a transaction only by once again introducing a set of dual perspectives. For "what in our earthly life ... is ever only a *becoming*," he says with reference to the perfect moral disposition, is "credited to us exactly as if we were already in full possession of it" (75/70). One of the perspectives could accurately be called *sub specie dei*, though recognition of the perspective in no way commits Kant to any assertion about God. He apparently appeals to this dual perspective when he claims that this justification of a man who has changed his moral disposition comes "from grace" but is also "fully in accord with eternal righteousness" (76/70). It looks like grace from the human perspective, where only the "old man" is empirically experienced. From the supersensible vantage point, however – which reason

---

[15] On the importance of the concept of *Vorstellung* in Kant's theory of the imagination, see Green, *Imagining God*, pp. 14–16.

[16] Michalson puts the issue rather confusingly by speaking of a "surplus of moral debt" (*Fallen Freedom*, pp. 107ff.). (*Any* moral debt constitutes a surplus – or rather a deficit!) As in medieval theology, so in Kant, the real problem is how to achieve a surplus of *merit*. The Roman Catholic claim that such a surplus accrues to the church because of the merits of Christ and the saints became, of course, the presupposition for the doctrine of indulgences, the spark that set off Luther's Reformation.

represents as a practical idea – the justification is fully merited by the sacrifice of the "new man."

Kant no sooner completes this deduction of the idea of justification than he begins to fear its misuse. His misgivings about religious doctrines extend even to his own, and he is quick to put it into perspective. He denies that his deduction has any *"positive"*use at all (76/70).[17] It could not help one achieve a good disposition, since the premise of the deduction was that the person in question already possesses one. Likewise, it can be of no use in comforting such an individual, since the possession of a good disposition carries with it its own sense of comfort and hope. "Thus," Kant concludes, "the deduction of the idea has done no more than answer a speculative question," though it is not therefore unimportant. For if the question of a rational idea of moral justification were to be ignored, "reason could be accused of being wholly unable to reconcile with divine justice man's hope of absolution from his guilt – a reproach which might be damaging to reason in many ways, but most of all morally" (76/70). Hence negatively Kant's deduction becomes a bulwark against certain religious dangers to morality – dangers that Kant attributes to the positive elements of religion. Briefly, the lesson to be garnered is that nothing short of real moral change – no rituals, no dogmas, no worship – can bring about a person's justification.

But neither should we overlook the positive accomplishment of Kant's "deduction of the idea of a *justification*." At the very point where Christianity appears to be most definitively and hopelessly wedded to positivity – the doctrine of the satisfaction of divine justice through the sacrificial death of the Son of God – Kant has transformed the offensive teaching into the "idea" of "a" justification. In other words, even here at the heart of positive religion he has demonstrated an essential identity between Christian

---

[17] Here Kant evidently uses the term *positive* in its more common meaning as the antithesis of *negative* rather than in the technical sense of positivity, where it is opposed to *natural*.

doctrine and "religion within the limits of reason alone." Gone are the appeals to historical particulars and empirical examples; gone, most important of all, is the apparent violation of moral autonomy. Enlightened Christians can breathe a sigh of relief: Professor Kant, the destroyer of supernaturalist orthodoxy, has revealed himself to be the apologist for a new, *true* Christianity!

Kant as father of liberal theology
By arguing that the Christian religion is the closest historical approximation we have to pure rational faith, Kant establishes himself as the progenitor of a long and influential tradition in modern Christian thought. Unlike Hume, whose antimetaphysical skepticism had almost wholly negative implications for traditional belief, Kant swept away the old foundations in order to establish new, more secure ones. He, of course, had announced his intention to do precisely that at the outset of the critical philosophy, in the famous dictum in the second preface to the *Critique of Pure Reason* that he had "found it necessary to deny *knowledge*, in order to make room for *faith*."[18] His interpreters have not always appreciated the extent to which it is precisely the *Christian* faith for which he thinks he has made room. *Religion within the Limits of Reason Alone*, whatever else it may be, is a sophisticated apologetic for the truth of Christianity in an age of Enlightenment.

For this reason, one could plausibly argue that Kant, rather than Schleiermacher, is the first "post-Kantian" Christian thinker, the first of many successors to try to reformulate Christian doctrine in an intellectually defensible form after the demise of metaphysical supernaturalism. "There can be no doubt," Hans Frei has written, "that Kant's thought was the crucial dividing point for Protestant theology in the nineteenth century. His thought was like a prism, through which reflection upon all previous

---

[18] *Immanuel Kant's Critique of Pure Reason*, trans. Norman Kemp Smith, p. 29 (B xxx).

philosophy had to pass. All paths led to Kant."[19] The image also implies what Frei does not spell out: that all paths through the nineteenth century diverge again from their common point in Kant's thought. After gathering up the rays of precritical thought, the Kantian prism redirects them into strikingly new patterns.

The pattern to which I wish to call attention is one that shaped the methodology of theologians, especially liberal Protestants, throughout the nineteenth century and beyond. At the root of these methods is a distinction between the form and the content of Christian faith, and an accompanying conviction that for the timelessly valid *content* of Christian truth to become persuasive once again in the modern age, it must be translated out of the untenable *form* of precritical orthodoxy into a mode appropriate to critical modernity. Such theologians differ among themselves about how correctly to characterize the "bad" form of inherited Christianity, and *a fortiori* about how it ought to be transformed. Kant anticipates two of the most popular nineteenth-century metaphors for making the form/ content distinction: the image of positivity as "only a vehicle which finally can pass over into pure religious faith" (116/107); and the metaphor of the positive "husk" that both protects and obscures the essential "kernel" of religious truth.[20] By far the commonest tendency has been to call for what amounts to a "depositivizing" of Christian teaching, even though most of these thinkers did not make explicit use of the idea of positivity.

Two of the most striking examples are exceptional in their explicit appeal to positivity, however, and both claim

[19] Hans W. Frei, "The Academic Tradition in Nineteenth-Century Protestant Theology," in *Faith and Ethics: The Theology of H. Richard Niebuhr*, ed. Paul Ramsey (New York: Harper & Row, 1965), p. 17.

[20] See, for example, Kant's discussion of miracles in the second "General Observation." "We need not call in question any of these miracles and indeed may honor the husk [*Hülle*] which has served to bring into public current a doctrine whose authenticity rests upon a record indelibly registered in every soul and which stands in need of no miracle" (85/79–80).

to do justice to the positive aspects of religion. Schleiermacher devotes the fifth of the *Speeches* to the multiplicity and particularity of "the religions." He is scathing in his indictment of the Enlightenment prejudice against positivity. "The essence of natural religion consists almost entirely in denying everything positive and characteristic in religion"; he calls natural religion "this empty formless thing."[21] The irony of Schleiermacher's apology for positivity, however, is that he defends it *in general.* "Schleiermacher," writes one commentator, "develops even the necessity of the multiplicity of religions out of his concept of religion."[22] He defends the positivity not of Christianity, or of any particular religious tradition, but rather of religion itself.[23] In his own Christian systematic theology he follows a version of Kant's depositivizing methodology, first locating a religious essence in human affect or feeling and then interpreting Christian doctrines as "*accounts of the Christian religious affections set forth in speech.*"[24] Without minimizing the significance of Schleiermacher's rejection of the Kantian identification of religion with morality, his program can nevertheless be seen as a methodological variation on a theme by Kant. *The* great quarrel in modern Christian thought has been about rightly distinguishing form and content. Here both Kant and Schleiermacher are on the same side of the issue: both want to interpret scripture and doctrine as forms expressive of a prior content. That this content is rational for Kant and affective for Schleiermacher is no doubt a major difference for some purposes; but in terms of the great form/content debate they are in fundamental agreement.

[21] Friedrich Schleiermacher, *On Religion: Speeches to Its Cultured Despisers,* trans. John Oman (New York: Harper & Row, 1958), pp. 233–4.

[22] Friedrich Hertel, *Das theologische Denken Schleiermachers: Untersucht an der ersten Auflage seiner Reden "Ueber die Religion"* (Zurich: Zwingli Verlag, 1965), p. 137.

[23] A more complete analysis of Schleiermacher on positivity can be found in Green, "Positive Religion," pp. 264–74.

[24] Friedrich Schleiermacher, *The Christian Faith,* ed. and trans. H. R. Mackintosh and J. S. Stewart (New York: Harper & Row, 1963), vol. I, p. 76 (§15).

The other nineteenth-century thinker who attended explicitly to the issue of positivity was Hegel. In the early fragmentary essay on "The Positivity of the Christian Religion," with which we began, the youthful Hegel, still under the strong influence of Kant, argues for the elimination of positivity in favor of an ethical rationalism. More interesting is the change in his mature viewpoint, where he argues for the necessity of religion taking on positive forms. Religion, the second form of absolute spirit, is characterized by positivity in the mode of *Vorstellung*,[25] and Hegel argues that it achieves its supreme expression in Protestant Christianity. In the end, however, he calls for the *Aufhebung* of religious positivity – even in its absolute, Christian mode – into the pure intelligibility of the concept.[26] Hegel, too, in other words, offers us another variation on a theme by Kant, another version of the argument that the essential content of Christian truth can be translated without loss into the depositivized thought forms of modernity.

Further variations on the theological pattern initiated by Kant and exemplified by Schleiermacher and Hegel are to be found throughout the nineteenth century and beyond. In every case the rejection of positivity (whether called by that name or some other) is based on a concept of religion; and religion is typically conceived to be the definitive mark of humanity. In many of the cases, this argument is coupled with an apologetic claim for the superiority of the Christian religion: Christianity, the typical argument goes, is the truest religion because it is the *most religious* religion. The liberal theology of a figure like Adolf von Harnack represents the genre in its virtually pure form. Moreover, this

---

[25] *Vorstellung*, traditionally translated as "representation," is closer to "imagination" in Kant and the German Idealists. See Green, *Imagining God*, pp. 13–18.

[26] For a more extensive discussion of the young Hegel's treatment of positivity, see Green, "Positive Religion," chapter 5. For Hegel's later thought, see Stephen D. Crites, "The Problem of the 'Positivity' of the Gospel in the Hegelian Dialectic of Alienation and Reconciliation," Ph.D. dissertation, Yale University, 1961; and Crites' excellent and neglected article "The Gospel According to Hegel," *The Journal of Religion* 46 (1966): 246–63.

tradition has continued into the twentieth century and has come to include Roman Catholic as well as Protestant thinkers. On the Protestant side, Paul Tillich's conscious revision of Schleiermacher's program once again employs a general concept of religion (called "faith" by Tillich) to show how Christianity (especially in its Protestant manifestation) is identical with the pure form of religion itself. Catholic variations on the theme can be found in the thought, for example, of Karl Rahner and David Tracy. Kant, in other words, is not only the "father" of mediating Protestant theology in the nineteenth century but also the "grandfather" of what can be termed the "ecumenical liberalism" of the twentieth century.

Nietzsche thinks Kant is an "underhanded Christian" because he divides reason into theoretical and practical aspects. "With his notion of 'practical reason . . .,'" Nietzsche writes, "he invented a special kind of reason for cases in which one need not bother about reason – that is, when morality, when the sublime command 'thou shalt,' raises its voice."[27] One such instance, of course, is religion – that special application of Kantian practical reason. As is so often the case, Nietzsche, approaching the matter from the side diametrically opposed to Christian orthodoxy, sees things more clearly than those with apologetic interests. He sees in Kant the very epitome of his contention that "the Protestant parson is the grandfather of German philosophy." Kant, exemplifying the "theologians' instinct," manages in the name of rational modernity to betray the very ideal of that modernity: "A path had been found on which one could sneak back to the old ideal."[28]

What Nietzsche here describes in unflattering terms as Kant's "Schleichweg zum alten Ideal" is what I have been calling Kant's Christian apologetic. More generally, we can

---

[27] Friedrich Nietzsche, *The Antichrist*, § 12, trans. Walter Kaufmann, *The Portable Nietzsche*, rev. edn. (New York: Viking Press, 1968), pp. 578–9; KSA, vol. VI, p. 178.
[28] *The Antichrist*, § 10; *Portable Nietzsche*, pp. 576–7; KSA, vol. VI, p. 176.

say that Kant and the tradition that follows the pattern begun by him are proposing a theological accommodationism, a method that seeks to preserve the essence of Christianity by translating it into the modern idiom. Nietzsche's discomfiture, of course, stems from his suspicion that Kant has betrayed the project of secular modernity. Christian theologians, far from finding solace in that situation, have reasons of their own for being suspicious of the Kantian program and its later imitators. For if Nietzsche suspects that Kant has sold out modern rationality, theologians may wonder whether he has not sold out Christianity. (Note that one must not necessarily choose between these opposed critiques of Kant: it is possible that both are correct!)

I want to suggest by way of conclusion some reasons why theologians in the late twentieth century ought to be suspicious of the Kantian apologetic, and by extension, of its subsequent theological variants. One of the ironies of the Kantian legacy in religious thought is that the apologetic appeal to universal reason and common human experience has led to some of the most imperialistic modern claims on behalf of Christianity. Kant speaks of "that church which contained within itself, from its first beginning, the seed and the principles of the objective unity of the true and *universal* religious faith, to which it is gradually brought nearer" (125/116). (Such claims, especially in the nineteenth century, were frequently linked to correlative treatments of Judaism as the archetypical "bad religion".)[29] Even in the mid-twentieth century, Tillich could argue for the superiority of specifically Protestant Christianity on the grounds that it incorporates within itself a self-critical purification of the impulse to faith.[30]

---

[29] See, for example, Kant's contention that "the *Jewish faith* was, in its original form, a collection of mere statutory laws upon which was established a political constitution; for whatever moral additions were then or later *appended* to it in no way whatever belong to Judaism as such." From this he concludes that "Judaism is really not a religion at all" (125/116).

[30] See, for example, Paul Tillich, *Dynamics of Faith* (New York: Harper & Brothers, 1957), pp. 97–8.

Finally more serious than the tendency to triumphalism is the way in which theologies of accommodation so fundamentally distort the very Christian message they seek to save. By targeting the positivity of the gospel – its concrete embodiment in historical and physical particularity – these thinkers have made a fatal misdiagnosis: intending to save the patient by excising a cancer, they set about removing the heart. The root error, I believe, lies in the false dichotomy of form and content. As theologians have increasingly come to recognize, the "essence" of Christianity – that which makes it what it is, and without which it either dies or becomes something else – lies in a particular configuration of symbolic elements, a paradigmatic structure that is unique and irreducible to other terms. The futility of projects like Kant's that seek to translate the essential content of the gospel into other terms can be compared to that of a teacher trying to teach students Chinese by offering them only texts in translation. As cultural anthropologists have shown us, religions are symbolic systems that are implicated in culture in complex and unpredictable ways, not mere systems of thought that can be abstracted from their cultural context. Theologians like Hans Frei and George Lindbeck have begun to show how Christian theology might incorporate this view of religion. If they are right – and I am persuaded that on the key issues they are – theologians can now hope to articulate the grammar of Christian faith in ways that remain open to dialogue with modern, and even postmodern, secular thought without falling into the errors of accommodationism. As in Kant's day, the theological and secular worlds today are full of voices urging us to abandon the particularity of revelation for the sake of reason and morality ("openness," "pluralism," and "inclusivity" are the preferred terms today). The theological task is to show the futility of such accommodation while reaffirming the integral "positivity" of Christian faith and practice.

At least one eighteenth-century thinker understood this challenge from the start. He was in fact a friend and neighbor of Kant, Johann Georg Hamann. This enigmatic man, who abandoned the Enlightenment after a mysterious conversion experience in London in 1758, who never held an academic post yet influenced not only his contemporaries but later figures like Goethe and Kierkegaard – this odd but orthodox Christian thinker diagnosed with uncanny foresight the errors of accommodationist theology in ways not widely recognized until two centuries later.

3

Against purism: Hamann's metacritique of Kant

... the heart beats before the head thinks.

Hamann

... the proponents of competing paradigms practice their trades in different worlds.

Kuhn

After beginning with a look at Ricoeur's notion of the hermeneutics of suspicion, and attempting to locate ourselves historically in what I am calling the "twilight of modernity," we zeroed in on that watershed figure of modern thought, Immanuel Kant. His book *Religion within the Limits of Reason Alone*, one could argue, was the first book ever written on *religion* – that is, on religion *as such*, as distinct from the Christian or any other of the "positive religions." Our analysis showed us that Kant does not after all simply leave Christianity behind in favor of a rationalized "natural religion"; rather, he seeks to convince us *both* of the necessity of what he calls "pure rational faith" *and* that it is best embodied historically in the Christian reli-

---

The first epigraph is taken from Hamann's Letter to Hans Jacob von Auerswald, 28 July 1785, in *Briefwechsel*, vol. VI, p. 27; translated from W. M. Alexander, *Johann Georg Hamann: Philosophy and Faith* (The Hague: Martinus Nijhoff, 1966), p. 177. The second is from Thomas S. Kuhn, *The Structure of Scientific Revolutions*, 2nd enlarged edn. (Chicago: University of Chicago Press, 1970), p. 19.

gion. To make his case, however, he must subject the Christian gospel to a kind of distillation or winnowing process, in order to separate out the pure kernel of rational faith from the husk of mere "positivity." By so doing, Kant exemplifies a pattern that was to be emulated many times over the following two centuries, a pattern that I have dubbed "accommodationist theology": the endeavor to present Christianity in a form acceptable to the enlightened sensibility of modern people by removing its offensive "positivity." The accommodationist project, however, is fraught with difficulties that have become all too obvious since Kant wrote his book in the waning years of the German Enlightenment. Those difficulties will become more apparent as we follow the origins and development of the hermeneutics of suspicion in the course of the nineteenth century. Only then will we be in a position to consider what response theologians today ought to make to suspicious readings of their tradition.

We will begin once more with Kant, but this time as seen through the insightful and penetrating eyes of his friend and contemporary Johann Georg Hamann: that remarkable and enigmatic figure dubbed by an admirer "the Magus from the North," a modern wise man who sought to follow the star of Bethlehem from his own position in eighteenth-century Königsberg, at the heart of the German Enlightenment.

The central metaphor of enlightenment

When Kant announced his famous definition of enlightenment in 1784, he enshrined a metaphor that had long been a favorite self-definition of European modernity and was destined – in large part as a result of Kant's essay – to become the quasi-official criterion of what it means to be modern. Kant defines *Aufklärung*, as virtually every textbook tells us, as "man's emergence from his self-incurred immaturity" and goes on to explain immaturity as "the inability to use one's own understanding without the guidance of another."[1] At the heart of Kant's definition is a metaphor – or, as we shall see, a combination of two interrelated metaphors. Enlightenment, Kant is saying, is analogous to the passage from the status of minor child to that of adult: enlightened modernity is the adulthood of the human race.

When Hamann, in the same month that Kant's essay on enlightenment appeared, wrote a thank-you note to a friend for sending him a copy, he raised profound questions about the assumptions of the *Aufklärer*, and he did so precisely in terms of Kant's central metaphor of the passage from childhood to adulthood. Hamann's comments in this remarkable letter[2] exemplify what has often been said about him: that he anticipates, in sometimes uncanny ways, criticisms of the Enlightenment that were not generally recognized until long after his lifetime.[3] Indeed, as I hope to demonstrate, Hamann's letter in December 1784 adumbrates several themes that have been elaborated by leading theorists of the twentieth century. Without the benefit of historical hindsight, Hamann recognized the limitations and dangers lurking in Kant's optimistic endorsement of enlightenment, especially as embodied in his focal metaphor. Hamann's own term for that image – *Gleichnis*, a word that entered the German language as the translation of Latin *parabola* and has never lost its biblical associations – already sets him apart from Kant, who surely did not understand himself to be speaking in parables but

---

[1] Immanuel Kant, "An Answer to the Question: 'What Is Enlightenment?'," original German in *Kant's Gesammelte Schriften*, ed. Königlich preussischen Akademie der Wissenschaften, vol. VIII (Berlin: Walter de Gruyter, 1910), p. 35 (hereafter cited as AA, followed by volume and page numbers); translated by H. B. Nisbet in *Kant's Political Writings*, ed. Hans Reiss, trans. H. B. Nisbet, 2nd edn. (Cambridge: Cambridge University Press, 1991), p. 54 (hereafter cited as Reiss, followed by the page number).

[2] An annotated translation of Hamann's letter appears as an appendix to this volume, pp. 207–15.

[3] The comment of Frederick C. Beiser is representative: "Judged by twentieth-century standards, Hamann's thought is often striking for its modernity, its foreshadowing of contemporary themes." *The Fate of Reason: German Philosophy from Kant to Fichte* (Cambridge, MA: Harvard University Press, 1987), p. 17.

rather in clear philosophical concepts. Acknowledging his willingness to be guided by Kant in matters of the understanding (though, significantly, "with a grain of salt"), Hamann identifies the metaphor as the focus of his disagreement with Kant. He can "tolerate gladly," Hamann writes, "seeing enlightenment, if not explained, at least elucidated and expanded more aesthetically than dialectically, through the analogy [*Gleichnis*] of immaturity and guardianship." Before examining Hamann's own "aesthetic" reading of the analogy, we need to attend to the imagery that it employs.

Readers of Kant in English translation are likely to misconstrue the controversial metaphor, or even to overlook it entirely. The crucial concept, *Unmündigkeit*, is generally rendered in English as "immaturity." The trouble with that translation is that it subtly shifts the underlying analogy from a legal[4] to a psychological context. Likewise unavailable to the English reader is the common image linking the correlative terms *Vormund* ("guardian" or "tutor" in most English translations) and *Unmündige* ("immature ones"). Their common root – *Mund* ("mouth") – indicates that the underlying meaning of *unmündig* is being unable to *speak* on one's own behalf. For that purpose one has need of a *Vor-mund*, a legally sanctioned "mouthpiece" to stand *in front of* (*vor*) him – or her – as official spokesman. The closest equivalent in English is the status of being a *minor*, a term with the appropriate legal connotations and for which *guardian* is indeed the correlative term. Not only minor children, however, are *unmündig*. A senile old person might also be assigned a legal guardian. Even more important, *Unmündigkeit* (unlike minority) is tied not only to age but also to gender. As both Kant and Hamann make explicit in their comments on the "fair sex," women were considered

---

[4] Elfriede Büchsel notes that "*Mündigkeit* and *Unmündigkeit* are primarily concepts from the legal world." "Aufklärung und christliche Freiheit: J. G. Hamann contra I. Kant," *Neue Zeitschrift für systematische Theologie* 4 (1962): 141.

unmündig and therefore (in Kant's view) prime candidates for enlightenment. Hamann's intriguing (if cryptic) comments about Kant, women, and his own daughters suggest that one of the later theoretical perspectives he anticipates is feminism.

A major drawback of translating *Unmündigkeit* as "immaturity" is its pejorative implication of childish demeanor. It may be the case that persons deprived of the legal right to speak for themselves suffer the psychological consequence of immature behavior, but the German term emphasizes the legal rather than the psychological or behavioral nuances of immaturity. The absence of adequate English equivalents also obscures the persistence of the metaphor in modern thought and culture. English speakers are unlikely to suspect a connection, for example, between Kant's definition of enlightenment and Dietrich Bonhoeffer's reflections from a Nazi prison about the "world come of age." Yet Bonhoeffer's language is the same as Kant's: he speaks of *die mündiggewordene Welt* in which we moderns live, a world that has exchanged its minority status for responsible adulthood.[5]

The politics of maturity
Hamann's letter of 18 December 1784 to his friend Christian Jacob Kraus,[6] professor of practical philosophy and political science in Königsberg, contains an indictment of the basic enlightenment program expressed in terms of Kant's own metaphors. Hamann finds the key to the root metaphor of immaturity and guardianship (*Unmündigkeit*

---

[5] See, for example, Bonhoeffer's comments in his letter to Eberhard Bethge of 8 June 1944 from Tegel prison. Dietrich Bonhoeffer, *Letters and Papers from Prison*, ed. Eberhard Bethge, enlarged edn. (New York: Macmillan, 1972), pp. 324–9.

[6] According to James C. O'Flaherty, "An especially warm friendship obtained between Hamann and Christian Jakob Kraus, who became professor of practical philosophy and of economics at the university of Königsberg, and who was, next to Kant, the most brilliant docent there. Although much younger than Hamann, Kraus was probably closer to him in his later life than anyone except Herder." *Johann Georg Hamann* (Boston: Twayne Publishers, 1979), p. 33.

and *Vormundschaft*) in a second, unacknowledged metaphor with which it is associated. Kant's essay on enlightenment identifies the problem as "*self-incurred* immaturity." Here too, significant connotations of Kant's language disappear in English translation. The root of what Hamann calls "that accursed adjective *selbstverschuldet*" – *Schuld* – can mean "guilt," "debt," or "fault." Kant is saying that those in need of enlightenment are immature, deprived of the right to speak for themselves, through their own fault; and it is this claim that most arouses Hamann's ire. He returns to the issue repeatedly in the letter, and his language is peppered with allusions to *Schuld* in its various connotations. Employing one of his favorite Greek phrases, he finds the *proton pseudos*, the basic or original error of Kant's program for enlightenment, in that "accursed adjective."

Never questioning the claim that immaturity is the fundamental issue, Hamann presses the question of who is to blame for it. He uncovers a contradiction in Kant's opening words. No sooner has Kant defined *immaturity* as the *inability* to reason on one's own than he calls it *self-incurred*. But, Hamann points out, "inability is really no fault [*Schuld*]," as even Kant will acknowledge. Kant makes it into a fault, Hamann notes, by introducing categories of the *will* in his next sentence. Immaturity, Kant writes, "is *self-incurred* if its cause is not lack of understanding, but lack of resolution and courage to use it without the guidance of another . . . Laziness and cowardice are the reasons why such a large proportion of men . . . gladly remain immature for life." Hamann seizes on the two terms of Kant's indictment of the immature, their lack of resolution (laziness) and their lack of courage (cowardice), and turns them against the accuser.

Those whose wills in fact lack resolution and courage – the truly lazy and cowardly ones – turn out to be not the immature ones but their "enlightened" guardians, among whom is Kant himself. Hamann arrives at this conclusion by pursuing the identity of the one he calls the "indeterminate other" in Kant's essay. If, as Kant had written, "immaturity is the inability to use one's own understanding without the guidance of *another*," this "other" is by definition the guardian, the *Vor-mund* who speaks for the immature. Hamann's suspicions are aroused by the fact that this significant figure appears *anonymously* in Kant's account, evidence for the fact that "the metaphysicians hate to call their persons by their right names." The reason for Kant's reluctance to identify the anonymous "other," Hamann surmises, is that "he reckons himself to the class of guardians," thereby exalting himself above the immature candidates for enlightenment.

Hamann now attacks the project of enlightenment head-on, calling into question the image contained in the term itself, through a series of ironic allusions to darkness and light, blindness and sight, night and day. He contrasts his own "pure & healthy human eyes" to the "moonlight-enlightened eyes of an *Athene glaukopis*," owl-eyed Athena who sees in the dark. The "*inability* or *fault* of the falsely accused immature one" comes not from his own laziness or cowardice but rather from the "blindness of his guardian, who purports to be able to see, and for that very reason must bear the whole responsibility for the fault." Immaturity only becomes culpable, "self-incurred," when "it surrenders to the guidance of a blind ... guardian and leader" – in other words, to an "enlightened" guardian like Kant. Hamann closes his letter with a volley of ironic plays on "en*light*enment": he calls the Enlightenment of his century "a mere northern light," suggesting that the rationalists' program, like the aurora borealis, is both frigid and illusory – "a cold, unfruitful moonlight without enlightenment for the lazy understanding and without warmth for the cowardly will." Such nocturnal enlightenment is a "blind illumination" for the everyday citizen deprived of legal maturity, "who walks at *noon*." In closing Hamann notes that he is writing at dusk ("*entre chien et loup*"), the liminal state between light and darkness. The French phrase was a favorite of Hamann's, for whom the "realm between day and night became a symbol of his eschatological existence between the times."[7]

Recovering the legal context of the metaphor of maturity and immaturity provides a clue to the important political dimensions of the controversy between Hamann and Kant. Both would agree that the enlightenment of individuals is inevitably implicated in a network of social and political forces. Kant's essay defining enlightenment puts the whole question quite explicitly in political terms, most pointedly in his announcement that "our age is the age of enlightenment, the century of *Frederick*."[8] Hamann, writing to a political scientist whom he addresses as *Domine Politice*,[9] does not overlook the implications of Kant's testimonial to their common monarch, toward whom their attitudes could hardly stand in sharper contrast. Büchsel notes that the importance of Frederick the Great as opponent in Hamann's writings has won increasing acknowledgment by scholars.[10] When Frederick assumed the throne from his father in 1740, no less an authority than Voltaire had pronounced him "Le Salomon du Nord," appointed to enlighten the eyes of the Prussian *barbares*. Voltaire's epithet, identifying the king with the Old Testament paradigm of the wise man, places Frederick in symbolic rivalry with Hamann, whom Karl von Moser had dubbed "Magus in Norden" after those other biblical wise men, the New Testament magi.[11] Hamann, who accepted the epithet gracefully, signs the letter containing his critique of Kant with the variant *Magus in telonio*, which calls attention to

---

[7] Oswald Bayer, "Selbstverschuldete Vormundschaft: Hamanns Kontroverse mit Kant um *wahre* Aufklärung," in *Der Wirklichkeitsanspruch von Theologie und Religion*, ed. Dieter Henke, Günter Kehrer and Gunda Schneider-Flume (Tübingen: J. C. B. Mohr [Paul Siebeck], 1976), pp. 27–8.

[8] Kant, "What Is Enlightenment?" (AA, vol. VIII, p. 40; Reiss, p. 58).

[9] Büchsel interprets this form of address to mean that Hamann sees Kraus as one "qualified and authorized to judge political problems." "Aufklärung und christliche Freiheit," p. 145.

[10] Ibid., p. 134, note 4.

[11] See the references cited by O'Flaherty, *Johann Georg Hamann*, p. 25.

his own position as Frederick's unwilling civil servant in the Königsberg customs house.

Hamann's political critique of Kantian enlightenment goes directly to the issue of power. Kant's flattering description of Frederick as "the man who first liberated mankind from immaturity"[12] betrays the *proton pseudos*, the root error of the enlighteners, and it has to do with the question of culpability introduced by Kant's "accursed adjective" *self-incurred*. The telling phrase occurs in Kant's almost incidental remark that the enlightened ruler "has at hand a well-disciplined and numerous army to guarantee public security."[13] In Hamann's sarcastic paraphrase, the purpose of the guardian's army is "to guarantee his infallibility and orthodoxy." As the "anonymous other," Hamann fingers the guardian implied by the very existence of the immature, the *Vormund* whose job it is to speak for the *Unmündige*, and singles him out for the severest censure: he twice calls him "the man of death." Without ever naming the king directly, Hamann lets Kraus know exactly whom he has in mind. The first clue, not decisive by itself, is the epithet "man of death," which apparently alludes to King David's encounter with the prophet Nathan in 2 Samuel 12. This supposition becomes more likely in light of Hamann's predilection for parables as the most appropriate genre for telling the truth. In the same paragraph Hamann casts Kant in the ironic role of prophet: "who is the *other*, of whom the cosmopolitical chiliast prophesies?" But it is surely Hamann himself who intends to play Nathan to Frederick's David, prophesying in parable, allusion, and "maccaronic style" in an effort to catch the conscience of the king – or, if that is expecting too much, at least to warn the consciences of his immature compatriots against the wiles of the "man of death" who has appointed himself their guardian. Such *political* pretension – backed

---

[12] Kant, "What Is Enlightenment?" (AA, vol. VIII, p. 40; Reiss, p. 58).
[13] Kant, "What Is Enlightenment?" (AA, vol. VIII, p. 41; Reiss, p. 59).

up by "a large well-disciplined army" – is the real fault: "the self-incurred guardianship and not immaturity." A more direct clue to the identity of the "other" is Hamann's allusion to him as "this lad Absalom," another figure in the Davidic royal history, who leads an unsuccessful rebellion against his father. Hamann is surely speaking parabolically about Frederick, who as crown prince had (like Absalom) plotted against his own father, King Frederick William, and (again like Absalom) had failed. In one regard, however, Frederick fared better than his biblical prototype: although he spent some time in prison, he – unlike Absalom – survived to become king in the more conventional manner, by waiting out his father's death.

Hamann's political critique takes special aim at Kant's distinction between public and private discourse. Kant had defined their relative spheres in such a way as virtually to reverse their meaning as ordinarily understood. In Hamann's view, Kant's distinction amounts to taking away with the left hand the freedom that he has just granted with the right. "The *public* use of man's reason must always be free, and it alone can bring about enlightenment among men," Kant argues; "the *private use* of reason may quite often be very narrowly restricted, however, without undue hindrance to the progress of enlightenment."[14] Kant's odd use of these terms is governed not by the size of one's audience but rather by one's employer. Reason is used publicly, he writes, by "*a man of learning* addressing the entire *reading public*" – that is, by the self-employed intellectual. It is used privately, on the other hand, by someone performing "in a particular *civil* post or office with which he is entrusted" – that is, by an employee of the political establishment. Kant's three examples of such civil offices – the military officer, the tax collector, and the clergyman – become grist for the mill of Hamann's irony. Kant affirms the right to "argue" (*räsonniern*) to one's heart's content so long as one

---

[14] Kant, "What Is Enlightenment?" (AA, vol. VIII, p. 37; Reiss, p. 55).

obeys one's political masters: "The officer says: Don't argue, get on parade! The tax-official: Don't argue, pay! The clergyman: Don't argue, believe!" The parenthetical tribute to Frederick that Kant appends is hardly calculated to reassure Hamann: "Only one ruler in the world says: *Argue* as much as you like and about whatever you like, *but obey!*"[15] Hamann's sarcastic rejoinder in the letter to Kraus goes right to the underlying political and economic relations:

> So doesn't it all come to the same thing? – believe, get on parade, pay, if the d— is not to take you. Is it not *sottise des trois parts*? And which is the greatest and most difficult? An army of priests [*Pfaffen*] or of thugs, henchmen, and purse snatchers?

For Hamann, here speaking in his proto-Marxist voice, it all comes down in the end to "the financial exploitation of immature persons" by their self-appointed political guardians. This "enlightened" political arrangement is what Hamann, in the phrase that pithily sums up his whole critique of Kant, calls "a supremely *self-incurred guardianship*." The guilt, in other words, has been attributed to the wrong party; Kant is blaming the victims. The onus of guilt should be removed from the oppressed and imputed to the oppressors – including their philosophical apologists.

Hamann's extended commentary on public and private comes in a postscript that is at once the most trenchant and the most difficult passage in the letter. He calls Kant's distinction "comical," but he doesn't appear to be laughing. He sees it as a distinction without a difference, but one that is nevertheless politically dangerous because it gives aid and comfort to "enlightened" tyrants. In language suggestive of the Chalcedonian definition of Christ's "two natures in one person," Hamann identifies the problem as that of "unifying the two natures of an *immature person &*

---

[15] Ibid.

guardian," though not in the way Kant wants to do it. "Here," he says, "lies precisely the nub of the whole political problem." What follows, however, is a character-istically "maccaronic" barrage of metaphor and allusion, involving a New Testament parable and passages from St. Paul, Boethius, and Kant. Apparently borrowing imagery from Jesus' parable of the king's wedding feast in Matthew 22, Hamann first asks rhetorically: "What good to me is the *festive garment* of freedom when I am in a slave's smock at home?" Kantian "public" freedom is of little use to a civil servant like Hamann, who is "privately" enslaved in the king's service.

There follows the most arcane passage in the letter, in which Hamann's proto-Marxian political critique in terms of money and power appears to take on a feminist colora-tion as well: "Does Plato [i.e. Kant] too belong to the *fair sex*[?] – which he slanders like an old bachelor." The inter-pretive puzzle here is why Hamann would infer a similarity between Kant and women. Has he not already demon-strated that Kant wants to set himself up as the enlightened guardian of women and other immature persons? The key lies in Hamann's allusion to the passage in 1 Corinthians where Paul argues that "women should keep silence in the churches" (1 Corinthians 14.35). It is essential to bear in mind that Hamann, unlike many feminists today, acknowl-edges the authority even of scriptural passages that seem to oppose his own opinions. So the Pauline passage is presum-ably cited in earnest. Hamann appears, in fact, to remove any suggestion that the apostle is deprecating women by juxtaposing Boethius' association between keeping silent and being a philosopher. The implication would seem to be that women, by remaining silent in accordance with the biblical precept, behave more like philosophers than those (like Kant?) who are full of words.

Even harder to explain, however, is the apparent contra-diction in the passage that immediately follows. Still speaking of women, Hamann writes:

At home (i.e., at the lectern and on the stage and in the pulpit) they may chatter to their hearts' content. There they speak as guardians and must forget everything & contradict everything as soon as, in their own self-incurred immaturity, they are to do indentured labor for the state.

According to Kant's classification, the professional activities of teachers ("at the lectern"), actors ("on the stage"), and preachers ("in the pulpit") are *private*, since they involve performance "in a particular *civil* post or office" entrusted to them. But that would imply that they are *not* free to "chatter to their hearts' content" in those situations. The key to the apparent contradiction lies in the phrase "at home" (*daheim*), which Hamann has used twice already in the postscript. Kant, speaking specifically of religion, had written that the ecclesiastical teacher's use of reason is private, "since a congregation, however large it is, is never any more than a domestic [*häusliche*] gathering."[16] This identification of the congregation as domestic makes clear how Hamann could use *daheim* to refer to activities such as those "in the pulpit." Applying Kant's logic to the Pauline passage, Hamann shows the absurdity of Kant's position by drawing the conclusion that women should be able to chatter away in such "domestic" (private) places as the lectern, the stage, and the pulpit. But in those very roles, according to Kant, people speak as guardians and thus have to give up their freedom of speech as good, "private" servants of the state – thereby becoming immature through their own fault. This bizarre reversal comes about by superimposing the Pauline distinction between congregation and home on the Kantian one between public and private. Paul says that women must remain silent in the congregation but may speak at home; Kant, by making the congregation "domestic," identifies it with the realm of free speech. Here the contradiction at the heart of Kant's distinction stands

---

[16] Kant, "What Is Enlightenment?" (AA, vol. VIII, p. 38; Reiss, p. 57).

exposed, for rather than allowing freedom of speech in the congregation, he subjects it to the constraints of "private" reasoning. Hamann has thus demonstrated not only the absurdity of Kant's distinction between public and private but also his violation of scriptural authority. Kantian sleight of hand has turned the "public" free use of reason into a mere "sumptuous dessert," while enslaving the "private" use, which is "the *daily bread* that we should give up for its sake." This phrase resonates with the language of the Lord's Prayer, which includes both a petition for "our daily bread" and a plea to "forgive us our debts [*Schuld*]," by which allusion Hamann returns to the underlying issue of culpability.

The feminist twist comes just at this point: "The *self-incurred immaturity is* just such a sneer as he makes at the whole fair sex, and which my three daughters will not put up with." Hamann has shown that Kant's linkage of guilt with the social status of immaturity amounts to a slander against women, who thus come to stand for all those deprived of a political voice. By falsely blaming these victims for their *Unmündigkeit*, Kant implicitly makes himself their *Vormund*, thus acquiring the actual guilt of the "self-incurred" guardian. Hamann's transfiguration of Kant's enlightenment – his *Verklärung* of *Aufklärung*, as he puts it – leads to his radically different definition of "*true enlightenment*" as the "emergence of the immature person from a supremely *self-incurred guardianship*." Kant is right that the problem is the liberation of the immature, but he chooses the wrong target for his critique: it is not the women and other voiceless groups who incur guilt but rather the "enlightened" monarchs and their court philosophers.

Hamann's critique of Kantian purism
For all its immediacy and the specificity of the issues it handles, Hamann's letter to Kraus is also a key to more general and fundamental differences between these two contemporaries. One significant clue appears near the

beginning of the letter, when Hamann first speaks of Kant. In calling attention to the *Gleichnis*, the parable or metaphor at the heart of Kant's definition of enlightenment, Hamann is at the same time demonstrating his own critical method, which he calls "aesthetic," in contrast to the "dialectical" method preferred by Kant. "Poetry is the mother-tongue of the human race," Hamann writes in his *Aesthetica in nuce*; and "parables [*Gleichnisse*] [are] older than reasoning."[17] Oswald Bayer notes the irony in this situation: "The strict 'dialectician' Kant, 'professor of logic and critic of pure reason,' employs a metaphor [*Gleichnis*] without being aware of it, thus explaining the 'Enlightenment' aesthetically."[18] Today we might say that Hamann *deconstructs* Kant's argument, for he shows how Kant implicitly depends on a kind of reasoning that he explicitly rejects; Hamann demonstrates an "aesthetic" subtext subverting the "dialectical" text of the Kantian critical philosophy. No better example could be found to illustrate Hamann's relationship to Kantian philosophy, the relationship expressed technically in the title of Hamann's best-known treatment of Kant, the "Metacritique on the Purism of Reason."[19]

Hamann composed this brief but trenchant analysis of Kant's *Critique of Pure Reason* in the same year as the letter to Kraus, 1784, but did not publish it during his lifetime because of his friendship with Kant. Largely on the basis of Hamann's "Metacritique," Frederick C. Beiser calls him "the most original, powerful, and influential critic" of Kant's attempt to vindicate the "Enlightenment faith in the universality and impartiality of reason."[20] The radicalness of Hamann's critique of the Kantian critical philosophy is

---

[17] J. G. Hamann, *Sämtliche Werke*, ed. Josef Nadler (Vienna: Herder, 1949–57), vol. II, p. 197; translated in *German Aesthetic and Literary Criticism: Winckelmann, Lessing, Hamann, Herder, Schiller, Goethe*, ed. H. B. Nisbet (Cambridge: Cambridge University Press, 1985), p. 141.

[18] Bayer, "Selbstverschuldete Vormundschaft," pp. 17–18.

[19] Hamann, "Metakritik über den Purismum der Vernunft," in *Sämtliche Werke*, vol. III, pp. 281–9; trans. Kenneth Haynes, in Schmidt, ed., *What Is Enlightenment?*, pp. 154–67.

[20] Beiser, *Fate of Reason*, pp. 8–9.

concentrated in the prefix "meta-," which Rudolf Unger credits him with introducing into German philosophical discussion.[21] For that tiny syllable does to Kant's project the one thing it cannot tolerate: it relativizes the critical philosophy by placing it within a more comprehensive context of interpretation. As Beiser puts it, "The tribunal of critique spoke with such awesome authority not only because its principles were self-evident, but also because they were universal and impartial."[22] If a *meta*critique is possible, the critique loses its claim to these qualities, and thus to its foundational status.

Hamann's principal objection to Kant's philosophy, expressed in the title he chose for his treatment of it, is its "purism" – that is, its attempt to rid knowledge of any intrinsic connection with tradition, experience, or language. The first "purism," Hamann writes, is the "attempt to make reason independent of all tradition and custom and belief in them," while the second seeks "independence from experience and its everyday induction." By far the most interesting and fateful of Kant's attempted purifications is the desire to free reason from "*language*, the only, first, and last organon and criterion of reason, with no credentials but *tradition* and *usage*."[23] Hamann recognizes that language is not only the foundation of rational thought but "also the *center of reason's misunderstanding with itself*," and he therefore concludes that "*sounds* and *letters* are then pure forms a priori." Here Hamann foreshadows a broad range of twentieth-century thinkers who have found in language the key to philosophical conundrums. His stress on tradition likewise presages the attention of later thinkers to the

---

[21] Rudolf Unger, *Hamann und die Aufklärung: Studien zur Vorgeschichte des romantischen Geistes im 18. Jahrhundert* (Jena: Eugen Diederichs, 1911), vol. I, p. 526. It should be noticed, however, that Hamann himself is ironic in his use of "meta-," calling it "the accidental synthesis of a Greek *prefix*" (*Sämtliche Werke*, vol. III, p. 285; *What Is Enlightenment?*, p. 155).

[22] Beiser, *Fate of Reason*, p. 8.

[23] Hamann, "Metacritique" (*Sämtliche Werke*, vol. III, p. 284; *What Is Enlightenment?*, p. 155).

cultural location of ideas and systems of thought. Hamann affirms the "genealogical superiority of *language* ... over the *seven* holy functions of logical propositions and inferences."[24] Kant's wish to "purify" philosophy of its dependence on language rests, according to Hamann, on "nothing more than an old, cold prejudice for mathematics."[25] He expresses with particular clarity the antithesis between the foundational role of language in his own thought and of reason in Kant's in a letter to Jacobi written in 1784, the same year as both the "Metacritique" and the letter to Kraus:

> For me the question is not so much What is reason? as What is language? It is here I suspect the basis of all paralogisms and antinomies can be found which are ascribed to reason: it comes from words being held to be concepts, and concepts to be the things themselves.[26]

This stress on language above reason is the basis of Hamann's "metacritique" of the Kantian critical philosophy, and it is one of the aspects of his thought that anticipates twentieth-century philosophical issues in a most surprising way for an eighteenth-century figure.

Hamann's appeal to language and experience as the ground of reason rests on a still more basic disagreement with Kant. For if one asks why language should be the criterion of reason, Hamann appeals to the priority of the sensual over the intellectual, which amounts to an appeal to the bodily – and even sexual – basis of human language, experience, and thought. Here we encounter the most surprising of Hamann's anticipations of later thinkers. A century before Freud, the pivotal importance of sexuality was

---

[24] Hamann, "Metacritique" (*Sämtliche Werke*, vol. III, p. 286; *What Is Enlightenment?*, p. 156); emphasis altered to agree with original.

[25] Hamann, "Metacritique" (*Sämtliche Werke*, vol. III, p. 285; *What Is Enlightenment?*, p. 156).

[26] Johann Georg Hamann, *Briefwechsel*, ed. Arthur Henkel (Frankfurt: Insel-Verlag, 1965), vol. V, pp. 264–5. I have revised the translation in Ronald Gregor Smith, *J. G. Hamann, 1730–1788: A Study in Christian Existence* (New York: Harper & Brothers, 1960), p. 249.

acknowledged by a thinker whose life, values, and philosophical principles are about as far from Freud's as one could possibly imagine. Hamann's emphasis on sexuality follows from his insistence on the priority of sense over intellect.[27] Language, rather than "pure" reason, has philosophical priority because "the entire faculty of thought [is] founded on language"; but language in turn depends on the body. "The oldest language was music," he claims, "and next to the palpable rhythm of the pulse and of the breath in the nostrils, it was the original bodily image of all *temporal measurements* and ratios."[28] Hamann's point in stressing the bodily foundation of thought is not to exalt sense over reason; he intends, rather, to restore the original integrity that Kant's purism threatens. Since "sensibility and understanding spring as two branches of human knowledge from one common root," he writes, Kant errs by perpetrating "an arbitrary, improper and self-willed divorce of that which nature has joined together."

Hamann's treatment of sexuality differs from other writers who use sexual imagery and analogies because, as James C. O'Flaherty points out, "his allusions stem from an epistemological principle."[29] That principle is rooted in Hamann's holistic conception of human nature, which, W. M. Alexander argues, has been "secularized in Romanticism and distorted in Kierkegaard and existentialism."[30] Hamann's point is not to exalt will over intellect or emotions over reason but rather to respect the integrity of what nature – and God – has joined together. The error of Kantian purism is that it violates the bodily basis of that integrity: "*Sensus,*" he writes, "is the principle of all *intellectus*";[31]

---

[27] For an instructive treatment of the theme of sexuality in Hamann, see O'Flaherty, *Johann Georg Hamann*, chapter 2, especially pp. 38–42.

[28] Hamann, "Metacritique" (*Sämtliche Werke*, vol. III, p. 286; *What Is Enlightenment?*, p. 156).

[29] O'Flaherty, *Johann Georg Hamann*, p. 40.

[30] Alexander, *Johann Georg Hamann*, p. 177.

[31] Letter to Jacobi, 14 November 1784, in *Briefwechsel*, vol. VI, p. 27.

"the *heart* beats before the *head* thinks."[32] But Hamann is also capable of making the point in explicitly sexual terms. "The *pudenda* of our nature," he wrote to Johann Friedrich Hartknoch (once again in 1784), "are so closely connected with the chambers of the heart and the brain that too strict an abstraction of such a natural bond is impossible."[33] Some years earlier he had confessed to Herder that "my crude imagination has never been able to picture a creative spirit without genitalia."[34] Hamann's unflinching insistence on the importance of sexuality – its *epistemological* importance, in particular – sets him apart from all the major voices of his time, whether those of Enlightenment rationalism, theological orthodoxy, or the "neologians," the theological progressives of his day.

Hamann's unfashionable attention to sex turns out to provide an unexpected clue to the underlying motive of his attack on Kant and the Enlightenment. At the root of his philosophical and political critique is a theological commitment to biblical revelation. The earthiness of his view of human nature and human knowledge probably owes more to his immersion in the Bible and the writings of Luther than to any contemporary influences. Hamann's break with the Enlightenment had come, after all, as a direct result of his own dramatic, if rather mysterious, conversion in London in 1758. From the day he arrived back in Königsberg to the end of his life, he demonstrated an unflagging tenacity in his adherence to a Christian sensibility that left him immune to the endeavors of his enlightened friends, including Kant, to win him back to the cause, and made him remarkably independent of the spirit of the age.

Hamann liked to describe his own vocation as "spermalogian," a term whose ambiguity links the theological and

---

[32] Letter to Hans Jacob von Auerswald, 28 July 1785, in *Briefwechsel*, vol. VI, p. 27; translated from Alexander, *Johann Georg Hamann*, p. 177.

[33] *Briefwechsel*, vol. IV, p. 167; I have revised the translation in Alexander, *Johann Georg Hamann*, pp. 177–8.

[34] Letter of 23 May 1768, in *Briefwechsel*, vol. 2, p. 415.

sexual themes in his thought. It is first of all a biblical term (Acts 17.18), whose literal meaning ("picking up seeds," used of birds) had come to be used metaphorically of persons to mean "gossip," "chatterer," or "babbler."[35] Interpreters of Hamann are in general agreement, however, that he intends the sexual implications of the word as well. In his biblical commentary written shortly after his conversion in London, Hamann comments that "our reason should be impregnated by the seed of the divine word . . . and live as man and wife under one roof." The devil endeavors, he says, to disrupt this marital bliss, seeking not only "to put asunder what God has joined together" but "in our times to institute a formal divorce between them, and to titillate the reason through systems, dreams, etc."[36] The Bible should be our criterion, "our dictionary, our linguistics, on which all the concepts and speech of the Christian are founded."[37] Reason, on the other hand, plays a role for the Christian analogous to that of the law for the apostle Paul. Hamann puts it this way in 1759:

> the commandment of reason is holy, just, and good. But is it given to us – to make us wise? No more than the law of the Jews was given to justify them, but rather to convince us of the opposite: how unreasonable our reason is; that our errors are to be increased by it, just as sin was increased by the law. If everywhere Paul speaks of the law one puts *reason* – the law of our century and the watchword of our wise men and scribes – then Paul will speak to our contemporaries.[38]

Twenty-four years later he uses the same analogy in a letter to Jacobi: "You know that I think of reason as St. Paul does of the whole law and its righteousness – that I expect of it

---

[35] William F. Arndt and F. Wilbur Gingrich, *A Greek–English Lexicon of the New Testament and Other Early Christian Literature* (Chicago: University of Chicago Press, 1957), p. 769.

[36] *Sämtliche Werke*, vol. I, pp. 52–3.

[37] Ibid., p. 243.

[38] Letter to Johann Gotthelf Lindner, 3 July 1759, in *Briefwechsel*, vol. I, pp. 355–6. I have revised the translation in Alexander, *Johann Georg Hamann*, p. 153.

nothing but the recognition of error, and do not regard it as a way to truth and life."[39] Human reason unfertilized by the Word of God, concludes the self-professed "spermalogian," is like the law without the gospel, like the letter without the life-giving spirit: while retaining its formal validity, it nevertheless kills.

Given the vast difference between Hamann's theologically grounded "linguistics" and Kant's philosophical commitment to a critical "purism," their disagreement about the Enlightenment quest for maturity was inevitable. The gulf separating Hamann from Kant and his contemporaries has not always been sufficiently taken into account by his interpreters. Even Oswald Bayer, who as a theologian himself is aware of the theological basis of Hamann's critique, tries to portray him as a radical *Aufklärer*, one in whom "the Enlightenment is driven further, radicalized."[40] But when a position is so radicalized that its basic premise and criterion of truth is called into question, that amounts to a new position, not an extension of the old. This becomes even clearer in Hamann's attack on the ideal of "purism" so fundamental to the whole project of critical philosophy. Such a position is not just a correction of Kant but a fundamental rejection in favor of another and more adequate criterion. Hamann's method is more like Hegel's practice of showing how the dialectical tensions within a position finally cause it to collapse into its opposite. A more contemporary comparison might be deconstruction, which tries to subvert the text by turning its own unacknowledged premises against it. As Bayer himself repeatedly emphasizes, Hamann's objective is not to reform Kant but to *convert* him. It is a battle between advocates of rival paradigms, not a disagreement among fellow *Aufklärer*. Bayer is right in rejecting the interpretation of Hamann as an

[39] Letter of 2 November 1783, in *Briefwechsel*, vol. V, p. 95, following the translation in Smith, *J. G. Hamann*, p. 248.
[40] Oswald Bayer, *Zeitgenosse im Widerspruch: Johann Georg Hamann als radikaler Aufklärer* (Munich: Piper, 1988), p. 145.

"irrationalist."[41] But he apparently assumes that the only alternative to enlightenment is "irrationality." Since this term does not adequately describe Hamann's position, Bayer is forced to see him as some kind of enlightener. But Hamann speaks on behalf of a radically *different* concept of reason from that of the *Aufklärer* – one based not on human autonomy but on the "fear of the Lord."

Incommensurability in science and theology

Borrowing a concept from the new philosophy of science, I have said that Kant and Hamann differ so radically because they are committed to rival paradigms. Thomas Kuhn, trying to characterize the discontinuities that periodically appear in the history of science when a new paradigm arises to challenge the authority of an established one, actually says at one point that the only way for a scientist to move from one paradigm to another is through a "conversion."[42] When Bayer proposes that Hamann wants to *convert* Kant, he is pointing to just such a radical discontinuity between their ways of thinking, for they imagine the world according to irreconcilable paradigms.

The issues involved in cases of radical paradigm change have led to a particularly intense debate in recent philosophy of science – one with important implications for theology as well – centering on the notion of *incommensurability*. The controversy concerns the logical discontinuities that Kuhn discovered in the history of science – most notoriously in his idea of scientific revolutions – and which many philosophers now take to be an essential aspect of the scientific investigation of nature. The corresponding notion in theology is *fideism*, a religious standpoint that makes no attempt to justify itself in rational terms that might persuade outsiders to the faith, a description that has

---

[41] A notable example of this misreading of Hamann is Sir Isaiah Berlin's book *The Magus of the North: J. G. Hamann and the Origins of Modern Irrationalism*, ed. Henry Hardy (London: J. Murray, 1993).

[42] Kuhn, *Structure of Scientific Revolutions*, p. 19.

sometimes been applied to Hamann. My contention is that the underlying issue concerns the positivity of gospel, and that the issues of incommensurability and fideism are therefore crucial topics in the late modern crisis of hermeneutics. The charge brought against Kuhn and others who stress the incommensurability of paradigms is that they introduce an element of irrationality into the heart of the scientific enterprise, a move that both undermines the legitimate work of scientists and offers aid and comfort to the enemies of science. The corresponding charge in theology is that such relativistic concepts lead to an irrational fideism that severs the essential link between faith and reason while leaving believers immunized against criticism and therefore isolated from serious intellectual inquiry in the modern world. Such charges, however, in both science and theology, misunderstand the logic of incommensurability by confusing it with two related but quite different concepts, incomparability and incompatibility. Logical holism, which entails the incommensurability of paradigms, far from being irrational, is essential to a right understanding of the rationality of both science and religion. The positivity of the Christian gospel is a consequence of its logical holism that cannot be abandoned, for apologetic or any other reasons, without betraying its central message.

According to its critics, the idea of incommensurability, taken by many to be "the most exotic, controversial, and perhaps vaguest theme" in recent discussions of science, "opens the door to everything that is objectionable – subjectivism, irrationalism, and nihilism."[43] These critics have in mind certain statements made by Kuhn in *The Structure of Scientific Revolutions*. In describing aspects of "the incommensurability of competing paradigms," he made the following remark: "In a sense that I am unable to explicate

---

[43] Richard J. Bernstein, *Beyond Objectivism and Relativism: Science, Hermeneutics, and Praxis* (Philadelphia: University of Pennsylvania Press, 1985), p. 79, characterizing views of the opponents of postempiricist philosophy of science.

further, the proponents of competing paradigms practice their trades in different worlds."[44] No statement by Kuhn has had so polarizing an effect on the discussion as this one, and none has been subject to a wider range of interpretation. The notion of multiple worlds has inspired enthusiastic emulation by some and irritable dismissal by others. William E. Paden, in his religious studies textbook entitled *Religious Worlds*, describes the concept of *world* as "the comparative category par excellence," preferring it explicitly to *beliefs* as a way of characterizing the differences among religious traditions.[45] The opposite response to the idea of a plurality of worlds is represented by the philosopher Donald Davidson, who, after citing Kuhn and a similar point by Strawson, comments, "Since there is at most one world, these pluralities are metaphorical or merely imagined."[46] Leaving aside for the moment Davidson's tendentious attribution of "merely" to "imagined," I want to examine the conceptual issue that lies behind the metaphor of multiple worlds.

The debate about incommensurability has been plagued by rhetorical excess and philosophical unclarity. Richard Bernstein shows how incommensurability has often been confused with two related but quite different terms, *incomparability* and *incompatibility*. He argues that critics of Kuhn and Feyerabend have taken their "remarks about incommensurability . . . to mean that we cannot *compare* rival paradigms or theories," an assumption that Bernstein finds "not only mistaken but perverse."[47] His rejoinder, that the whole point of introducing the concept of incommensurability was to aid in comparing rival paradigms, is right on the mark. Not only critics but also enthusiastic proponents

---

[44] Kuhn, *Structure of Scientific Revolutions*, p. 150.
[45] William E. Paden, *Religious Worlds: The Comparative Study of Religion*, 2nd edn. (Boston: Beacon Press, 1994), pp. xiii and 7.
[46] Donald Davidson, "On the Very Idea of a Conceptual Scheme," in *Inquiries into Truth and Interpretation* (Oxford: Clarendon Press, 1984), p. 187.
[47] Bernstein, *Beyond Objectivism and Relativism*, p. 82 (Bernstein's emphasis).

of incommensurability have sometimes identified it with incomparability. Religious thinkers have been especially prone to this move, which appears to offer a useful apologetic device against the relativism of comparative religion. This attitude is well expressed in the quip (whose author I don't recall) that "comparative religion makes people comparatively religious." The assumption behind this remark raises the issue of relativism, which I will take up explicitly in the final chapter. Leaving that matter aside for the moment, I want to focus on the defensive strategy that some have employed against it: namely, to insist that religions are incommensurable, with the (usually implicit) assumption that they are therefore incomparable.

The religious position to which this strategy leads has frequently been labeled *fideism*. The tension in Christianity between those who stress the rationality of Christian truth and those who base theology on faith, of course, runs throughout the history of Western thought. Religious thinkers from Tertullian in the patristic age to the theological admirers of Wittgenstein in our own time have been labeled fideists. The high point of premodern fideism came in the late Middle Ages, when extreme skepticism about the ability of human reason to attain knowledge of God led some Christian thinkers – especially those influenced by William of Ockham – to assert that only faith in divine revelation allows human beings to know anything of God. The effect was to undermine the rational foundations of faith, thus severing the link between faith and reason. "At one and the same time," in the words of historian Gordon Leff, "a growing empiricism was giving rise to a growing fideism."[48]

In view of the importance of fideism as an issue in ancient and medieval theology, the term itself is surprisingly recent. The *Oxford English Dictionary* places the

---

[48] Gordon Leff, *Medieval Thought: St. Augustine to Ockham* (London: Merlin Press, 1958), p. 291.

earliest occurrence of the word in 1885. So it is a modern term, one that has been formulated in the context of Enlightenment oppositions between religion and science, authority and autonomy, faith and reason. One encounters it especially among Roman Catholic traditionalists and positivist philosophers. What these groups have in common is a conviction that faith and reason represent two distinct avenues to knowledge and truth. Among the canons of the Vatican Council of 1870–1 is the following:

> If any one shall say that divine revelation cannot be made credible by outward signs, and therefore that men ought to be moved to faith solely by the internal experience of each, or by private inspiration: let him be anathema.[49]

Catholic neoscholasticism, taking up themes from medieval Thomism and adapting them to a world dominated by modern science, insisted that the truths of faith could not in principle be opposed to science properly conceived. The complement to the doctrine that reason cannot be invoked against the Church's faith is the teaching that faith must not be presented as something irrational. To base one's convictions on sheer faith as opposed to reason thus constitutes the error of fideism. The theologian most responsible for the identification of this error was Joseph Kleutgen, chief architect of the First Vatican Council's Apostolic Constitution on Faith.[50] He contrasted fideism, the error of denying a role to unaided reason in human knowledge of God, to semirationalism, which allowed reason too great a role. For positivists the logic is similar even though their evaluation of faith is negative. Since faith is an illegitimate claim to knowledge without rational warrants, any position appealing to faith as a source of knowledge falls into the error of fideism.

---

[49] Schaff, *Creeds of Christendom*, vol. II, p. 253.
[50] Gerald A. McCool, *Catholic Theology in the Nineteenth Century: The Quest for a Unitary Method* (New York: Seabury Press, 1977), p. 2.

In an effort to clarify what is meant by fideism, I want to suggest that the term has three distinct, if not entirely separate, senses in its modern context. The first and most obvious type of fideism claims that theological statements can be justified only by direct appeal to the authority of revelation. This view, which we can call *authoritarian* fideism, is the kind that was first identified as an error by Roman Catholic dogmaticians in the late nineteenth century. It is typically equated with the traditionalism of figures like De Bonald and Lammenais. A Protestant version is sometimes identified with critics of the Enlightenment such as Hamann and Jacobi.[51] A second variety of fideism claims that theological statements can be verified only by appeal to the immediate experience of individuals or groups. This position, which might be called *experiential* fideism, is characteristic not of theological conservatives or traditionalists but rather of liberals. Unless you have had the experience, the argument goes, you cannot understand or evaluate the doctrine. Here the appeal is not to objective or established authority but rather to private or privileged experience. The most recent and controversial type of fideism, which I will call *relativistic*, involves the claim that theological statements have meaning only within their own paradigm, conceptual scheme, or language game. It is therefore impossible to evaluate them according to any external criterion. This is the position dubbed "Wittgensteinian Fideism" by Kai Nielsen in the title of his well-known 1967 article.[52] Attributing the doctrine to a number of Wittgenstein's disciples, including Peter Winch and Norman Malcolm, Nielsen stops short of blaming the master himself. He agrees with the Wittgensteinians that

---

[51] See the article on "Fideismus," in *Die Religion in Geschichte und Gegenwart: Handwörterbuch für Theologie und Religionswissenschaft*, 3rd rev. edn., ed. Kurt Galling (Tübingen: J. C. B. Mohr [Paul Siebeck], 1957–1962), vol. VI, pp. 985–6; and James C. Livingston, *Modern Christian Thought*, 2nd edn. (Upper Saddle River, NJ: Prentice-Hall, 1997), pp. 142–61.

[52] Kai Nielsen, "Wittgensteinian Fideism," *Philosophy: The Journal of the Royal Institute of Philosophy* 42 (1967): 191–209.

"to understand religious discourse one must have a participant's understanding of it," but he does "*not* agree that the first-order discourse of religion is in order as it is" or that "philosophy cannot relevantly criticise religions or forms of life." He is particularly critical of Winch for arguing that "an ongoing form of life . . . guarantees intelligibility and reality to the concepts in question."[53] He complains about the "compartmentalization of language," claiming "that there is no separate religious language," and that people "can and do come to doubt the very coherence of this religious mode of life and its first-order talk."[54] Nielsen's critique has been seconded by a number of philosophers and theologians who object to the use of cultural relativism as an apologetic device to immunize religious discourse against outside critique.

The "faith" appealed to in the three kinds of fideism thus varies markedly: institutional religious authority, personal experience, and insider status. The opponents of fideism, whether neo-Thomist theologians or positivist philosophers, nevertheless agree that the alternative to faith is reason, conceived as a faculty unencumbered by authority, dogma, or experience. But it is just that assumption that marks the discussion so clearly as *modern*. If all data are theory-laden, then the purity to which the opponents of fideism aspire is illusory. But this point is precisely the one made in the eighteenth century by Hamann against Kant in the "Metacritique on the Purism of Reason." Hamann's response to Kant shows both why he has been labeled a fideist and why his insights call into question the very presuppositions of the notion of fideism. If Hamann and the new philosophers of science are right that no theoretical constructions can or ought to be kept "pure" of cultural and linguistic commitments, then we are left to wonder

---

[53] Ibid., pp. 193, 199. The key texts by Winch are "Understanding a Primitive Society," *American Philosophical Quarterly* 1 (1964): 307–25, and *The Idea of a Social Science and Its Relation to Philosophy* (New York: Humanities Press, 1958).

[54] Nielsen, "Wittgensteinian Fideism," pp. 205–7.

what has become of fideism. Either there is no such thing
as a fideist, or we are all fideists, since all of us necessarily
employ concepts forged in the foundry of tradition,
custom, and language.

Does the concept of fideism have any coherent and legitimate use in a postmodern world? I believe there is a kernel
of truth in the notion that can be salvaged by reconceiving
fideism as an ethical rather than a methodological issue.
What the three rather different types of fideist arguments
have in common is the avoidance of rational accountability
for theological statements. The fideist ought to be blamed,
not for appealing to faith rather than reason, but for refus-
ing to engage in critical dialogue with those who do not
share his faith. It is one thing to insist that one's faith is
incommensurable with another position; but it is quite
another to claim exemption from criticism on the grounds
that incommensurability implies incomparability. Paradigms, because they are holistic in character, force the critic
into a kind of all-or-nothing position: *either* one must think
on the basis of this paradigm, *or* one must replace it with
another paradigm. But one may wish to do just that –
replace the paradigm in question with another – and may
be able to adduce good reasons for doing so. The point is
that it cannot be done piecemeal, because the "pieces"
belong to a larger pattern, and it is to that pattern as a
whole that analysis and criticism must be directed. Here we
encounter the so-called hermeneutical circle in a form that
allows us to see what is at stake. The mutual interdepen-
dence of parts and whole implies not that the pattern they
constitute is immune from critique but rather that it is precisely the constitutive pattern that must be the object of
criticism. It is illegitimate to examine the "parts" in
abstraction from the whole pattern that makes them parts
in the first place. So the issue is not *whether* one can compare competing paradigm commitments but *how*. And the
holistic nature of paradigms implies that the comparison
must take place at the level of the *whole*, not that of the

parts. Incommensurability does not imply incomparability.

The situation is more complicated in the case of incompatibility. Or rather, the *reality* is more complicated, for the philosophical point can be stated quite simply: it all depends! Negatively, the point can be put this way: from the fact of the incommensurability of two paradigmatic wholes, we cannot conclude anything at all about their compatibility or incompatibility; the issue must be decided on a case-by-case basis. The shifting-*Gestalt* figure called the duck-rabbit, made famous by Ludwig Wittgenstein, is a case in point. That the two figures, duck and rabbit, are incommensurable can be demonstrated by the fact that both "wholes" lay claim to the same territory: those looping lines on the right may be seen *either* as the rabbit's ears *or* the duck's bill but not as both at the same time. As soon as one names a part ("ears," "bill") one already signals commitment to one of two incommensurable wholes ("rabbit," "duck"). The very fact that one can choose, however, shows that the two figures are *compatible*. This particular set of lines allows either of two incommensurable figures to be imagined. The two figures therefore appear to be compatible with one another. One has a choice; and the choice is precisely one of imagination: I can imagine the figure as a duck, or I can imagine it as a rabbit. The importance of the duck-rabbit figure is that it isolates the act of imagination so that we may see it for what it is. All that differentiates duck from rabbit is imagination, the ability to grasp the figure *as* one particular coherent whole-in-parts rather than another.

Scripture and incommensurability

But are they really compatible? The issue of compatibility is difficult to abstract from real-life situations. Take a religious example – one that concerns the canon of scripture and raises hermeneutical questions. The thirty-nine writings that Jews call Bible or Tanakh and Christians call the Old Testament have been appropriated by the two traditions in different ways. They are paradigmatic for both traditions, and the paradigms appear to be incommensurable in a way similar to the duck-rabbit. To read these texts as containing a promise that finds fulfillment in Jesus as the Messiah of Israel is incommensurable with reading it as the story of the Jewish people coming to live as an independent nation in their own land and looking forward to the time when all Jews will return under the rule of God's Messiah. The former reading, of course, is the one that became normative in the church, the latter in the synagogue. Viewed in the real-life context of historical Judaism and Christianity, the paradigms of Tanakh and Old Testament appear to be incompatible as well as incommensurable, as evidenced by the fact that a community seeking to live by one of these paradigms must necessarily reject the other. The visual paradigms of duck and rabbit appear compatible to us precisely because they make no claims on us beyond our field of vision. Within that field, however, they are in fact incompatible, as evidenced by the fact that one cannot simultaneously see both duck and rabbit. Only in this way does the duality duck/rabbit model the duality Tanakh/Old Testament. The historical moment at which the duality became manifest is epitomized by a passage in Justin Martyr's *Dialogue with Trypho*, which may well be based on an actual encounter. At one point in the argument the Christian Justin says to Trypho the Jew that passages about Christ "are contained in your Scriptures, or rather not yours, but ours."[55] As Kuhn says of scientists on opposite sides of a revolution, "the proponents of competing paradigms practice their trades in different worlds." Here, where the religious worlds of Judaism and Christianity diverge, the hermeneutical issue becomes visible.

The issue of the scriptural canon is no mere illustration of the issue of incommensurability and incompatibility but

---

[55] Justin Martyr, *The Dialogue with Trypho*, in *The Fathers of the Church* (Washington, DC: The Catholic University of America Press, 1948), vol. VI, p. 191.

rather the critical point at which the hermeneutics of suspicion calls into question the interpretation of scripture. One of the most corrosive effects of the growing relativism of late modern culture has been the undermining of authoritative texts, especially scriptures. Disputes about canon, of course, have not been confined to the canon of scripture. The often bitter culture wars over the question of the canon of normative texts to be read in schools and universities began in the field of literary criticism but have now engulfed the whole of liberal education in the West. In a pluralistic world no canon may simply be taken for granted, including the church's canonical scriptures. It is therefore an urgent theological task to clarify what it means to affirm the authority of the canon, not only to ourselves but also to those who do not share our faith.

The whole paradigm-shift associated with the cultural movement from modern to postmodern – more specifically, with the emergence of post-Kuhnian philosophy of science and the turn to antifoundationalism in philosophy – the major issues emerging from this shift can be focused on the discovery of incommensurability, or at least the discovery of its significance at all levels of human knowledge and experience. The term is often attacked or dismissed (perhaps even by the "later" Kuhn himself) on the assumption that it signifies irrationality, or that it promotes "a plurality of unrelated languages."[56] From there it is a short jump to charges of "fideism," Wittgensteinian or otherwise. But this account of incommensurability misrepresents the issues. There is nothing inherently irrational about incommensurability, and it need not lead to the radical separation of spheres of knowledge. It is an extremely common

[56] J. Wentzel van Huyssteen, "Theology and Science: The Quest for a New Apologetics," in *Essays in Postfoundationalist Theology* (Grand Rapids, MI: William B. Eerdmans Publishing Co., 1997), pp. 221–2. Van Huyssteen argues for a unified epistemological theory of knowledge that eschews both the "absolutism of foundationalism" and the "relativism of antifoundationalism" (p. 235) while affirming "a common ground of rationality" that nevertheless insures that "nothing that is part of, or the result of, natural scientific explanation need ever be logically incompatible with theological reflection" (p. 236).

phenomenon; we live with all kinds of incommensurables all the time. The key task is to show that *incommensurability* does not entail *incomparability* or (necessarily) imply *incompatibility*. You cannot add apples and oranges, as your arithmetic teacher used to say; but you can live quite unproblematically in a world containing both. Incommensurables cannot be *directly* compared, measured in the same units (that's what the word means!); to try to do so is to commit a logical error. Thus, for example, an evolutionary account of human origins is incommensurable with a theological account, but they are nonetheless compatible. The postmodern turn means that we give up the illusory goal of finding a common framework for everything, the quest for universal commensurability (which might even do as a definition of Enlightenment modernity). Thus religion and science are very different, utterly incommensurable, and quite compatible. The dialogue between them will focus on those points at which they appear to be *incompatible* or *contradictory*. The same holds true for the relations among the world's religions, except that it may not be so easy to exclude incompatibility in those cases.

The old issue of the positivity of the gospel reemerges at just this point. The vision of reality that Christians glimpse in Holy Scripture has the kind of specificity, particularity, and uniqueness that resists reduction to systematic principles and is incommensurable with other ways of organizing the world. Like Galileo gazing through his newfound telescope at the moons circling Jupiter, we claim that our biblical lenses grant us a vision of the world that challenges and questions the assumptions of those who use different lenses. Our appeal – our apologetics, if you prefer that language – will take the form of a Wittgensteinian "Look and see!" Our claim is that just this collection of ancient writings, the canon of the Old and New Testaments, uniquely embodies the paradigm that allows our mortal minds to imagine, not just an ideal world, but the *real* world! Such a paradigm, though not reducible to some more general or "natural" schema, is not irrational. Incommensurable as it may be with other paradigms, it enables us to envision what could not otherwise be imagined. Like the old gospel hymn *Amazing Grace*, we can only attest we once were blind, but now can see; like Galileo, we can invite others to look through our lenses, but we cannot predetermine or control what they will see.

4

Feuerbach: forgotten father of the hermeneutics of suspicion

... an object first takes on its true intrinsic dignity when the sacred nimbus is stripped off; for as long as a thing or being is an object of religious worship, it is clad in borrowed plumes, namely, the peacock feathers of the human imagination.

Feuerbach

We ... need be afraid of no Feuerbach.

Barth

Ludwig Feuerbach appears condemned to play the historical role of "influence." We read other thinkers of the nineteenth century today – Hegel, for example, or Kierkegaard, or Marx – for their ideas, for the insights they continue to bring to contemporary issues even at the end of the twentieth century. But Feuerbach is nearly always studied primarily because of the influence he has exercised on other thinkers – the ones who still attract readers today. James

The opening epigraph is taken from Ludwig Feuerbach, *Lectures on the Essence of Religion*, trans. Ralph Manheim (New York: Harper & Row, 1967), p. 38; *Vorlesungen über das Wesen der Religion: Nebst Zusätzen und Anmerkungen*, ed. Wolfgang Harich, *Gesammelte Werke*, ed. Werner Schuffenhauer, vol. VI (Berlin: Akademie-Verlag, 1967), p. 47. I have followed Van A. Harvey's practice of using shortened titles in references to this work, first to the English translation (*Lectures*) and then to the German original (*Vorlesungen*). The second epigraph is from Karl Barth, *Church Dogmatics*, ed. G. W. Bromiley and T. F. Torrance, trans. G. W. Bromiley, vol. IV, part 3 (Edinburgh: T. & T. Clark, 1961), p. 85. For the German original, see *Die kirchliche Dogmatik*, vol. IV, part 3 (Zurich: TVZ, 1959), p. 94.

Livingston, for instance, concludes his treatment of Feuerbach in *Modern Christian Thought* by noting how his "influence on modern thought far exceeds that of thinkers of much greater reputation and popularity." He mentions Feuerbach's contributions to now familiar themes in existentialism, to the psychological theories of Sigmund Freud and Erich Fromm, and to the I–Thou philosophy of Martin Buber, before coming at last to the "most significant of all" the influences: the role that Feuerbach's ideas played in the development of Karl Marx's thought both early and late.[1] Even the critical edition of Feuerbach's works (produced, significantly, in the Berlin of the German Democratic Republic) pays tribute to him primarily as "one of the most outstanding philosophical materialists of the pre-Marxist period . . . and above all as one of the immediate philosophical predecessors of Marx and Engels."[2]

Feuerbach's role in the development of the "hermeneutics of suspicion" has largely been overlooked – in part, no doubt, because Paul Ricoeur, who coined the phrase, went on to anoint Marx, Nietzsche, and Freud as the classic modern "masters of suspicion." But Feuerbach is in fact the true founder of the modern suspicious interpretation of religion, not only through his influence on Marx and the other "masters," but also because of the enormous influence exercised by his critique on modern religious thought generally, ever since *The Essence of Christianity* first appeared in 1841. To make the case, I want to look in some detail at Van Harvey's recent study *Feuerbach and the Interpretation of Religion*.[3] Convinced that Feuerbach has

---

[1] James C. Livingston, *Modern Christian Thought*, 2nd edn. (Upper Saddle River, NJ: Prentice Hall, 1997), pp. 228–9.

[2] Preface to Ludwig Feuerbach, *Gesammelte Werke*, ed. Werner Schuffenhauer (Berlin: Akademie-Verlag, 1981), vol. I, p. vii. In the same opening sentence, the editor also pigeonholes Feuerbach as "one of the prominent representatives of classical German *bourgeois* philosophy."

[3] Van A. Harvey, *Feuerbach and the Interpretation of Religion* (Cambridge: Cambridge University Press, 1995); page references to this work will be given parenthetically in the text.

been the victim of persistent misunderstandings, Harvey wants to rehabilitate him so that his voice can be heard in the dialog about the meaning of religion today. To this end, he proposes to undertake a "rational reconstruction" of Feuerbach's philosophy of religion, not simply an historical account of his thought in the context of his own time and place (116ff.). Two themes in particular emerge from his attempt to reconstruct Feuerbach's treatment of religion that have implications for the hermeneutics of scripture. The first theme highlighted in Harvey's reading of Feuerbach is *suspicion*. He claims, in effect, that Feuerbach is the forgotten founder of the hermeneutics of suspicion, whose omission from the canonical list of "masters of suspicion" stems from a failure to understand and appreciate his mature theory of religion. The second theme to emerge from Harvey's retrieval of Feuerbach is the central role played by *imagination* in his account of the origin and continuing power of religion in human life and history. Especially significant is the way in which these two themes converge to give to Feuerbach's account of religion its characteristic emphasis.

Why, asks Harvey, is Feuerbach not included along with Marx, Nietzsche, and Freud as one of the "masters of suspicion," those revolutionaries of nineteenth-century thought who changed for ever the way we read the authoritative texts of our traditions, including especially our religious traditions? He notes that Ricoeur is not alone in denying to Feuerbach a place among the suspicious elite and offers some reasons why this should be so. First of all, Feuerbach's influence on subsequent thinkers has not been as great as that of Marx, Nietzsche, and Freud; and second, his critique "was not part of a larger theoretical framework that was widely appropriated by secular intellectuals and integrated into what we now call the behavioral sciences" (7). More important than either of these factors, however, are a number of widely held misinterpretations of Feuerbach's critique of religion, and it is largely to show that they *are* misinterpretations that Harvey has written his book. He is persuaded that "all of these conventional judgments are partial and misleading truths," and he proposes "to challenge and, if possible, to correct them" (11). Chief among the misreadings of Feuerbach, according to Harvey, is the exclusive identification of his theory of religion with *The Essence of Christianity*, an interpretation that leads either to the neglect of his later works or else to the assumption that they merely refine or clarify the theory already articulated in the 1841 book. In fact, according to Harvey's interpretation, in the mature Feuerbach religion "is no longer explained in terms of self-consciousness alone but in terms of a contingent self confronted with an all-encompassing nature upon which it is absolutely dependent" (162). And Harvey is quite definite in his judgment that the later theory is better (163); it is new and "truly original" (169), he claims, and best of all it breaks finally with the lingering Hegelianism of *The Essence of Christianity*. The later theory "assumes, as the earlier did not, that believers have intellectual grounds, albeit mistaken, for their beliefs" (199). Harvey thinks that Feuerbach makes a useful contribution to the modern academic study of religion because he really "listen[s] to what believers themselves say" (309). (Harvey's hermeneutical "charity" toward Feuerbach may occasionally overreach itself; believers might be excused for not fully appreciating a careful listener who concludes that their hymns, prayers, hopes, and beliefs all amount in the end to no more than "the religious illusion.") But Harvey's point is that Feuerbach deserves a hearing for his mature attempt to "let religion itself speak" and then to offer his own interpretation.

Feuerbach and the theologians

One of the criteria for rational reconstructions that Harvey borrows from Richard Rorty (whom he credits with originating the distinction between rational and historical reconstructions) is that "they are dominated by questions that have come to prominence in some recent work." He assures us that his reconstruction of Feuerbach's thought springs from just such contemporary concerns; he is also explicit about the fact that in his own case the questions arise "in the field of religious studies in contrast to theology." Despite his own disinterest in theological questions, he nevertheless makes an intriguing observation about Feuerbach's reception by the theologians. "Strangely enough," he remarks, "Feuerbach's work for the most part has been taken seriously only by Marxist philosophers and Protestant theologians and has been virtually neglected by scholars in religious studies" (20). For just this reason he undertakes to explore the implications of Feuerbach's thought for religious studies, by which he evidently means nontheological religious studies. Since I have a rather different take on what properly constitutes the field of religious studies (and how it is related to theology), I want to remove the brackets that Harvey has placed around theological questions. Religious studies is the legitimate domain of all scholars who – out of whatever religious, antireligious, or extrareligious motivations and interests – wish to engage in the serious, public, and academic investigation into the nature, function, and value of religion. For this reason I do not find it strange that theologians (not to mention Marxist philosophers) should be among the first to take Feuerbach's critique of religion seriously. They, after all, are the ones with the biggest stake in the outcome. The attempt to separate the study of religion from theological questions (something, incidentally, that Feuerbach never dreamed of doing) inevitably leads to the neglect of the inescapable question of the *truth* of religious teachings, and hence the integrity of religious believers. Nowhere are these issues more sharply focused than in the themes of suspicion and imagination, especially at their point of convergence. Harvey's rational reconstruction of Feuerbach's interpretation of religion, perhaps in spite of his own intentions, sheds a revealing light on just these issues, including their theological implications.

Harvey's observation about theological interest in Feuerbach requires some qualification as soon as we look more closely at the theological landscape since the nineteenth century. Of the leading twentieth-century theologians, only Karl Barth has devoted serious attention to Feuerbach.[4] More remarkable than the general theological neglect of Feuerbach, however, is the character of this one exception: for Barth's treatment of Feuerbach's theory of religion is overwhelmingly positive. The primary reason for Barth's affirmation of Feuerbach is that he sees him as an ally (though admittedly an unwitting one) in his struggle to free theology from its dangerous infatuation with religion. Barth takes him to be, in the words of John Glasse, "the man whose query does nothing less than locate the Achilles' heel of modern theology," a flaw that is most obvious in the case of Schleiermacher but which also afflicts other theologians, including Schleiermacher's critics.[5] Barth mentions specifically G. Menken, J. A. L. Wegscheider, W. L. De Wette, A. Tholuck, and P. Marheineke as other theologians of the day who left themselves open to Feuerbach's reduction of theology to anthropology. He does not stop with Schleiermacher's generation but includes as well later theologians who though having heard Feuerbach's critique, nevertheless persisted in doing theology in a way that perpetuated the "apotheosis of man," thus remaining vulnerable to the Feuerbachian reduction. This history of shame in nineteenth-century theology reaches its culmination in 1900 in the crowning irony of Adolf von Harnack's public lectures on *The Essence of Christianity*, the same title under which Feuerbach had already demonstrated the

---

[4] For bibliographical references to theological responses to Feuerbach in the first part of the century, see the superb article by John Glasse, "Barth on Feuerbach" (*Harvard Theological Review* 57 [1964]: 69–96), especially note 1.

[5] Ibid., p. 72.

disastrous consequences of the very path proposed by Harnack to his listeners.

Barth's endorsement of Feuerbach is decidedly qualified in one respect. While crediting him with drawing the inevitable consequence of the theological enterprise of his day, he nevertheless refers to it as "Feuerbach's trivial conclusion," wondering how these theologians could have left themselves vulnerable "to that mean insinuation," that "slander."[6] Feuerbach may be right in important respects, says Barth, but his theory of religion remains shallow, "a platitude," "at bottom trite beyond compare."[7] It is surely overstating the case, however, to say, as Harvey does in his introduction, that Barth treats Feuerbach simply "as a *reductio ad absurdum* of liberal theology since Schleiermacher" (20). In the first place, Barth hardly thinks that the identification of religion with human projection is an absurdity, for he endorses this position himself as the negative moment of the dialectic of religion and revelation in his own theory of religion in the *Church Dogmatics*.[8] In the second place, Barth by no means restricts his appreciation of Feuerbach to his role in unmasking the error of modern[9] theology. For even his negative comments about Feuerbach are set in the context of a generous appreciation of the latter's intentions. He says, in effect, that if one is going to turn man into God Feuerbach's way of doing it is at least more honest than that of the theologians. Moreover, it does greater justice to the concrete reality of human life in the

[6] Karl Barth, "An Introductory Essay," in Ludwig Feuerbach, *The Essence of Christianity* (New York: Harper & Row, 1957), pp. xx–xxi. This essay, used as an introduction to the English translation of Feuerbach's most famous work, was translated by James Luther Adams from a lecture Barth gave in Münster in 1926, later published as a chapter in his *Die Theologie und die Kirche* (Zollikon-Zürich: Evangelischer Verlag, 1928).
[7] Barth, "Introductory Essay," p. xxvii.
[8] For an account of Barth's theological theory of religion, see Garrett Green, "Challenging the Religious Studies Canon: Karl Barth's Theory of Religion," *Journal of Religion* 75 (1995): 473–86.
[9] Harvey also errs in assuming that Barth thinks Feuerbach unmasks the secret only of *liberal* theology. Barth makes quite clear that the judgment falls on virtually all theologians, including many of the most conservative of the day.

world than do the spiritualizing abstractions of the theologians. Feuerbach has a "head start over modern theology" because of what Barth calls (negatively) "his resolute anti-spiritualism" or (positively) "his anthropological realism." Barth calls special attention to the communal nature of Feuerbach's humanism. Perhaps for this reason he treats Feuerbach with greater deference than that other notorious nineteenth-century despiser of Christianity, Friedrich Nietzsche. Whereas Nietzsche represents for Barth the great champion of the isolated individual, of "humanity without the fellow-man,"[10] Feuerbach affirms the unity of human bodily and spiritual reality "in the relation of the I and the Thou." ("It is just because religion is concerned with the assertion of this unity," Barth comments, "that it makes sense and not nonsense" for Feuerbach.)[11] The supreme example of this communal anthropology is surely Feuerbach's interpretation of the Christian doctrine of the Trinity, which Harvey cites. The Trinity, Feuerbach argues,

> is the secret of the *necessity of the "thou" for an "I"*; it is the truth that *no being* – be it man, God, mind or ego – *is for itself alone* a *true*, *perfect*, and *absolute* being, that *truth* and *perfection* are only the *connection* and *unity* of beings equal in their essence. The highest and last principle of philosophy is, therefore, the *unity of men with men*.[12]

This social understanding of the Trinity shows striking similarities to Barth's own theology, so his admiration is perhaps not surprising. Not only does Feuerbach work "with human honesty and real seriousness"; Barth is willing to say even that "he works, as it were, with a Christian

---

[10] Barth, *Church Dogmatics*, vol. III, part 2, ed. G. W. Bromiley and T. F. Torrance, trans. Harold Knight, G. W. Bromiley, J. K. S. Reid and R. H. Fuller (Edinburgh: T. & T. Clark, 1960), pp. 231–42. For the German original, see *Die kirchliche Dogmatik*, vol. III, part 2 (Zurich: TVZ, 1948), pp. 276–90.

[11] Barth, "Introductory Essay," p. xxiv.

[12] Feuerbach, *Principles of the Philosophy of the Future*, cited by Harvey (p. 179).

realism." So "Feuerbach – however badly he may have done his work – was and is really stronger than the great majority of modern and most recent theologians."[13] Barth's concern is finally not to pass judgment on Feuerbach – who, after all, does not claim to be doing Christian theology – but rather on those thinkers who do make such a claim. "Why has Christian theology," he asks, "not seen these things earlier and better than Feuerbach, things that it certainly must have seen if it really knew the Old and New Testament?" Barth is unwilling to join in the self-serving tut-tutting of the theologians about Feuerbach's atheism until they have put their own house in order. He agrees, in effect, with Harvey's judgment that Feuerbach "believed that religion was too important a subject to leave to the theologians" (6). Barth believes it too – rather, he believes that *theology* is too important a subject to leave to the theologians, for "the attitude of the anti-theologian Feuerbach was more theological than that of many theologians."[14]

Suspicion and imagination in Feuerbach's theory of religion

Feuerbach and the Interpretation of Religion ought to alter the way scholars henceforth understand the nineteenth-century roots of religious studies. For Harvey demonstrates convincingly that the hermeneutics of suspicion begins with Feuerbach – and not merely because of his influence on Marx. Indeed, Feuerbach's ideas on religion lead more directly to the Freudian than to the Marxian or Nietzschean version of suspicion.[15] The all-important concept of projection originates with Feuerbach, a debt acknowledged by

---

[13] Barth, "Introductory Essay," pp. xxiv–xxv.

[14] Ibid., p. x.

[15] Merold Westphal detects three layers in Feuerbach's critique of religion: an explicit Hegelian one, a proto-Freudian one, and a more obscure Marxian strain, later radicalized by Marx himself. See *Suspicion and Faith: The Religious Uses of Modern Atheism* (Grand Rapids, MI: William B. Eerdmans Publishing Co., 1993), pp. 123–33, especially p. 125.

Freud, who first turned it into a powerful and influential (if also problematic and controversial) tool in the interpretation of religion. (A portion of the credit also belongs to George Eliot, who rendered Feuerbach's cumbersome philosophical term *Vergegenständlichung* in the arresting metaphor of *projection*.)[16] Likewise pointing toward Freud's later theory is Feuerbach's emphasis on the role of desire in religion, eventuating in the *Glückseligkeitstrieb*, a term rife with proleptic Freudian overtones.

More important than these adumbrations of later nineteenth-century theory, however, is Feuerbach's account of the engine of religious projection. By identifying imagination as the "organ of religion," Feuerbach opened a perspective on religion whose significance is only beginning to be grasped at the end of the twentieth century. Had he possessed even an inkling of the possibilities inherent in this thesis – and nothing is more obvious from Harvey's book than that he did not – his treatment of religion might well have taken on a proto-Nietzschean cast. For the importance of Feuerbach's thesis that the imagination is the key to understanding how and why human beings are religious lies beyond the horizon of his own narrowly positivist epistemology and stolidly modernist temperament. All one has to do in order to bring out the possibilities of his thesis is to bracket just one unreflected assumption that Feuerbach always takes for granted and (therefore) never attempts to justify: the axiom that *imagination* and *reality* comprise an unproblematic duality, that they are opposed and mutually exclusive terms. In more fashionably contemporary terms, one could call this move a deconstruction of Feuerbach's concept of *Einbildungskraft/Phantasie*.

The crucial connection is the one that links suspicion to imagination. Feuerbach's descriptive thesis is that religion

---

[16] It is ironic testimony to the success of Eliot's translation that her term has found its way back into German discourse about religion in the twentieth century in the form of *projizieren* and *Projektion*.

is the product of imagination. But his evaluative thesis is more revealing: *because* religion is produced by imagination, he claims, we are justified in treating it with suspicion. Why is Feuerbach suspicious of religious ideas and sentiments? Because they are the fruits of imagination and *therefore* cannot be true. Nothing could have been more obvious to Feuerbach; and nothing makes it more obvious to us how much the world of ideas has changed in a century-and-a-half. In reviewing his intellectual development at the start of the *Lectures on the Essence of Religion*, Feuerbach contrasts his own position with Hegel's in a way that brings out forcefully the dualism of reason and imagination in his thought. Philosophy, he writes, deals with thought (*Denken*) or reason (*Vernunft*), while religion has to do with emotion (*Gemüt*) and imagination (*Phantasie*). Whereas in Hegel religion "merely translate[s] speculative ideas into emotionally charged images," Feuerbach insists on a sharp dichotomy between them. For he believes that Hegel missed something important in religion, "an element that is distinct from thought" and which constitutes the "very essence" of religion, which he calls sensuousness (*Sinnlichkeit*).[17] In Hegel, religion occupies precisely the mediating position between the pure sensuousness of art and the pure conceptuality of philosophy; its defining feature is this ability to mediate between the realms of intellect and sense, a form that he calls *Vorstellung* – traditionally translated as "representation" but actually closer to "imagination" in English, as I have argued elsewhere.[18] From the vantage point of the late twentieth century (whether one thinks of post-Kuhnian philosophy of science or of postmodern critiques of the metaphysical tradition), Feuerbach's move hardly seems an advance over Hegel. For although Hegel can be faulted for ultimately subordinating

---

[17] Feuerbach, *Lectures*, p. 12; *Vorlesungen*, p. 18.
[18] See Garrett Green, *Imagining God: Theology and the Religious Imagination* (Grand Rapids, MI: William B. Eerdmans Publishing Co., 1998), pp. 14–16.

religious *Vorstellung* to the philosophical *Begriff*, thus perpetuating the long-standing Western prejudice for intellect over sense, Feuerbach does it undialectically and from the outset. For him the essence of religion is sensuousness, *not* intellect; and since "emotion and imagination are ... rooted in sensibility," imagination can yield *only* illusion, leaving the field of truth to pure reason, now stripped of sensuousness – that is, of all relation to the body. So Feuerbach's sensuous anthropology, much praised even by Karl Barth, is not quite what it seems. After wisely noting that *Sinnlichkeit* includes "not only the belly, but the head as well," Feuerbach proceeds to exempt the head from the limitations of *Sinnlichkeit* by presupposing a disembodied faculty of purely intelligible *Denken* and *Vernunft* that evidently gazes directly upon the truth. So in the end, for Feuerbach – *Sinnlichkeit* notwithstanding – the head thinks truth, while the belly imagines illusion.

The beam of projection and the grid of imagination
Harvey titles his book *Feuerbach and the Interpretation of Religion* – rather than, say, *Feuerbach's Interpretation of Religion* – for good reason. His interest is not simply an historical one, for he thinks that studying Feuerbach not only illumines the origins of religious studies in the nineteenth century but can also help us understand religion today. This constructive and contemporary motivation comes most clearly to the fore in chapter 7, the book's longest, entitled "Feuerbach and Contemporary Projection Theories." Here Harvey attempts to cash out the new and improved critique of religion in the later Feuerbach by showing its usefulness for the theory of religious projection, a task he carries out by bringing his "ideal Feuerbach" into "the modern conversation" about the meaning and truth of religion. For reasons that I find puzzling, Harvey has chosen to modernize Feuerbach by focusing on projection – the very concept on which Feuerbach relied so heavily in *The Essence of Christianity* but then abandoned in his

later theory (the one Harvey himself finds to be superior). Harvey's strategy – as I hope to demonstrate – leads him to make a problematic distinction between two types of projection, which he dubs the "Beam" theory and the "Grid" theory. I believe that the issues become clearer, both in the later Feuerbach and in the contemporary discussion, if we limit the term "projection" to the Beam model and see Grid theory as one way (a rather unclear one, in my judgment) of thematizing the role of imagination in religion. This approach recommends itself because it focuses on a term that was crucial for Feuerbach (late as well as early) and remains crucial for religious studies today. The term "imagination" not only describes religion more accurately but also does so in a less tendentious way than the problematic term "projection."

One of the most useful, and as far as I know original, aspects of Harvey's book is the careful distinction he draws between Feuerbach's early and late critiques of religion.[19] The well-known theory in *The Essence of Christianity* – the version that so impressed the young Karl Marx – was an "inversion of Hegel's philosophy of Spirit" in which religion is "regarded as an involuntary projection inherent in and necessary for complete self-consciousness." In the *Essence of Religion* and the *Lectures on the Essence of Religion*, Feuerbach (in Harvey's paraphrase) sees religion instead as "an erroneous, belief-like interpretation of the all-encompassing and mysterious nature upon which the self knows itself to be dependent, an interpretation that springs out of the confrontation of the I with the not-I and the desire for recognition by this other" (229). The twofold occurrence of the word "interpretation" is not accidental; rather, it captures the main thrust of the new theory as Harvey presents it. Two other, briefer summary statements

---

[19] It should be noted, however, that Glasse anticipated Harvey's thesis over thirty years ago: "In the latter work [*Lectures on the Essence of Religion*] Feuerbach viewed God not so much as the essence of man as the essence of Nature" ("Barth on Feuerbach," p. 93, note 47).

make the point even more directly. Whereas in *The Essence of Christianity*, Harvey summarizes, "Feuerbach proposed that religion is a stage in the development of self-consciousness and must, therefore, evolve into philosophy," the later Feuerbach sees religion as "not an involuntary reflex of the self but an interpretation . . ." Even more pithily, Harvey can say that the early theory was "largely a function of . . . the notion of projection," while in the later theory "religion is an interpretative response" to external forces (231). Note that in Harvey's own most careful formulations "projection" is a feature of the early Feuerbach, while his later theory is described by "interpretation." The contrast, in other words (this time mine, not Harvey's), is between two ways of imagining God: in the projected ideal image of the human species, or in the image of a personified nature. Harvey is surely right that these two theories are incompatible with one another, though he is less convincing in his claim that the later one is more persuasive. What remains problematic is Harvey's persistence (unlike Feuerbach) in trying to conceive the issues in terms of projection. In projecting, one begins subjectively and then moves to conceive external reality – precisely the direction of religious "alienation" in the early Feuerbach. What is new about the later theory is the reversal of direction: Feuerbach now sees the religious person as beginning with an experience of the outside world ("nature") and then "processing" or organizing that experience in a particular way. Such a move is rightly called (by Harvey, in discussing Feuerbach) interpretation, not projection. As Harvey says, this kind of religion is an "interpretive response" rather than an "involuntary reflex of the self." Feuerbach's own term *imagination*, despite some serious problems in the assumptions he makes about it, therefore offers a more promising way of talking about religion and its relation to human life and thought.

The "Beam metaphor" requires little comment, since it encapsulates just what Feuerbach, Freud, and most other people have long meant by "projection." Something inward, unconscious, or subjective is displaced as something outward and taken (i.e. *mis*-taken) by the intending subject to be objective. That, after all, is just what the early Feuerbach said: his word was *vergegenständlichen*, "to objectify." The assumption that such a move produces illusion rather than truth appears to be so directly implied by the Beam metaphor itself that attempts to use "projection" to describe religion without at the same time precluding its truth have had a difficult time of it.

More interesting and far more problematic is what Harvey calls the "Grid theory." The problem appears in his very first sentence about it, where he describes this option as "another type of projection theory," an assumption that begs the question at stake. He defines Grid theory accordingly in terms of "the symbolic or conceptual forms that human beings *superimpose* on their experience in order to make it intelligible" (246; my emphasis). Implied by this metaphoric language is the assumption that people first have experience that is *un*formed (outside "symbolic or conceptual forms") and then proceed to "superimpose" forms upon it – forms that are evidently alien to the "experience itself," that is, qualitatively other than the "pure" experience prior to the act of imposition. Simply putting the issues this way should make plain why I find Harvey's presentation of Grid theory unsatisfactory. Such appeals to unformed prelinguistic experience have (for good reason) not had an easy time of it in recent philosophical and social scientific thought.[20] Whether one appeals to

---

[20] For an insightful treatment of the relationship between experience and the concepts used to interpret it, see Wayne Proudfoot, *Religious Experience* (Berkeley and Los Angeles: University of California Press, 1985). Though Proudfoot, like Harvey, is concerned to expose the errors of "religious apologists," the argument cuts both ways: just as it is illegitimate to appeal to religious experience to justify the concepts that believers use to interpret it, so it is equally untenable to presuppose an essentially nonreligious experience lying behind the language of piety. If "religious beliefs and practices are interpretations of experience, and . . . themselves fit objects of interpretation" (ibid., p. 41), the same holds for non- or antireligious interpretations of experience, such as those

Wittgenstein's refutation of private language and demonstration of the *Gestalt*-like holism implicit in our perception and language; or to philosophers of science like Kuhn, Lakatos, and Feyerabend, who have shown the essential role of models and paradigms in the natural sciences; or to post-Heideggerian philosophers like Gadamer, Rorty, and Derrida, who have exposed the inherent contradictions in appeals to "pure presence" and other claims to have "unformed" access to reality apart from linguistic commitments to already existing traditions and forms of life – whichever of these voices one attends to will make it extremely difficult ever again to think of our relation to the world in terms of merely "subjective" images imposed upon an "objective" reality, however it may be conceived.

Feuerbach's two theories of religious imagination

One of the most common concepts found in Feuerbach's writings, especially in English translation, is *imagination*, which persists through all the twists and turns of Feuerbach's developing philosophy of religion. Worthy of particular note is the fact that imagination plays the key role in *both* the early projection theory *and* the late "existential" theory. So pronounced is this consistency in Feuerbach that it ought to relativize our understanding of the change of position highlighted by Harvey. It is no doubt both interesting and important that Feuerbach changed his mind about *how* religious people imagine the world; but even more significant is the fact that Feuerbach never wavered in his conviction *that* religion is fundamentally imagination – *and* that for this very reason it is suspect. To see how basic this strain of Feuerbach's thought really is, we need to look at what he says about religion and imagination both in *The Essence of Christianity* and in his later theory, presented most fully in the *Lectures on the Essence of Religion*.

proposed by Feuerbach – and by Harvey himself. *All* data are theory-laden, not just the data cited by religious apologists. For Harvey's treatment of Proudfoot, see pp. 93ff.

First, a comment on terminology. In discussing German philosophical texts in English, one often faces the difficulty that various German terms – *Einbildungskraft* and *Phantasie* are the most important – correspond to "imagination" in English. In Kant, for example, the technical term for imagination is *Einbildungskraft*. In Hegel (and also in the thought of the Young Hegelians, such as David Friedrich Strauss), religious imagination is characterized as *Vorstellung* (in contrast to the conceptual purity of the *Begriff*).[21] Feuerbach employs all of these terms (though *Phantasie* is his favorite), and Eliot has rendered all of them "imagination" in most cases. The question therefore arises, whether the translation might be obscuring distinctions made in the original, and whether he might have used the terms differently in his earlier and later writings. Fortunately, Feuerbach himself provides compelling evidence for identifying all of these terms, especially *Einbildungskraft* and *Phantasie*, under the single concept *imagination*. Not only does he alternate in his use of the terms, but more than once he places them in an apposition that clearly shows they are meant as synonyms. This sentence from *The Essence of Christianity* is typical: "God exists in heaven, but is for that reason omnipresent; for this heaven is the imagination."[22] In the first two editions, Feuerbach uses *Phantasie*; but in the third and final edition of 1849 he appends the word *Einbildungskraft*, so that heaven is identified as "*die Phantasie, die Einbildungskraft*" – obviously two words for the same thing. One could cite numerous other passages where both terms are employed, but none is plainer than this one. Furthermore, the same usage appears repeatedly in the later Feuerbach. In the twentieth *Lecture on the Essence of Religion*,

---

[21] See Green, *Imagining God*, chapter 1.

[22] Ludwig Feuerbach, *The Essence of Christianity*, trans. George Eliot (New York: Harper & Row, 1957), p. 203, n.; *Das Wesen des Christentums*, ed. Werner Schuffenhauer and Wolfgang Harich, *Gesammelte Werke*, ed. Werner Schuffenhauer, vol. V (Berlin: Akademie-Verlag, 1973), p. 345, n. I have followed Harvey's practice of using shortened titles in references to this work, first to the English translation (*Christianity*) and then to the German original (*Christentums*).

for example, where he is ridiculing the "fetishism" of what he calls "savages [*die Wilden*]," he asks, "what impels men to make gods of snail shells, crab claws, flags, and pennants?" His answer: "Their imagination, whose power is proportional to their ignorance." The one word "imagination" in the translation stands for "*Die Phantasie, die Einbildungskraft*" in the original; and he repeats the appositive when he generalizes the example to all religion: "The theoretical cause or source of religion and of its object, God, is therefore the imagination [*die Phantasie, die Einbildungskraft*]."[23]

A passage from *The Essence of Christianity* cited by Harvey (42) is characteristic of the younger Feuerbach's theory of religious imagination. After referring to "the impression which the imagination [*Phantasie*] makes upon the feelings [*das Gemüt*]," he specifically declares that the "imagination is the original organ of religion."[24] Feuerbach's actual words are "organ and essence [*Organ und Wesen*] of religion." Eliot's omission from the translation of the key word *Wesen*, the title concept of the book, is a rare but significant lapse, for Feuerbach announces here that the essence of religion – all religion, and not just Christianity – is the imagination. Specifically, he locates religion at the point where the emotions impact the imagination. The job of the imagination is to *represent* the contents of emotion, a task that it carries out by means of images taken from the world of the senses. Another passage, not cited by Harvey, makes clear just how central this imaginative task is to Feuerbach's view of human nature. "Man, as an emotional and sensuous being," he writes, "is governed and made happy only by images, by sensible representations."[25] Feuerbach in fact uses the singular and emphasizes it: human beings are satisfied, he insists, "only [by] the *image* [*Bild*]." Then follows

---

[23] *Lectures*, p. 178; *Vorlesungen*, p. 201.
[24] *Christianity*, p. 214; *Christentums*, p. 360.
[25] *Christianity*, p. 75; *Christentums*, p. 153.

the definition that Harvey cites (43): "Mind [*Vernunft*] presenting itself as at once type-creating [*bildlich*], emotional [*gemütlich*], and sensuous [*sinnlich*], is the *imagination*."[26] Here is the hinge where Feuerbach's description of religion turns to suspicion, for this triple characterization of the imagination – *bildlich*, *gemütlich*, and *sinnlich* – provides three reasons for Feuerbach's prejudice against it. Harvey's language is not too strong: imagination *cheats* reason. Feuerbach, he writes, believes that the "imagination . . . is deceptive in the nature of the case, especially when it becomes allied with feeling and wishing. It can and often does cheat the reason" (43). Even this paraphrase is not strong enough: for Feuerbach, imagination can and *always* docs cheat reason. Feuerbach's hermeneutic of suspicion, in other words, is rooted in his prejudice against images, feelings, and – most striking of all in this philosopher of sensuousness – the senses as sources of truth. This prejudice, as we will see, in no way disappears or even diminishes in Feuerbach's later theory of religion.

One more feature of the early Feuerbach's interpretation of the religious imagination is worth noting; and this point is onc that he will abandon in his later thought. The context for the definition of imagination cited above from *The Essence of Christianity* is christological. It appears as part of Feuerbach's treatment of "The Mystery of the Logos and Divine Image." Immediately following the tripartite definition of imagination, he makes this comment: "The second Person in God, who is in truth the first person in religion, is the nature of the imagination made objective."[27] More literally translated, Feuerbach says that the Second Person of the Christian Trinity "is the *objective essence of the imagination* [*das gegenständliche Wesen der Phantasie*]" (Feuerbach's emphasis). So Christ is the projection of the human imagination; in Christ the imagination imagines

[26] Ibid.; Harvey cites the passage on p. 43.
[27] Ibid.

itself as divine. (It is intriguing passages like this one in *The Essence of Christianity* that make me hesitant to agree with Harvey that Feuerbach's later theory is necessarily an improvement.) Here is an interpretation that might indeed provide the basis for a productive dialogue between Feuerbach and Christian theologians today, especially after Feuerbach's overhasty dismissal of the imagination is called into question.

When we turn to the later Feuerbach with the question of imagination in mind, we discover the same basic premise at work. As Harvey notes, "Although the concept of the imagination plays an important role in the *Lectures*, as it did in *Christianity*, it is not treated any more systematically in the latter, unfortunately, than in the former" (181). It is nevertheless quite clear that the theory of religion presented in the *Lectures on the Essence of Religion* presupposes the very duality of emotion and thought, imagination and truth, that runs throughout *The Essence of Christianity*. Summarizing his own views in the second lecture, for example, Feuerbach maintains that "the difference between religion and philosophy is ineradicable, for philosophy is a matter of thought, of reason, while religion is a matter of emotion and imagination."[28] Later on, in a discussion of animal cults, he argues for his new theory that underlying all religion is "the feeling of dependency," which causes religious believers to propose "a chaos of the most baffling contradictions." "For what reason?" he asks rhetorically. The answer: "Out of superstition." Then follows the familiar dualism: In religion "the alternative between fortune and misfortune, well-being and suffering, sickness and health, life and death depends in *truth* and *reality* [*in Wahrheit und Wirklichkeit*] on certain objects of worship, and on others only in *imagination*, in *faith*, in the *mind* [*in der Einbildung, im Glauben, in der Vorstellung*]."[29] Feuerbach is

[28] *Lectures*, p. 12; *Vorlesungen*, p. 19.
[29] *Lectures*, pp. 43–4; *Vorlesungen*, p. 53 (Feuerbach's emphasis).

able to distinguish with such alacrity between superstition (*Aberglaube*) and truth because he presupposes that the former employs imagination (*Einbildung*, which he immediately equates with *Glaube* and *Vorstellung*) while the latter conforms to "truth and reality."

Feuerbach reconstructed: implications for religious studies and theology

What would it take to make of Feuerbach a genuine dialog partner in our own late twentieth-century attempts to interpret religion? In conclusion, I want to suggest some points at which Harvey's "ideal Feuerbach" might contribute to our own theorizing as scholars of religion. Like most theorists, his chief virtues are closely linked with his vices; but even the vices of great thinkers can be instructive.

Feuerbach's greatest contribution (his chief "virtue"), I take to be his insight into the fundamentally imaginative nature of religious belief and practice. In his passion to reverse the effects of Hegelian spiritualizing, he saw with refreshing clarity the concrete, sensuous substance of religious life – its intrinsic connection to the earth, the body, and the natural world generally. Both secular religion scholars and theologians can surely applaud this emphasis in Feuerbach, for it is a trait as rare in the philosophers of his day as in the theologians. He knew and taught what it has taken religious studies another century to discover, that religion is not first of all a matter of ideas and ideals but of images and practices. The corresponding "vice" has already been noted: his unquestioned assumption (so typical of his age in this regard) that such a product of the sensuous imagination could not possibly be the bearer of truth. So the scholar of religion must say to Feuerbach: Yes, the imagination is indeed the source of religion, but No, religion is not thereby disqualified from the search for truth. In a time when we have learned that even the physicist, not to mention the anthropologist, must engage the imagination in order to gain rational insight into the world, the scholar of religion today will be more reluctant than Feuerbach to preface "imagination" with "mere." The dialog between Feuerbach and the theologians will be more complex and even more interesting, for he will remind them that religious teachings, whatever their truth value, can never be exempt from critical examination, because they are rooted in imagination and therefore implicated in the complex tangle of human desires and mixed motives. Theologians, in turn, will want to ask Feuerbach how he can be so sure that believers do not imagine the world rightly. Here Barth has shown the way – praising Feuerbach for his "Christian realism" while chastizing him for his trivialization of the Christian imagination. But Feuerbach will also be a warning to theologians not to suspend their suspicion too hastily in the endeavor to "retrieve" the religious truths of the past. Along with Marx, Nietzsche, and Freud, Feuerbach offers a salutary reminder to theologians that imagination and desire are inevitably intertwined in a complex web of conflicting motives, not all of which lead to truth. Imagination is surely more than a garb of "peacock feathers" adorning mundane reality; but the temptation to strut about in "borrowed" religious finery must always be resisted. The issue that emerges from this dialog, therefore, is the hermeneutics of imagination. If the imagination not only is the source of error, as Feuerbach believed, but can serve the cause of truth as well – indeed, is necessary to our apprehension of truth – how can we tell the difference? Suspicion of imaginative excess is deeply rooted in religious tradition: "The heart is deceitful above all things," says the prophet (Jeremiah 17.9). Not whether to imagine but how to imagine rightly is the central theological question to emerge from the conversation with Feuerbach.

Another potential contribution that a reconstructed Feuerbach could make to religious studies and theology involves a less obvious but nevertheless intriguing theme in his writings. Like others before and after him who were influenced by Hegel, Feuerbach understands religion in the framework of an historical process. This theme too reveals both strengths and weaknesses in his interpretation of religion. Potentially useful to scholars of religion is an historical-cultural thesis, evident in a number of passages from both the early and the later Feuerbach, which represents a kind of parallel to Nietzsche's meditations on the "death of God." One of the strongest indications that religious objects are unreal, Feuerbach argues, is that each religion demythologizes the gods of earlier ages. "What the present regards as reality [*für Wirklichkeit hält*], the future recognizes to be imagination [*erkennt . . . für Phantasie, für Einbildung*]," he writes in the *Lectures*. "Some day it will be universally recognized that the objects of Christian religion, like the pagan gods, were mere imagination [*nur Einbildung waren*]."[30] Setting aside for a moment the epistemological questions raised by this statement, we can extract an historical thesis that there has been a progressive weakening of the religious imagination over time, something akin to Max Weber's demystification of the world. The thesis that the imaginative force of religion (presumably only in Europe and North America?) has been progressively replaced by rational explanations could be investigated empirically by scholars of religion without necessarily accepting Feuerbach's deprecation of imagination. Less acceptable today, surely, is the evolutionary scheme and cultural prejudice that form one aspect of Feuerbach's historical thesis. He assumes that "naïve primitive peoples . . . were close to the origin and hence to nature."[31] Such assumptions, of course, were nearly universal among scholars of the nineteenth and early twentieth centuries, including many of those theorists most influential in the development of religious studies as a discipline, and they can no more be used to discredit his entire theory of religion than theirs.

---

[30] *Lectures*, p. 195; *Vorlesungen*, pp. 219–20.
[31] *Lectures*, p. 89; *Vorlesungen*, pp. 102–3. The English translation makes the problem worse: Feuerbach speaks not of "primitive peoples" but of *Naturvölker*; in other passages (see above) he does, however, refer to *die Wilden* and regularly assumes their ignorance.

As in the case of Nietzsche, the implications of Feuerbach's "death of God" (or "cooling of religion") theme are especially interesting and potentially fruitful for the dialog with theology. Like Nietzsche, Feuerbach frequently shows more sympathy for orthodox believers than for rationalizing modernist theologians. He compares them as follows:

> The more man is dominated by his imagination, the more sensuous is his god . . . The difference between the Christian God of the rationalists, of those whose faith is tempered by thought, and the Christian God of the older total believers, is merely that the rationalists' God is more sophisticated, more abstract, and less sensuous than the God of the mystics or orthodox believers, that the rationalists' faculty of abstraction restricts their imagination, whereas the old believer's imagination is stronger than his powers of conceptual thinking. In other words: the rationalist's faith is determined, or rather limited, by reason . . . whereas the orthodox believer's reason is dominated by his faith.[32]

In the *Essence of Christianity* he even goes so far as to insist that the "Church was perfectly justified in adjudging damnation to heretics and unbelievers." In a wonderfully apt phrase, he accuses "the believing unbelief of modern times" with hiding "behind the Bible" while opposing "the biblical dicta of dogmatic definitions, in order that it may set itself free from the limits of dogma by arbitrary exegesis." In this situation, he notes, "faith has already disappeared, is become indifferent, when the determinate tenets of faith are felt as limitations."[33] Here, too, we might ask (with Barth) why the theologians did not discover this truth for themselves, rather than learning it from the mouths of their secular opponents.

---

[32] *Lectures*, p. 192; *Vorlesungen*, pp. 216–17.

[33] *Christianity*, pp. 251–2; *Christentums*, p. 416–17. Eliot omits one important term from her English translation: Feuerbach speaks of "*die Charakterlosigkeit, der gläubige Unglaube der neuern Zeit*," thus explicitly identifying the bad faith of theologians as a character flaw.

More than three decades after his initial engagement with Feuerbach's critique of religion in the 1926 lecture, Karl Barth returned to the topic in volume IV of the *Church Dogmatics*.[34] At the culmination of his discussion he remarks (according to the published translation) that we can venture the "good confession of the prophecy of Jesus Christ . . . without embarrassment, and need be afraid of no Feuerbach."[35] In fact, Barth's reference is not to fear but to shame: ". . . *und werden wir uns . . . vor keinem Feuerbach zu schämen haben*." The brief excursus that follows this remark offers a clue to its meaning, for Barth mentions the so-called ontological argument of Anselm of Canterbury and frankly acknowledges the circularity of theological argument against skeptical critics like Gaunilo and Feuerbach. But this circle, he maintains, is not vicious but virtuous, "a *circulus virtuosus*." Our examination of Feuerbach's theory of religious imagination suggests why the believer can affirm the truth of revelation, without shame or embarrassment, in spite of its imaginative character. Feuerbach saw clearly that imagination was the engine of religion, but he also – like so many others, including theologians of his own time and ours – found the imagination to be a source of embarrassment. Now it is time to subject this suspicious thesis itself to a dose of suspicion. This "deconstructive" move will make it harder for secular scholars to dismiss theological claims out of hand, just as Harvey's book makes it harder for theologians to dismiss Feuerbach out of hand.

[34] For a detailed analysis of the continuities and differences in Barth's early and late treatments of Feuerbach, see Glasse, "Barth on Feuerbach," especially pp. 82–91. Also to be commended are Glasse's thoughtful concluding remarks (pp. 92–6).

[35] Barth, *Church Dogmatics*, ed. G. W. Bromiley and T. F. Torrance, trans. G. W. Bromiley, vol. IV, part 3 (Edinburgh: T. & T. Clark, 1961), p. 85. For the German original, see *Die kirchliche Dogmatik*, vol. IV, part 3 (Zurich: TVZ, 1959), p. 94.

5

Nietzschean suspicion and the Christian imagination

Is the cross an argument?

Nietzsche

For the word of the cross is folly to those who are perishing, but to us who are being saved it is the power of God.

1 Corinthians 1.18

Several years ago in an introductory religious studies class I was reading aloud the famous "death of God" speech by Nietzsche's madman.[1] Midway through the passage, I looked up to notice a young African-American woman at the back of the classroom who had both hands clamped firmly over her ears, which she kept in place until I finished reading. She left the classroom hurriedly at the end of the hour and never returned after that day. One part of me found her response gratifying. She, at least, got Nietzsche's point, unlike the other blasé undergraduates (most of whom were white, well-to-do products of Christian, Jewish, or secular liberalism). For her it *mattered* whether God is the God of the living or the dead. On the other

---

The epigraph from Nietzsche is from *The Antichrist*, §53, *The Portable Nietzsche*, rev. edn., trans. Walter Kaufmann (New York: Viking Press, 1968), p. 637; Kritische Studienausgabe (hereafter KSA), ed. Giorgio Colli and Mazzino Montinari (Berlin and New York: Walter de Gruyter, 1967–77), vol. VI, p. 235.

[1] Friedrich Nietzsche, *The Gay Science*, §125, trans. Walter Kaufmann, *Portable Nietzsche*, pp. 95–6; KSA, vol. III, pp. 480–2.

hand, her gesture epitomized all too graphically an attitude common among modern believers (though rarely exhibited so concretely): they are unwilling to hear challenges to the truth of their faith, and at the root of that unwillingness is cowardice; they do not believe that they can meet the challenge, and they are afraid to try.

In previous chapters I have been exploring the development in modern thought that Ricoeur has christened the hermeneutics of suspicion – so far, by means of a largely historical investigation of its origins in the philosophy of religion of the Enlightenment, and the theological response to the new intellectual and cultural climate of modern European thought. Despite my use of Ricoeur's felicitous label, I have so far avoided (oddly, some may think) focusing on those very thinkers dubbed by Ricoeur himself the "masters of suspicion." One reason has been my conviction that to understand the suspicious projects of Marx, Nietzsche, and Freud, we need to look behind them to discover their preconditions and origins. We therefore examined Kant's paradigmatic attempt to translate the "positive" religion of Christian orthodoxy into an "accommodationist" theology acceptable to modern sensibilities, and I argued that Feuerbach is the originator of the hermeneutics of suspicion, even though his project lacks the subtlety and sophistication of Marx's transformation of it. Indeed, the very straightforwardness of Feuerbach's program, in both its earlier and later versions, makes unmistakable the unique place of imagination as the focus of hermeneutical suspicion. Both Kant and Feuerbach are important not only in their own right but also as the originators of patterns that have been widely emulated by others. Kant shows us the paradigm of accommodationist theology, which has both misrepresented the Christian gospel by its ill-advised flight from "positivity" and (ironically enough) made theology more vulnerable to the hermeneutics of suspicion in that very attempt to defend it against modern critique. Feuerbach introduced the immensely influential idea of religious belief as "projection" and made the religious imagination the specific target of suspicious interpretation.

Another reason for neglecting the "masters" has been a desire to avoid repeating what others have already said. Especially in the cases of Marx and Freud, I think, their suspicious critiques of religion have been well analyzed by other scholars, beginning with Ricoeur's own work.[2] The case of Nietzsche is different, however, for his hermeneutics of suspicion is both more complex and more interesting than that of either Marx or Freud. Freud, as important as his psychological insights and cultural impact have been on modern society, is hardly to be taken seriously as a philosopher, and his views on religion often verge on caricature, in part because of his ignorance of the theological tradition and unfamiliarity with the scholarly study of religion generally. The same can certainly not be said of Marx; and yet his influence, so powerful in the century following his own lifetime, now appears to be waning on all fronts. In particular, the brief but enthusiastic infatuation of theologians with Marxism shows signs of coming to an end. Again the case of Nietzsche is decidedly different, for among both philosophers and Christian theologians interest in his ideas and influence continues to increase and to generate new, postmodern philosophical departures. Nietzsche, in other words, represents the culmination of the *modern* hermeneutics of suspicion and foreshadows a distinctly *postmodern* style of suspicion. The task of the present chapter is to consider the hermeneutics of suspicion of the modern Nietzsche; his postmodern side will be reflected in the next chapter.

---

[2] See especially Ricoeur, *Freud and Philosophy: An Essay on Interpretation* (New Haven, CT and London: Yale University Press, 1970) and Merold Westphal, *Suspicion and Faith: The Religious Uses of Modern Atheism* (Grand Rapids, MI: William B. Eerdmans Publishing Co., 1993). Of many useful studies of the individual "masters of suspicion," I mention in particular Denys Turner's work on Marx (including his relation to Feuerbach) in *Marxism and Christianity* (Oxford: Blackwell, 1983) and his more recent unpublished essay "Mysticism or Mystification? How To Tell the Difference" (1997).

Nietzsche as enemy

As the young woman in my religious studies class discovered, Friedrich Nietzsche was an uncompromising enemy of the Christian faith. But his hostility was not simply arbitrary or incidental to his point of view. For Nietzsche believed in the importance of choosing one's enemies wisely. One of the great triumphs of "we immoralists and Antichristians," he asserted, "is our spiritualization of *hostility* ... [which] consists in a profound appreciation of the value of having enemies." He pointedly contrasts this principle with the historic behavior of the church, which "always wanted the destruction of its enemies."[3] On this score, at least, Nietzsche was wiser than the church, and theologians would do well to emulate him. The *Christian* grounds for a doctrine of hostility is to be found in Jesus' commandment "Love your enemies" (Matthew 5.44). For those modern Christians, including many a theologian, who believe that we ought not to have any enemies, it should be noted that people cannot very well love their enemies unless they have some. The commandment to love one's enemies thus implies as its corollary: "Thou shalt have enemies." Refusal to acknowledge one's enemies as such amounts to a violation of the injunction to love them, since (as we all know in this "therapeutic" age) one of the more effective if insidious ways of expressing hostility toward other people is by ignoring them. Christians, accordingly, are bound by obedience to their Lord to take their enemies seriously.

It behooves us, therefore, like Nietzsche, to choose our enemies with care; and Christianity has had no more formidable opponent in the modern world than Nietzsche himself. One might suppose that everyone would agree in classifying this thinker as an enemy of Christianity – who could write so passionately anti-Christian a tract as *The Antichrist*, accusing Christians of inhabiting a fictional

---

[3] *Twilight of the Idols, Portable Nietzsche*, p. 488; KSA, vol. VI, p. 84.

world rooted in hatred of reality and of everything natural
and life-promoting. But surprisingly enough, some com-
mentators claim to find, precisely in *The Antichrist*, the basis
for new theological, and even christological, construction.
Peter Köster, in a useful survey of responses to Nietzsche
by twentieth-century theologians,[4] describes this strategy as
"Christian occupation." Repeatedly over the century since
Nietzsche wrote, theologians have appealed, more or less
directly, to the notion that "Nietzsche *basically* (ultimately,
in spite of all the misunderstandings or even in them) *represented genuinely Christian 'concerns' or thoughts*," which it is
the duty of the theological exegete to recover and articulate.[5] As a particularly egregious, though nonetheless representative, example of this strategy, Köster cites the views
of Enno Rudolph and Georg Picht, who claim to find
within the polemics of *The Antichrist* a "combination of
faith and thought to which the name 'theo-logy' points in
a previously unclarified meaning."[6]

In contrast to the dubious strategy of "occupying" the
enemy's territory and claiming it for theology, I propose to
take Nietzsche seriously, which means to acknowledge him
as the enemy of Christian faith and theology that he intended to be. Such an approach grants Nietzsche the respect
he deserves as a thinker and fellow human being in accordance with the Christian imperative to love one's enemies.
But it also treats theology with greater respect than does
the strategy of occupation, by forcing it to face up to the
criticisms directed against it and thereby granting it the
opportunity to mount an effective defense. The great
danger of the strategy of occupation, so popular with the
theologies of accommodation over the past two centuries,

---

[4] Peter Köster, "Nietzsche-Kritik und Nietzsche-Rezeption in der Theologie des 20.
Jahrhunderts," *Nietzsche-Studien* 10/11 (1981/82): 615–85.

[5] Ibid., pp. 627–8; Köster's emphasis.

[6] Enno Rudolph, "Nietzsches Kritik an der Metaphysik und am Christentum" and
"Antwort von Georg Picht," in *Theologie – was ist das?*, ed. Georg Picht and Enno
Rudolph (Stuttgart: Kreuz Verlag, 1977), pp. 289–309, 311–2.

is that it so often turns out to be the strategy of the Trojan horse: anti-Christian arguments, "baptized" and invited within the theological precincts, end up attacking Christian doctrine from within. The strategy of open acknowledgment and confrontation of the enemy, on the other hand, offers theology the opportunity to bear witness to the gospel entrusted to it, to learn from its mistakes, and to develop new weapons in defense of the faith. The military metaphor, by the way, is both biblical and Nietzschean, and thus especially appropriate to the present discussion. The New Testament urges Christians to "put on the full armor of God" (Ephesians 6.11), and Nietzsche offers an aphorism *"Out of life's school of war:* What does not destroy me, makes me stronger."[7]

Taking Nietzsche seriously as the enemy and critic of Christianity that he set out to be illumines Christian doctrine from an unusual angle, revealing aspects not easily visible from the more common perspectives of academy and church. The Nietzschean hermeneutics of suspicion, applied to Christianity, can shed light on theological issues with results that Nietzsche himself would no doubt have found appalling. By focusing on the symbol of the cross, I will show how Nietzsche's endeavor to destroy the credibility of Christian faith can become a catalyst for recognizing a genuinely *theological* hermeneutics of suspicion, one that calls Nietzsche's own position into question and suggests a strategy for interpreting Christian belief in the modern world.

Power and weakness: Nietzschean virtues and vices

At the center of Nietzsche's attack on Christianity is the issue of power, arguably the major focus of his thought as a whole. At one time he apparently intended *The Antichrist* – which contains the most sustained treatment of

---

[7] *"Aus der Kriegsschule des Lebens. –* Was mich nicht umbringt, macht mich stärker." *Twilight of the Idols,* "Maxims and Arrows," §8, *Portable Nietzsche,* p. 467; KSA vol. VI, p. 60.

Christianity of any of his published works – as the first of four books comprising a volume to be titled *The Will to Power*.[8] It is clear, at any rate, that Nietzsche's animus against Christianity is not simply gratuitous or peripheral but springs directly from the deepest source of his own values. He sees faith, most especially Christian faith, as the doctrine diametrically opposed to his own; and contrasting views of power are the key to the opposition. Nietzsche sounds the keynote near the beginning of *The Antichrist* in characteristically uncompromising terms:

> What is good? Everything that heightens the feeling of power in man, the will to power, power itself.
> What is bad? Everything that is born of weakness. (A 2)[9]

If the "will to power" expresses Nietzsche's primary value, he conceives its negative under the rubric of *decadence*. Christianity is virtually defined by Nietzsche as the religion of decadence. "Life itself is to my mind the instinct for growth, for durability, for an accumulation of forces, for *power*," he writes: "where the will to power is lacking there is decline [*Niedergang*]" (A 6). He generally prefers the connotations of the French term *décadence*,[10] which he applies very broadly indeed, contending that "all the values in which mankind now sums up its supreme desiderata are *decadence-values*."

Before we turn to Nietzsche's explicit critique of religion,

---

[8] The book published posthumously under the title *The Will to Power* is definitely not the volume that Nietzsche had envisioned under that name but rather a selection of passages assembled from his late notebooks. For the tortuous history of that text, see the editor's introduction to Friedrich Nietzsche, *The Will to Power*, trans. Walter Kaufmann and R. J. Hollingdale, ed. Walter Kaufmann (New York: Random House, 1967); a briefer account can be found in Walter Kaufmann, *Nietzsche: Philosopher, Psychologist, Antichrist*, 4th edn. (Princeton, NJ: Princeton University Press, 1974), pp. 6–7.
[9] Citations from *The Antichrist* (indicated parenthetically by "A" followed by the section number), unless otherwise noted, follow Walter Kaufmann's translation in *Portable Nietzsche*, pp. 565–656. The German text can be found in KSA, vol. VI, pp. 165–254.
[10] Because of the similarity of the French and English terms, I will normally employ the English. The reader should bear in mind, however, that Nietzsche's use of the French term carries a particular set of associations, including literary ones.

it will be instructive to take a closer look at the values on which that critique is based. We can learn at least as much about those values from his polemics against their opposite, the "decadence-values," as from his explicit praise of power and its associated attributes. Nietzsche is a thinker who thrives on polarities, on starkly opposed pairs of concepts. In the continuation of the passage just cited he makes reference to the medieval Christian schema that contrasts an explicit set of virtues with a corresponding set of vices. But he wants to amend that schema by advocating "not virtue but fitness [*Tüchtigkeit*]," understood in the Renaissance sense of *virtù* (A 2). Were it not for the fact that Nietzsche insists that this quality be "moraline-free" (i.e., free of morality, "beyond good and evil," in one of his favorite phrases), we would be tempted to refer to Nietzsche's *morality* in describing his sharply differentiated table of "virtues" and "vices." It is not hard to imagine Nietzsche in the guise of an anti-Moses, returned from the heights (one of his favorite metaphors) carrying tablets inscribed with the values of *virtù* and prohibitions against *décadence-Werthe*. At the head of the tablets would stand the rubrics *power* and *weakness*. All the Nietzschean virtues and vices can be interpreted as implications or elaborations of this fundamental dichotomy. Next to power (*Macht*) and its synonym *strength*, Nietzsche's most important values appear in his language about the *natural*, the *real*, and the *healthy*. I want to look briefly at each of them in turn.

One of the headings in *Twilight of the Idols* describes "Morality as Anti-Nature." The context makes it clear that "natural" for Nietzsche means the instinctual, the passionately felt, the bodily – what he sometimes refers to simply as "life." "Every naturalism in morality," he writes, "– that is, every healthy morality – is dominated by an instinct of life." Here the notions of nature, life, and health converge. By contrast, most of the moralities that have actually been taught are "*anti-natural . . . against* the instincts of life," and their appeal to religious sanction therefore "posits God as the *enemy of life*."[11] A somewhat different use of *natural* places it close to *rational*. In his critique of the history of Israel as the "denaturing of natural values," Nietzsche accuses "the Jewish priesthood" of systematically over-turning "the natural concepts of cause and effect" by sub-stituting a pseudo-causality of "spiritual" forces by means of such concepts as sin, revelation, holy scripture, and the will of God (A 22–6). The opposition between religious lies and natural "cause and effect" occurs repeatedly in Nietzsche's polemics. Christian moral concepts are a par-ticular focus of his ire. "The concept of guilt and punish-ment," he maintains, "including the doctrine of 'grace,' of 'redemption,' of 'forgiveness' – *lies* through and through, and without any psychological reality – were invented to destroy man's *causal sense*: they are an attempt to assassinate cause and effect" (A 49).

This sense of *natural* overlaps with a second Nietzschean value, *reality*. "In Christianity," he charges, "neither moral-ity nor religion has even a single point of contact with real-ity"; and he refers specifically to "imaginary *causes* ('God,' 'soul,' 'ego,' 'spirit,' 'free will' . . .)" and "imaginary *effects* ('sin,' 'redemption,' 'grace,' 'punishment,' 'forgiveness of sins')." The corresponding negative term (the "decadence-value" opposed to "reality") is *fiction*. The Christian "*world of pure fiction*," he writes, "is vastly inferior to the world of dreams insofar as the latter *mirrors* reality, whereas the former falsifies, devalues, and negates reality." His critique is essentially psychological: "this whole world of fiction is rooted in *hatred* of the natural (of reality!); it is the expres-sion of a profound vexation at the sight of reality" (A 15). Christianity is "a form of mortal enmity against reality that has never yet been surpassed" (A 27). Nietzsche makes of this thesis a definition of Christianity: he identifies "the instinctive hatred of reality" as "the only motivating force at the root of Christianity" (A 39).

[11] *Twilight of the Idols, Portable Nietzsche*, pp. 486–90; KSA, vol. VI, pp. 82–5.

A third Nietzschean value that figures centrally in his critique of Christianity is *health*. "At the bottom of Christianity," he charges, "is the rancor of the sick, instinct directed *against* the healthy, *against* health itself." This diseased instinct is offended by everything "successful [*wohlgerathen*], proud, high-spirited [*übermüthig*] – above all, [by] beauty" (A 51).¹² Since Christianity stands opposed to "all *spiritual* success [*geistigen Wohlgerathenheit*]," the only kind of reason it can employ will necessarily be "sick reason." Like the oppositions between the natural and the unnatural, and between reality and fiction, Nietzsche's polarity of health and sickness is merely one dimension of the overriding contrast between power and weakness. Sickness by its very definition is that which weakens, just as everything promoting power is healthy. Thus "sickness belongs to the essence of Christianity," and "faith" must itself be a "form of sickness" (A 52).¹³ In one of his notebooks Nietzsche puts it even more directly:

> Christianity has absorbed diseases of all kinds from morbid soil: one can only reproach it for its inability to guard against any infection. But that precisely is its essence: Christianity is a type of decadence.¹⁴

Decadence, Nietzsche's category for all these forms of weakness taken together, is the tendency diametrically opposed to the will to power. It represents the downward trajectory, away from the heights of power toward weakness, toward everything that is unnatural, unreal, and unhealthy.

---

¹² Walter Kaufmann, generally a skillful translator of Nietzsche, renders *wohlgerathen* as "turned out well," which is accurate but unduly awkward English. One of his few serious slips is his insistence on translating *übermüthig* as "prankish," which conveys too narrow and too frivolous a connotation in English; the word means "high-spirited" in a sense not confined to mischief but connoting the effects of excess energy generally: self-assertive, playful, "cocky."
¹³ I have slightly altered Kaufmann's translation.
¹⁴ *Will to Power*, §174 (p. 105); KSA, vol. XII, p. 511.

Nietzsche's Jesus

It is easier to know what Nietzsche thought about Christianity, and why, than what he thought about Jesus. Sometimes he appears to exempt Jesus from responsibility for what Christians, starting with the Apostle Paul, did in his name; but other passages suggest that the problem begins with Jesus himself. Before considering what response theologians ought to make to Nietzsche, it will be useful to examine his views of Jesus Christ.

In the days immediately following Nietzsche's collapse on a Turin street in January 1889 – but before insanity put an end to his writing altogether – he fired off a series of mad missives to friends around Europe, signing some of them "Dionysus" and others "The Crucified." Whatever he may have meant, assuming we could make any sense of it, the duality echoes language used many times previously by a quite sane Nietzsche. Considerable scholarly attention has been devoted to his use of Dionysus, but – rather surprisingly – his many references to Jesus Christ have received less satisfactory treatment. Köster offers this observation: "Remarkably, in the literature on Nietzsche there has been to date, so far as I am aware, no general portrayal, thorough and undistorted by bias, of Nietzsche's interpretation of Jesus."[15] This judgment may be overstated, for several scholars over the years have written informative, if not comprehensive, essays on Nietzsche's Jesus,[16] and I want to look briefly at one of them.

---

[15] Köster, "Nietzsche-Kritik und Nietzsche-Rezeption," p. 679. One reason for Köster's negative evaluation of the available scholarship is that he deliberately limits his scope to German-language publications, and within that group to theological publications (see p. 617, note 4). Walter Kaufmann – a nontheologian writing in English – offers one of the better treatments of Nietzsche's Jesus-interpretation in *Nietzsche: Philosopher, Psychologist, Antichrist*, chapter 12.

[16] In addition to the chapter by Kaufmann mentioned in the previous note, see Eugen Biser, "The Critical Imitator of Jesus: A Contribution to the Interpretation of Nietzsche on the Basis of a Comparison," trans. Timothy F. Sellner, in *Studies in Nietzsche and the Judaeo-Christian Tradition*, ed. James C. O'Flaherty, Timothy F. Sellner, and Robert M. Helm, University of North Carolina Studies in the Germanic Languages and

The most interesting and significant attempt to recover Nietzsche's Jesus is contained in a 1944 article by Martin Dibelius on the "psychological type of the redeemer," a phrase that Nietzsche employs in section 29 of *The Antichrist*.[17] Dibelius begins with the apparently most shocking of Nietzsche's religious judgments, his attribution to Jesus (in the same section of *The Antichrist*) of "the word *idiot*." Few readers were even aware of the passage until long after Nietzsche's death, since his sister (who after his breakdown appointed herself her brother's keeper, publicity agent, and literary executrix), kept it out of the published versions of *The Antichrist*. Dibelius demonstrates that Nietzsche uses the term *idiot*, not in the familiar pejorative sense, but rather in a way closer to its original meaning in Greek and Latin, "as designating a person without culture."[18] Used in this way, the word is not exactly complimentary, but Dibelius argues persuasively that Nietzsche (who was, after all, a well-trained classical philologist) intended not to condemn Jesus for stupidity but rather to classify him according to social type, using a term that also appears elsewhere in Nietzsche's writings from this final creative period. These passages, Dibelius summarizes,

> have this in common: that the "idiot" type, in consequence of a failure or distortion of instinct, lacks something actually belonging to full humanity. They differ according to what is lacking: the understanding of art, the scientific sense of reality,

Literatures, no. 103 (Chapel Hill, NC: University of North Carolina Press, 1985), pp. 86–99; Gerhard Sauter, "Nietzsches Jesusbild als Frage an eine 'Theologie nach dem Tode Gottes'," in *Neues Testament und christliche Existenz: Festschrift für Herbert Braun zum 70. Geburtstag am 4. Mai 1973*, ed. Hans Dieter Betz and Luise Schottroff (Tübingen: J. C. B. Mohr [Paul Siebeck], 1973), pp. 401–19; Klaus Schäfer, "Zur theologischen Relevanz der Jesus-Deutung Friedrich Nietzsches," in *Wort Gottes in der Zeit: Festschrift Karl Hermann Schelkle zum 65. Geburtstag*, ed. Helmut Feld and Josef Nolte (Düsseldorf: Patmos-Verlag, 1973), pp. 319–29; and the article by Martin Dibelius discussed below.

[17] Martin Dibelius, "Der 'psychologische Typ des Erlösers' bei Friedrich Nietzsche," *Deutsche Vierteljahresschrift für Literaturwissenschaft und Geistesgeschichte* 22 (1944): 61–91.

[18] Ibid., p. 67.

culture in general, or the healthy life instinct. The philistine or *décadent* – that is the idiot.[19]

The context of Nietzsche's attribution of the "idiot-type" to Jesus is his critique of two other popular categories, the hero and the genius, used to characterize Jesus in the nineteenth century – preeminently by Ernst Renan, whose *Life of Jesus* was one of the century's bestsellers. Nietzsche is convinced that the *hero* is the precise opposite of the "psychological type" represented by Jesus, whose attitude he finds epitomized in a saying from the Sermon on the Mount: "Resist not evil" (Matthew 5.39 KJV). The hero defiantly opposes his will to the forces of the enemy, but in Jesus "the incapacity for resistance becomes morality" (A 29). "To make a *hero* of Jesus!" Nietzsche scoffs. Renan's other favorite concept, *genius*, he finds equally unsuited to Jesus. At just this point Nietzsche proposes his alternative: "Spoken with the precision of the physiologist, a quite different word would instead be appropriate here – the word *idiot*."[20] These last three words are the ones suppressed by his sister when *The Antichrist* was first published in 1895 and were not made public until 1931. According to Dibelius, the context makes clear that Nietzsche is using "idiot," not as an insult, but rather as a technical term describing the "psychological type of the redeemer." As such, it combines two qualities – Nietzsche calls them "two *physiological realities*" (A 30): the "*instinctive hatred of reality*" and the "*instinctive exclusion of any antipathy, any hostility, and boundaries or divisions in man's feelings.*" If the latter is epitomized in Jesus' motto "Resist not evil," the former is encapsulated in the other saying of Jesus that Nietzsche takes as definitive of his attitude: "The kingdom of God is within you" (Luke 17.21).

---

[19] Ibid.
[20] I have used my own translation here in place of Kaufmann's uncharacteristically awkward rendering.

Nietzsche's critique of Christ and Christianity

About Nietzsche's hostility toward Christianity there can be no doubt, especially if one looks at *The Antichrist*, which, along with *Twilight of the Idols* and the autobiographical *Ecce Homo*, he dashed off in a final furious burst of literary activity late in 1888, finishing just days before his breakdown. *The Antichrist*, which bears the subtitle *A Curse on Christianity*, is Nietzsche's most sustained discussion of both the Christian religion and its founder. The fury of Nietzsche's attack becomes understandable when one realizes that he sees in Christianity the precise opposite of his own most cherished values. Christianity, he charges, "has waged deadly war against this higher type of man," that is, against Nietzsche's *Übermensch*, who thrives on the will to power. "Christianity," on the other hand, "has sided with all that is weak and base, with all failures; it has made an ideal of whatever *contradicts* the instinct of the strong life to preserve itself" (A 5).

Nietzsche formulates his case against Christianity in predominantly psychological terms. The supreme Christian value is *pity*, a sentiment that saps one's strength and "makes suffering contagious." It is no mere sentiment, however, but rather "the *practice* of nihilism," because it "persuades men to *nothingness*"; it is "*hostility to life*" (A 7). The stance that arises out of this religion of pity is called *faith*, which, as we have seen, amounts to a denial of all that is real, rational, and natural.

The psychological origin of this hostility to reality – and the heart of Nietzsche's rejection of Christianity – is what he calls *ressentiment*. The polemic against resentment runs throughout Nietzsche's writings. Zarathustra laughs "at the weaklings who thought themselves good because they had no claws."[21] In *The Genealogy of Morals* Nietzsche makes his strongest case against resentment, and here Jews and

---

[21] Nietzsche, *Thus Spoke Zarathustra*, part 2, *Portable Nietzsche*, p. 230; KSA, vol. IV, p. 152.

Christians are lumped together as targets of his scorn. "With the Jews," he writes, "there begins *the slave revolt in morality*: that revolt which has a history of two thousand years behind it and which we no longer see because it has been victorious."[22] Jesus becomes the epitome of all that is Jewish:

> This Jesus of Nazareth, the incarnate gospel of love, this "Redeemer" who brought blessedness and victory to the poor, the sick, and the sinners – was he not this seduction in its most uncanny and irresistible form, a seduction and bypath to precisely those *Jewish* values and new ideals? Did Israel not attain the ultimate goal of its sublime vengefulness precisely through the bypath of this "Redeemer," this ostensible opponent and disintegrator of Israel?

With this move, Nietzsche (no doubt greatly enjoying it) manages to insult both Jews and Christian anti-Semites at the same time! This and other passages in *The Genealogy of Morals* leave little room for doubt that Jesus – Nietzsche even says "Jesus of Nazareth" as if to emphasize that he means the actual historical figure – bears responsibility for initiating this religion of vengeance against the noble, the strong, and the healthy.

A rather different Jesus emerges, however, from the pages of *The Antichrist*, despite its equally devastating portrayal of Christianity. Here Nietzsche accuses the first Christians of misunderstanding the meaning of Jesus' death, whose "main point" and "exemplary character" he identifies as "the freedom, the superiority over any feeling of *ressentiment*" (A 40). Here he emphasizes the Jewishness, not of Jesus, but of his followers, those "little superlative Jews, ripe for every kind of madhouse, [who] turned all values around in their own image . . ." In another plague-on-both-your-houses generalization, Nietzsche announces:

[22] Nietzsche, *On the Genealogy of Morals and Ecce Homo*, trans. Walter Kaufmann and R. J. Hollingdale (New York: Random House, 1967), p. 34; KSA, vol. V, p. 268.

"The Christian is merely a Jew of 'more liberal' persuasion" (A 44).

The Antichrist is where Nietzsche utters his best-known statement about Jesus: "In truth," he writes, "there was only *one* Christian, and he died on the cross" (A 39). In distinguishing between the Christianity of the church and what he calls "the *genuine* history of Christianity," Nietzsche indulges in his own version of a device often employed (especially in the nineteenth century) by critics of the church: driving a wedge between the New Testament gospels and the letters of Paul. The interpreter typically attributes his own values to Jesus, whose "genuine" teachings were suppressed and distorted by St. Paul, who thus became the founder of a "Christianity" at odds with the teachings of Christ.[23] The circularity of the argument no more discouraged Nietzsche than other practitioners of the Jesus-versus-Paul genre, but his version is perhaps more ingenious than most.

The genuine Jesus, the "psychological type of the redeemer" that Nietzsche believes he can still perceive behind the "extensive distortion" of the gospel writers, is a "holy anarchist," a naive "idiot" innocent of all culture, "who summoned the people at the bottom, the outcasts and 'sinners' . . . to opposition against the dominant order – using language, if the Gospels were to be trusted, which would lead to Siberia today too" (A 27). Nietzsche's Jesus is a rebel, but one not motivated by resentment, whose actions threatened the politically powerful and "brought him to the cross" (Nietzsche sees proof of the political nature of his execution in the inscription on the cross). "He died for *his* guilt," Nietzsche insists. "All evidence is lacking," he adds, "however often it has been claimed, that he died for the guilt of others" (A 29). Nietzsche seems to

---

[23] On Nietzsche's interpretation of Paul, see Jörg Salaquarda, "Dionysus versus the Crucified One: Nietzsche's Understanding of the Apostle Paul," in O'Flaherty, Sellner, and Helm, eds., *Studies in Nietzsche and the Judaeo-Christian Tradition*, pp. 100–29.

show a kind of grudging respect for Jesus, whose death was a willingly accepted consequence of the way he lived. His message, the true "gospel" that died with him on the cross, was "not a faith, but a doing; above all, a *not* doing of many things, another state of *being*." The closest Nietzsche ever comes to praising Jesus is his claim that "such a life is still possible today, for certain people even necessary." Moreover, he adds, "genuine, original Christianity will be possible at all times" (A 39).

More than this ambivalent, ambiguous, and even contradictory account of Jesus we cannot expect from Nietzsche. For he is finally less interested in the "historical Jesus" than in the Christ created by Christians, starting with St. Paul. "The history of Christianity," he tells us, "beginning with the death on the cross, is the history of the misunderstanding, growing cruder with every step, of an *original* symbolism" (A 37). But that is another story – not of Nietzsche's Jesus but of the church's.

Nietzsche's Jesus and the Christian Jesus
Aside from biographical interest or simple curiosity, why should we care a century later about Nietzsche's view of Jesus? We will surely learn nothing reliable of a scientific or historical-critical nature about Jesus of Nazareth or the events of earliest Christianity. Nietzsche's speculations are an idiosyncratic amalgam of the popular prejudices and academic fads of his day, together with his own deep antipathy toward Christianity and everything it stands for. Even as sympathetic an interpreter as Walter Kaufmann concedes that "historically, he is often ignorant . . . and his conception of Jesus . . . is quite unconvincing."[24] It is hard to avoid the impression, in reading the more vituperative passages of *The Antichrist*, of a rather adolescent quality in Nietzsche's overwrought attempts to be shocking. There are

[24] *Portable Nietzsche*, p. 567. He adds, however, ". . . though no more so than most such portraits" (p. 568).

nevertheless sound reasons for taking Nietzsche seriously, even sound *theological* reasons why *Christians* should take him seriously, including his portrayal of Jesus.

To begin with, Nietzsche can be brilliant and illuminating even when he is historically inaccurate and morally outrageous. As Kaufmann comments after making his own criticisms of *The Antichrist*, "The errors of great men are more fruitful than the truths of little men."[25] Reading Nietzsche can be heuristically valuable for anyone who wants to understand the significance of Jesus for his own time or ours. Nietzsche can be philosophically, even theologically, provocative even when he is wrong – not least because of his dazzling command of metaphor and hyperbole. It is no accident that scholars of German literature pay almost as much heed to Nietzsche as do philosophers. His literary and philosophical brilliance, however, are not two different attributes but two aspects of one gift: an uncanny ability to put matters in strikingly new ways that stimulate the imagination and intellect to fresh insights. Thinking about Jesus under the type "idiot" jolts us out of the piously conventional categories through which he is usually seen, and offers at least the possibility of achieving a genuinely new insight into his significance.

But Nietzsche is important not simply because he is provocative. He also pays theology the supreme, if backhanded, compliment of taking its questions and its subject matter seriously. Whatever may have been the deep psychological motivation, Nietzsche cared passionately about Jesus Christ – surely no small matter to theologians. Ironically, Friedrich Nietzsche, that arch-foe of Christianity, stands in agreement with orthodox Christians against the typically modern relativizing of Jesus. Nothing so infuriated Nietzsche as the spectacle of a "radical" critic of Christianity, like David Friedrich Strauss or George Eliot, who behaved as though everything else in modern

---

[25] *Portable Nietzsche*, p. 568.

bourgeois culture could remain unscathed – its morality, its politics, and even its religion. Nietzsche agrees with Christian orthodoxy on one fundamental point, at least: if God is dead, it makes all the difference in the world. That conviction, no doubt, explains his fascination with so passionately Christian a writer as Dostoyevsky. He wrote in a letter to Georg Brandes about the Russian novelist, "In a remarkable way I'm thankful to him, however much he always goes against my most basic instincts."[26] Like Dostoyevsky's Ivan Karamazov, Nietzsche knows that if there is no God, "everything is permitted." Nietzsche seems occasionally to be aware of his odd kinship with Christian believers. In *Ecce Homo* he maintains that his "war against Christianity" is not based on any personal grievance and that he is "far from blaming individuals for the calamity of millennia." In fact, he writes, "the most serious Christians have always been well disposed toward me."[27]

We can go even further: Nietzsche is in agreement with Christian orthodoxy not only about the *importance* of its teachings but in significant ways about the *content* as well. Nietzsche sees Jesus as "idiot," that is, Dibelius concludes, one whose God is "really a God for sick people, a savior [*Heiland*]" – i.e. one who heals (*heilt*). Could anything better describe Christian belief? Consider the following imaginary dialogue:

Nietzsche: One is not "converted" to Christianity – one has to be sick enough for it (A 51).
Jesus: Those who are well have no need of a physician, but those who are sick . . . For I came not to call the righteous, but sinners (Matthew 9.12–13).

But wait – surely the parallel is misleading, for Jesus' words were spoken without irony but Nietzsche finds them offensive, even scandalous! Yes, and even here Nietzsche

[26] Cited by Dibelius, "Der 'psychologische Typ des Erlösers', " p. 71.
[27] Nietzsche, *On the Genealogy of Morals and Ecce Homo*, p. 233; KSA, vol. VI, p. 275.

plays the unwilling part of *advocatus Christi*: when the disciples of John the Baptist came to Jesus, he first called their attention to his acts of healing, and then concluded: "And blessed is he who takes no offense at me" (Matthew 11.4–6). Here Nietzsche's kinship to another nineteenth-century critic of Christianity, Søren Kierkegaard, is especially apparent. Although one was the passionate defender of the gospel and the other its equally passionate foe, both are in agreement about its scandalous nature. According to Kierkegaard's Johannes Climacus – in full agreement with the New Testament on this point – only two authentic responses are possible for one who truly hears the message of Jesus: offense or faith.[28] St. Paul puts it in terms tailormade for Nietzsche: "we preach Christ crucified, a stumbling block (σκάνδαλον) to Jews and folly to Gentiles, but to those who are called, both Jews and Greeks, Christ the power of God and the wisdom of God" (1 Corinthians 1.23–4).

In hoc signo: the meaning of the cross
In the midst of Nietzsche's final vituperative broadside against Christianity during those last few months of furious literary productivity in 1888 before his collapse, he utters a rhetorical question that begs for a theological response. Railing against the damage done by martyrdom ("The martyrs have *harmed* the truth," he charges), he impatiently hurls this italicized challenge: "*Is the cross an argument?*" (A 53). Ever since I first encountered this passage I have felt certain that the only responsible answer a theologian can give is Yes – but on what grounds? The conclusion I have come to is that the cross implies a hermeneutic – a way of reading scripture that not only provides a key to our interpretation of the text but also reveals how and why the

---

[28] Søren Kierkegaard, *Philosophical Fragments* (Princeton, NJ: Princeton University Press, 1985), especially chapter 3, "The Absolute Paradox" and the Appendix to chapter 3, "Offense at the Paradox."

text interprets us and our world. To begin with, the question can be used to bring out the heart of Nietzsche's quarrel with Christian faith; but more important, it offers a heuristic clue to the meaning of the gospel at precisely the point where Nietzsche must say No to it.

It is no accident that the definitive Christian symbol for Nietzsche is the image of Christ on the cross. Here, as in so many cases, Nietzsche and Christian orthodoxy agree in identifying the most important matters, even while evaluating them oppositely. Nietzsche agrees with Paul that the gospel depends on "nothing . . . except Jesus Christ and him crucified" (1 Corinthians 2.2), even though Nietzsche thinks that Paul, not Jesus, was the author of that gospel. The cross becomes for Nietzsche, surprisingly enough, the key symbol of both Judaism and Christianity, the emblem of the decadence they have fostered in history. For he credits the victory of the Jewish "slave revolt in morality" – again in ironic agreement with Christians – to the cross of Christ. One should not imagine (as did so many Christians in Nietzsche's day) that Christianity represents the overcoming of Judaism. On the contrary, the church became the means by which the Jewish "slave revolt" conquered the world:

> . . . could spiritual subtlety imagine any *more dangerous* bait than this? Anything to equal the enticing, intoxicating, overwhelming, and undermining power of that symbol of the "holy cross," that ghastly paradox of a "God on the cross," that mystery of an unimaginable ultimate cruelty and self-crucifixion of God *for the salvation of man*?
>
> What is certain, at least, is that *sub hoc signo* Israel, with its vengefulness and revaluation of all values, has hitherto triumphed again and again over all other ideals, over all *nobler* ideals.[29]

By stressing the continuity of Christianity with Judaism, Nietzsche takes a position offensive to anti-Semites and

---

[29] Nietzsche, *On the Genealogy of Morals and Ecce Homo*, p. 35; KSA, vol. V, p. 269.

anti-Jewish Christians, but in agreement with Christian orthodoxy. Indeed, he sees not simply continuity but the fulfillment of Judaism in the church. Seldom has theology had a more unlikely ally on an important point of Christian doctrine!

Nietzsche develops what we might call his own hermeneutics of the cross, for the cross has come to symbolize for him the very heart of the Judeo-Christian lie. Gerhard Sauter paraphrases Nietzsche's antitheology of the cross in this way: "Christianity has brushed aside the provocation of the cross, has falsified it in order to discover a meaning where every meaning must come to nought."[30] Sauter's comment follows a citation from *The Genealogy of Morals* in which Nietzsche in effect articulates the Christian argument of the cross. He calls it

> that stroke of genius on the part of Christianity: God himself sacrifices himself for the guilt of mankind, God himself makes payment to himself, God as the only being who can redeem man from what has become unredeemable for man himself – the creditor sacrifices himself for his debtor, out of *love* (can one credit that?), out of love for his debtor![31]

It would be hard to fault Nietzsche's theology in that terse summary! So whatever he may have intended by that throwaway question in *The Antichrist*, Nietzsche already knew quite well that the cross *is* an argument – one that has proven very powerful, much to Nietzsche's chagrin! Using Nietzsche's essentially accurate but hostile

---

[30] "Das Christentum hat sich über die Provokation des Kreuzes hinweggesetzt, es hat sie verfälscht, um einen Sinn zu finden, wo jeder Sinn zuschanden werden muß." Sauter, "Nietzsches Jesusbild," p. 405.

[31] ". . . jenem Geniestreich des *Christentums:* Gott selbst sich für die Schuld des Menschen opfernd, Gott selbst sich an sich selbst bezahlt machend, Gott als der Einzige, der vom Menschen ablösen kann, was für den Menschen selbst unablösbar ist – der Gläubiger sich für seinen Schuldner opfernd, aus *Liebe* (sollt man's glauben? –), aus Liebe zu seinem Schuldner!" Nietzsche, *On the Genealogy of Morals and Ecce Homo*, p. 93; KSA, vol. V, p. 331.

account of the Christian "argument of the cross," we can illuminate it in stark perspective. He sees in the cross an emblem of the "revaluation of values" in which first Jews and then Christians inverted the noble virtues of classical antiquity. (The final words of *The Antichrist* are "Revaluation of all values!") He wants to effect another "revaluation" – the German *Umwertung* implies an overturning, an ethical inversion, a turning of values upside down, so as to return (i.e. re-turn) them to their original integrity. Nietzsche's reading of Christianity through the lens of the cross is thus *perverse* in the literal sense of the word: wrongly turned. The quarrel between Nietzsche and the Christian is over "which way is up." By engaging in a kind of theological *Umwertung* of Nietzsche, I hope to articulate a properly Christian hermeneutic of the cross, using Nietzsche's own table of virtues and vices as a guide. The best New Testament text for this exercise in *Umwertung* is Paul's meditation on power and wisdom in 1 Corinthians 1. He speaks explicitly of the *power* of the cross, but he interprets it through an ironic series of inversions, in which the dualities power/weakness and wisdom/folly are the predominant terms. The "word of the cross is folly to those who are perishing," he writes, "but to us who are being saved it is the power of God" (1 Corinthians 1.18). The most "Nietzschean" passage comes in verses 23–5, where the cross becomes the symbol of the divine inversion of power and wisdom. Unlike the Jews and the Greeks, Paul proclaims, "we preach Christ crucified, a stumbling block to Jews and folly to Gentiles, but to those who are called, both Jews and Greeks, Christ the power of God and the wisdom of God." But God's power and wisdom assume a strangely ironic form, "for the foolishness of God is wiser than men, and the weakness of God is stronger than men." For Nietzsche these words epitomize the biblical *ressentiment* of the weak against the powerful, but it is important to note that Paul does not exalt weakness but rather questions where true power is to be found. God manifests his strength in weakness, but it is nevertheless *strength* that is manifested.

The first of Nietzsche's virtues of power, the *natural*, becomes the grounds for rejecting Christianity as "unnatural." The exaltation of the natural has deep roots in Nietzsche's thought. Already in *The Birth of Tragedy* he had used the image of the satyr to distinguish between the "real truth of nature" and the "lie of culture."[32] His use of the nature/culture polarity has proved influential among his followers, some of whom have drawn conclusions from it that he would no doubt have rejected. Such latter-day Nietzscheans want to "deculturate" human beings, since culture inevitably distorts true ("natural") humanity. But here they are trapped in a romantic myth of the self as the innermost core of the individual, uncontaminated by the world. Contemporary hermeneutics of suspicion (for example, in some feminist theology) has adopted this romantic notion of the true inner self together with the anticultural bias. The New Testament has a quite different view of true selfhood, one that defines the self in external rather than internal images: the Christian "puts on" Christ like a garment.[33] Those who surround the throne in Revelation wear white robes, because "they have washed their robes and made them white in the blood of the Lamb" (Revelation 7.14). Nietzsche is suspicious of superficial skins, but for the Bible the *shape*, the external form, is everything. We are to be *conformed* to Christ, to put Christ on. For us the myth of the pure, uncultured self must yield to the insight that the alternatives are always *among cultures*, never between culture and no culture. We are inevitably shaped by our culture but seem to have considerable leeway in choosing the formative elements to which we will subject

---

[32] See Merold Westphal, "Nietzsche and the Phenomenological Ideal," *The Monist* 60 (1977): 280.

[33] Cf., for example, Romans 13.14, Galatians 3.27, Colossians 3.10, 1 Thessalonians 5.8.

ourselves. Nietzsche's ideal of the natural also calls to mind Karl Barth's anthropological distinction between "real man," created by God and restored in Christ, and "natural man" who vainly seeks to live apart from the grace of God. It is significant that Barth identifies Nietzsche as the prophet of "humanity without the fellow human,"[34] stressing the heroic isolation of the Nietzschean "natural" man in contrast to the co-humanity of "real" human nature as revealed in the humanity of Christ.

The second of Nietzsche's virtues, *reality*, pits him against the *fictional* world of the Christians. Once again, Nietzsche is perversely right. From the perspective of the cross, Christians do in fact question the ultimate reality of the present "real" world, viewing it in the light of the "world to come," that future destiny to which we are related by faith but not yet by sight. Nietzsche links the three Christian virtues of faith, hope, and love (he calls them "the three Christian *shrewdnesses*" [A 23])[35] to the denial of reality. His comment on love is especially revealing: "Love is the state in which man sees things most decidedly as they are not. The power of illusion is at its peak here." An echo of 1 Corinthians 13 can be heard in his language: "In love man endures more, man bears everything" (A 23).[36] The hermeneutics of the cross should teach us not to worry as much as theologians have done over the past two centuries about the "problem of history," the distinction between fact and fiction. The most intriguing of Nietzsche's terms is *imaginär*, which he attributes to

[34] "Nietzsche . . . war der Prophet jener Humanität ohne den Mitmenschen" (Karl Barth, *Die kirchliche Dogmatik*, vol. III, part 2 [Zurich: TVZ, 1948]), p. 277; *Church Dogmatics*, vol. III, part 2, ed. G. W. Bromiley and T. F. Torrance, trans. Harold Knight et al. (Edinburgh: T. & T. Clark, 1960), p. 232. Barth's entire excursus on Nietzsche elaborates this thesis with special attention to the antithesis between Dionysus and the Crucified (*Die kirchliche Dogmatik*, vol. III, part 2, pp. 276–90; *Church Dogmatics*, vol. III, part 2, pp. 231–42).
[35] ". . . die drei christlichen *Klugheiten*" (*Portable Nietzsche*, p. 592; KSA, vol. VI, p. 191).
[36] "Die Liebe ist der Zustand, wo der Mensch die Dinge am meisten so sieht, wie sie *nicht* sind. Die illusorische Kraft ist da auf ihrer Höhe . . . Man erträgt in der Liebe mehr als sonst, man duldet Alles" (*Portable Nietzsche*, pp. 591–2; KSA vol. VI, p. 191).

each item in the Christian *Fiktions-Welt* (A 15). Here, in contrasting the real with the imaginary, reality with illusion, Nietzsche sounds like Feuerbach, speaking in the tradition of the classical nineteenth-century hermeneutics of suspicion. From the perspective of late twentieth-century holistic philosophy of science, however, the contrast appears rather different. Once again, the proper theological response to Nietzsche is to accept his description without the value judgment that he attaches to it. Yes, the theologian must respond, the gospel appeals to the imagination. It is not part of the worldly "reality" of the everyday; and if viewed as such, it will appear illusory and fictional. The quarrel between the gospel and the world is about "reality"; the gospel affirms a reality whose source and destiny lie beyond this world. Accused by Pilate of treason, disloyalty to the powers of this world, Jesus responds that his "kingship is not of this world" but that he has "come into the world to bear witness to the truth" (John 18.36–7). Pilate's reply is like Nietzsche's, full of insight but full also of worldly wisdom: "What is truth?"

The third Nietzschean virtue of the powerful is *health*, contrasted of course with the sickness of Christianity. Here Nietzsche's perversely insightful analysis takes in even Jesus, that "most interesting of all decadents," whose message is "a mixture of the sublime, the sickly, and the childlike" (A 31).[37] Health for Nietzsche means unrestricted exercise of one's powers, bodily and spiritual. Health for the Christian, on the other hand, requires self-denial. Here the Christian and Nietzschean hermeneutics of the cross are most radically opposed to each other, for the issue of self-denial focuses the real alternatives between Nietzsche and the gospel like no other term. "If any man would come after me, let him deny himself and take up his cross and follow me," says Jesus. "For whoever would save his life

---

[37] ". . . dieses interessantesten décadent . . . einer solchen Mischung von Sublimem, Krankem und Kindlichem" (*Portable Nietzsche*, p. 603; KSA, vol. VI, p. 202).

will lose it, and whoever loses his life for my sake will find it" (Matthew 16.24–5). Here, too, Nietzsche hears the gospel – and rejects it – for self-denial is the heart of what he calls the ascetic ideal. *The Genealogy of Morals* concludes with a tirade against the ascetic ideal, "this hatred of the human, and even more of the animal, and more still of the material, this horror of the senses, of reason itself, this fear of happiness and beauty, this longing to get away from all appearance, change, becoming, death, wishing, from longing itself – all this means – let us dare to grasp it – *a will to nothingness*, an aversion [*Widerwillen*] to life." His final word is a typically Nietzschean word play: "lieber will noch der Mensch *das Nichts* wollen, als *nicht* wollen."[38]

Let me conclude by citing Nietzsche's own account of the threat he poses, and by indicating the kind of theological response implied by the hermeneutic of the cross. In the brief preface to *The Antichrist* Nietzsche announces: "One must be honest in matters of the spirit to the point of hardness before one can even endure my seriousness and my passion."[39] Christian theology stands today in need of the "hardness" to withstand the assault of Nietzsche and other suspicious interpreters. The moral softness, the intellectual laziness of accommodationist theologies, the whining tone of some political and liberation theologies, not to mention "therapeutic" ("pastoral") theology – all these exhibit the very faults identified by Nietzsche: intellectual dishonesty, cowardice, sentimentality. Rather than face the challenge of the question of truth raised by modern philosophy and science, too many theologians prefer to look for a "secular meaning of the gospel" – whether political, psychological, or moral – that can accommodate its message to the sensibilities of the prevailing secular culture.

The hermeneutics of the cross calls not for a more militant apologetics but rather for what we might call an

---

[38] Nietzsche, *On the Genealogy of Morals and Ecce Homo*, p. 163; KSA, vol. V, p. 412.
[39] *Portable Nietzsche*, p. 568; KSA, vol. VI, p. 167.

"apologetics of the cross." Nietzsche was convinced that the heart of Jesus' message was "Resist not evil," and once again he may be closer to the truth than we find comfortable. Nonresistance, whatever we may think about its ethical or political applications, has hermeneutical implications for Christian apologetics. Nietzsche was contemptuous of Renan for applying the concept of hero to Jesus because nonresistance is the utter antithesis of heroism. What would a policy of nonresistance look like translated into the mode of theological apologetics? Dietrich Bonhoeffer may have grasped something of it in his July 1944 prison letters. One takes the opponent (for example, secular modernity) with utter seriousness but refuses to defend the gospel against it, at least directly.[40] The affirmation implicit in this apparently negative stance is utter faith in the power of God, that power that appears as weakness in this world. God is strong enough to resist all the slings and arrows that the world can hurl against him, and the same is true of God's Word. The appropriate stance of the theologian is therefore "Widerstand und Ergebung," standing by God in his hour of need, as Bonhoeffer puts it. This is surely not the "hardness" Nietzsche had in mind, but it is the kind of hardness appropriate to those who seek to live under the sign of the cross.

Last Enlightenment man or first postmodernist?
Never before has attention to Nietzsche been greater or his name more frequently invoked than at present. Those who appeal to his example, however, do not always agree about his message or its contemporary significance. One prominent recent tendency has been to view him as a postmodernist – even as the primary source of postmodernism. Advocates of the "new Nietzsche," as Maudemarie Clark calls them, "take Nietzsche's claim that truths are illusions

---

[40] Here, in a nutshell, is the nub of my theological disagreement with John Milbank and his followers.

to state his ultimate position on truth, and . . . deny that he accepted the traditional understanding of truth as correspondence, or regarded his own doctrines as true in this sense."[41] These interpreters attribute to Nietzsche the "theory that there are no truths but only interpretations" and deny that he himself intended to make truth claims. Rather, Nietzsche's writings represent, in the words of Derrida, "the joyous affirmation of the play of the world and of the innocence of becoming, the affirmation of a world of signs without fault, without truth."[42] Clark denies that the "new Nietzsche" ever existed; and it is surely the case that Derrida's paraphrase is likely to strike readers of *The Antichrist* and his other anti-Christian polemics as implausible. The Nietzsche who utters "A Curse against Christianity"[43] sounds less like a postmodernist than a radical *Aufklärer*, one who knows exactly what truth and reality really are. More accurately, perhaps, he sounds like a *philosophe*, whose railings against "priestcraft" are reminiscent less of the German Enlightenment than of Diderot or Voltaire, one of Nietzsche's favorite authors. Nietzsche the critic of religion, fulminating against the lies of Jews and Christians, does indeed mark a turning point in the history of thought ("Drehscheibe der Moderne," in Jürgen Habermas' phrase), but his role might better be described as the Last Enlightener than the First Postmodernist. The image of Nietzsche joyously affirming the polysemic possibilities of language is difficult to square with the "unrelievedly vituperative"[44] invective of *The Antichrist* and the other late works. Far from holding that there is no truth, the modernist Nietzsche speaks as the passionate defender

---

[41] Maudemarie Clark, *Nietzsche on Truth and Philosophy* (Cambridge: Cambridge University Press, 1990), pp. 11–12.

[42] Jacques Derrida, *Writing and Difference*, trans. Alan Bass (Chicago: University of Chicago Press, 1978), p. 292; cited by Clark, *Nietzsche on Truth and Philosophy*, p. 18.

[43] The subtitle of *The Antichrist* (KSA, vol. VI, p. 65), omitted by Kaufmann in *The Portable Nietzsche*.

[44] Arthur C. Danto, *Nietzsche as Philosopher* (New York: Macmillan, 1965; New York: Columbia University Press, 1980), p. 182.

of truth against lies, of reality against fiction. Theology ought to take this Nietzsche seriously as an opponent, for he pays Christianity the compliment of taking seriously – with deadly seriousness, one can say – its claims to truth. Virtually his last word before plunging into the silence of his final illness is the ringing challenge at the end of *Ecce Homo*: "Have I been understood? – *Dionysus versus the Crucified*."[45] Dionysus, who became for the Hellenophile Nietzsche the embodiment of everything noble and Greek – this Nietzschean Dionysus takes offense at the Crucified. Nietzsche is perhaps the supreme modern example of the one who hears the gospel – really *hears* it – and rejects it as a scandal. And like Paul, he recognizes that *power* is the crucial issue. In this way, though surely against his every intention, Nietzsche is ideally suited to be the one to awaken Christians from their modernist slumbers. As a theologian, I can find no more appropriate words for coming to terms with the modern atheist Nietzsche than Nietzsche's own words about the modern Christian Dostoyevsky: "In a remarkable way I'm thankful to him, however much he always goes against my most basic instincts."[46]

Despite the powerful figure of the modernist Nietzsche that we have been exploring in this chapter – the Nietzsche who brings to fulfillment the nineteenth-century hermeneutics of suspicion that originated in Feuerbach and flourished in Marx and Freud – a strong case can be made for the postmodernist Nietzsche. Even if these two Nietzsches are ultimately irreconcilable, it does not necessarily follow that only one of them can be the "real" Nietzsche; for he may well have adopted contradictory stances, either at

---

[45] Nietzsche, *On the Genealogy of Morals and Ecce Homo*, p. 335; KSA, vol. VI, p. 374. In the brief period after the onset of his insanity and before it reduced him to utter silence, Nietzsche dashed off several bizarre letters to various correspondents, some of which he signed "Dionysus" and others "The Crucified." One can scarcely avoid the speculation that this final polarity not only divided Nietzsche from Christianity but in some inscrutable way marked a split within himself.

[46] See n. 26 above.

different times or even simultaneously. Fortunately, however, we need not adjudicate this debate among the interpreters of Nietzsche, for whether or not there was a postmodernist Nietzsche, there is undeniably a Nietzschean postmodernism. In the next chapter I will examine this other face of Nietzsche, the postmodern one, which is such a powerful cultural force today. Among several possible proponents of postmodernism, I have chosen Jacques Derrida – not least because of the surprising parallels between his philosophical hermeneutics and the theological hermeneutics of Karl Barth.

Part II

Christian imagination in a postmodern world

6

The hermeneutics of difference: suspicion in postmodern guise

The Word became flesh: that is the first, original, and governing sign of all signs.

Barth

We have this treasure in earthen vessels, to show that the transcendent power belongs to God and not to us.

2 Corinthians 4.7

So far we have followed the course of the hermeneutics of suspicion from its prehistory in the modern accommodationist theology first exemplified in Kant's *Religion within the Limits of Reason Alone*, through its founding by Feuerbach, and its flowering in the "masters of suspicion," Marx, Freud, and Nietzsche. The previous chapter focused on what might be called the modernist Nietzsche, who attacks Christian faith and morality in the name of nature, reality, and health. Despite great differences among the classic nineteenth-century varieties of suspicion, they can all be classified as variations on the theme of "false consciousness." As we have noted, however, the case of Nietzsche is different – more complicated but also more interesting – because he stands as a kind of Janus figure at

The opening epigraph is taken from Karl Barth, *Die kirchliche Dogmatik*, vol. II, part 1, p. 233; *Church Dogmatics*, vol. II, part 1, p. 199. See further note 9 for fuller details of the citation method for Barth's material in this chapter.

the threshold of postmodernity. His voice has come to be heard today, in the twilight of modernity, not as the radical *Aufklärer* denouncing the Christian fiction, but rather as one who declares that "there are no facts, only *interpretations*." Whether the two Nietzsches can be reconciled is an interesting question in its own right but not one that will concern us here. For both the modern and the postmodern Nietzsche have continued to be heard in the twentieth century, though the voice of the latter speaks more loudly in our late modern world. It is his legacy that will concern us in the present chapter, refracted through the thought of Jacques Derrida, who may well be the most controversial of those recent philosophers to claim Nietzsche as the prophet of postmodernism.

Barth and Derrida: unlikely bedfellows

One can be excused for reacting with skepticism to any proposal linking the names of Karl Barth and Jacques Derrida. Even a serious scholar familiar with the thought of both might understandably be doubtful that significant convergences can be found between two such unlikely bedfellows. Is not Barth – for whom the Bible represents the criterion and touchstone of theology, the definitive witness to the Word of God – an example of just what postmodernists mean by a "logocentric" thinker committed to a metanarrative? And even theologians devoted to the method of correlation are likely to find in Derrida's deconstruction a most unpromising candidate for correlation with theology. Yet three recent books, all by scholars with impressive credentials for undertaking the task, find significant and positive parallels between Christian theology and postmodern philosophy and suggest in particular that a comparison of Barth and Derrida is a promising project. Walter Lowe, in *Theology and Difference*, uses Barth's *Römerbrief* to argue that his theology offers us not a dualism rooted in the kind of oppositions that cry out to be deconstructed, but rather an "analogy of difference" with striking similarities to central themes in Derrida.[1] Kevin Hart's book *The Trespass of the Sign* attempts a more general reconciliation between theology and deconstruction but includes hints that Barth's nonmetaphysical language is a step in the right direction.[2] Hart does not pursue this option, however, since he finds more promise for dialogue with deconstruction in the tradition of negative theology. The most recent book to explore the relationship between theology and deconstruction is also the one that devotes the greatest attention to parallels and convergences between Barth and Derrida: Graham Ward's *Barth, Derrida and the Language of Theology*.[3]

Ward's book has already provoked a spirited response by Bruce McCormack,[4] who accuses him of an "illegitimate appropriation of Barth . . . for 'postmodern' concerns," based on a misunderstanding of Barth's doctrine of analogy and an insufficient knowledge of his life and thought generally. McCormack's resounding "*Nein!*" to Ward's attempt at "negotiation" between Barth's theology of the Word and Derrida's "economy of *différance*" concludes with an appeal for an "Either-Or" choice: either Barth's theology – on its own terms and without postmodern "supplement" – or what McCormack calls the "abyss of deconstruction." Bracketing for a moment the question of who offers the more compelling case, we can use their interchange to focus attention on the key issue raised by the linkage of Barth's name with Derrida's. For however far apart they may be in their outcomes, Ward and McCormack agree about the central theological question. Ward identifies "the immediacy of the Word in the mediation of words" as "the theological *and* linguistic hub around which the whole of

[1] Walter Lowe, *Theology and Difference: The Wound of Reason* (Bloomington and Indianapolis: Indiana University Press, 1993).
[2] Kevin Hart, *The Trespass of the Sign: Deconstruction, Theology and Philosophy* (Cambridge: Cambridge University Press, 1989); see especially pp. 257, 262–3.
[3] Graham Ward, *Barth, Derrida and the Language of Theology* (Cambridge: Cambridge University Press, 1995).
[4] Bruce L. McCormack, "Article Review: Graham Ward's *Barth, Derrida and the Language of Theology*," *Scottish Journal of Theology* 49 (1996): 97–109.

the *Church Dogmatics* circulates."[5] He speaks of the problem of "how the Word takes possession of human words and thoughts," or, put the other way around, the problem of "the capacity of language to communicate the Word."[6] As McCormack puts it succinctly, echoing Barth's own formulation in 1921,[7] the theological task is to provide "a coherent account of the Word in the words." If we take this issue as our point of entry for a comparison of Barth and Derrida, we must admit at the very least that there are some striking similarities between them. Whether these parallels are indications of a deep commonality or merely superficial affinities of expression between otherwise heterogeneous thinkers is the question to be explored here.

In order to evaluate the apparent convergences between Barth and Derrida, and then to see to what extent they are significant, I want to bring three deconstructionist rubrics – signs, presence, and *différance* – into conversation with Barth's theology. Following Ward, I will focus the inquiry on Barth's treatment of the knowledge of God in chapter 5 of the *Church Dogmatics*. In terms of McCormack's interests this choice also makes sense, since he argues that the final christological shift in the development of Barth's theology "first makes itself felt in the treatment of the doctrine of God in *Church Dogmatics* II/1" starting in the summer of 1937.[8]

The necessity of the sign

At the heart of Barth's treatment of the knowledge of God is a dialectical relationship of revealing and concealing, unveiling and veiling. So accustomed are we to associating

---

[5] Ward, *Barth, Derrida and the Language of Theology*, p. 14.

[6] Ibid., pp. 21, 25.

[7] Karl Barth, *Der Römerbrief, 1922* (Zurich: TVZ, 1989), p. xix (original edn. p. xii). The English translation (p. 8) has conflated Barth's description of the hermeneutical task, which should read, "to the extent possible, the relation of the words to the Word in the words must be uncovered" (my translation). See also Bruce L. McCormack, *Karl Barth's Critically Realistic Dialectical Theology: Its Genesis and Development, 1909–1936* (Oxford: Clarendon Press, 1995), p. 270.

[8] Ibid., p. 22.

the name of Karl Barth with "revelation," that it is easy to overlook the second, or negative, side of this dialectic. But without it we are left with an undialectical theology of the Word – one that would deserve the epithet "positivism of revelation." What saves Barth's theology from positivism is his attention to the play of differences within his concept of revelation, especially in the section on "The Limits of the Knowledge of God" (§27), where he stresses God's *hiddenness*. In a crucial passage, he locates the theological principle at stake in this way: "Precisely in his *revelation*, precisely in *Jesus Christ*, the hidden God has in fact made himself comprehensible" – *faßbar* is his word: God has made himself available, "graspable," tangible (223/199).[9] Barth goes on to qualify this assertion in three parallel ways: "Not directly, but indirectly. Not for sight, but for faith. Not in his being, but in sign." He then summarizes all three: "Not, then, by the sublimation [*Aufhebung*] of his hiddenness – but comprehensibly [*faßbar*]." So directness, sight, and being are all identified – and rejected – as descriptions of our epistemic relation to God; and indirection, faith, and *signs* are identified – and affirmed. "Revelation means *giving signs*," he can write; therefore, "Revelation means *sacrament*" (56/52). Karl Barth's theology can thus be accurately described as a semiology, a theological semiotics.

This move brings him into the arena of Derrida's central concerns – though whether for similar reasons cannot as yet be determined. As Geoffrey Bennington points out,

---

[9] References to Barth's chapter on the knowledge of God will be made parenthetically. The first page number refers to *Die kirchliche Dogmatik* (hereafter *KD*), vol. II, *Die Lehre von Gott*, part 1 (Zurich: Theologischer Verlag Zürich, 1940); the second number refers to *Church Dogmatics* (hereafter *CD*), vol. II, *The Doctrine of God*, part 1, ed. G. W. Bromiley and T. F. Torrance, trans. T. H. L. Parker et al. (Edinburgh: T. & T. Clark, 1957). I have freely altered the translation when appropriate, generally preferring to stay closer to the original German than is the practice in the published translation. I have also restored Barth's emphasis by the use of italics to indicate *gesperrte Schrift* in the original (Barth's frequent use of this typographic convention is often an important clue to his meaning).

"not only does Derrida begin with the sign in the order of his published work, *he asserts, from the beginning, that the sign is at the beginning.*"[10] The whole problematic leading to deconstruction can be derived from the differences implied in our use of signs: "The sign refers to the concept which refers to the world, allowing us a grasp of the world which is other than chaotic and evanescent." The sign, according to Derrida, makes possible a language that does not consist simply of proper names. Its difference from what it signifies allows us, in Bennington's phrase, to "call a cat a cat rather than Marmaduke."[11] But the difference between sign and signified also means that no sign ever succeeds in fully (i.e. unambiguously) identifying its intended object. Signs refer not to things directly but to other signs, which in turn refer to still other signs in an inconclusive and neverending deferral of meaning. Since we nevertheless *want* unambiguous meaning, we *desire* closure, this hermeneutical situation represents a continual temptation to falsify meaning by devious, and ultimately unsuccessful, attempts at fore-closure.

The question of presence
All of this sounds very much like Barth, except for one possibly decisive difference: Derrida is describing the grammar of signs in general, whereas Barth is talking about a *particular* use of signs, namely, to designate God. But in fact for Derrida "God" is not simply one more sign, subject to the vicissitudes and deferrals of all signs; rather, it holds (or we would like it to hold) a unique place in the hierarchy of signs. To understand the place of the signifier "God" in Derrida's account, we need to introduce a second major rubric: *presence*. As Kevin Hart points out, "the concept 'sign' presupposes a concept of presence: a sign is always

---

[10] Geoffrey Bennington and Jacques Derrida, *Jacques Derrida* (Chicago: University of Chicago Press, 1993), p. 24.
[11] Ibid., p. 25.

a *sign of* something present or presentable."[12] There is a polemical edge to Derrida's account of the distinction between sign and presence, for he is persuaded that the entire tradition of Western thought has been dominated by a quest for the illusory goal of complete presence and has consequently produced a long series of projects in what Derrida calls the "metaphysics of presence." Such misguided quests assume "the possibility of thinking a *concept signified in and of itself*, a concept simply present for thought, independent of a relationship to language . . . to a system of signifiers."[13] This goal Derrida dubs a "transcendental signified," something "which in and of itself, in its essence, would refer to no signifier, would exceed the chain of signs, and would no longer itself function as a signifier."[14] Although there are examples of nontheistic, and even atheistic, metaphysics of presence, "God" has been the favorite nominee for transcendental signified. Thus how a particular thinker treats the concept of God will be, from Derrida's perspective, an important clue to the thinker's semiotic assumptions and commitments.

In the case of Barth's theology, it quickly becomes apparent that God is no transcendental signified and that dogmatics, properly conceived, cannot possibly be a metaphysics of presence. Indeed, much of the thrust of chapter 5 of the *Church Dogmatics* is directed against any suggestion that our knowledge of God could be based on immediate experience, which is just what presence entails. Barth's distinction between the primary and secondary objectivity of God appears designed to head off any such conclusion. From our standpoint, God is objective only in this "secondary" way: indirectly, not directly; for faith, but not for sight; veiled under signs, not as being. To stress God's hiddenness, after all, is surely to deny God's presence, at least

[12] Hart, *Trespass of the Sign*, p. 5.
[13] Jacques Derrida, *Positions*, trans. Alan Bass (Chicago: University of Chicago Press, 1981), p. 19.
[14] Ibid., pp. 19–20.

in any usual or straightforward sense of the term. Hiddenness, of course, is not all that Barth has to say about God, or even the most important thing. But it is the first, the *terminus a quo* of our knowledge of God, and thus its limit: in this life we know God not as a presence "face to face" but in his "enigmatic" indirection (1 Corinthians 13.12), by which he offers himself to us "in, with, and under the sign . . . of other objects." This "clothed" knowledge of God is what Barth means when he says that our knowledge of God is a knowledge of faith. As the very distinction between "faith" and "sight" implies, the former is a relationship not of presence but of absence.

The economy of *différance*

But "absence" is not quite right either. For Barth does not say or imply that in faith we live in the *absence* rather than the presence of God. Faith is, after all, an analogical relationship, an *analogia fidei* – a relationship, in other words, characterized by likeness or similarity. By rejecting the "analogy of being" that Barth found operative in both Roman Catholic and Liberal Protestant theology, he was rejecting the thesis that our knowledge of God is based on a similarity of *being* shared by Creator and creature alike. His alternative, however, was not to deny the likeness, the analogy, but rather to deny that it is based on being. But that means that faith is itself an analogical relationship, one that involves both *Gleichheit* and *Ungleichheit* – equality and inequality, parity and disparity (as the English translation has it), identity and difference. In faith the Word of God is *neither* simply like our words *nor* simply unlike them; alternatively, in faith God's Word is *both* like *and* unlike ours. Barth is not simply glorying in paradoxes, however much his rhetoric may sometimes leave that impression. The key to resolving the apparent paradox of identity and difference, presence and absence, lies in what George Hunsinger calls Barth's actualism, the most distinctive trait of his theology. "It is present," writes Hunsinger, "whenever

Barth speaks . . . in the language of occurrence, happening, event, history, decisions, and act."[15] Barth's actualism is epitomized in his preference for *becoming* over *being*. At crucial points in the *Church Dogmatics* he contrasts the two verbs to make his point. In terms of the divine/human analogy, Barth puts it this way: strictly speaking there *is* no analogy between God's Word and ours; the word we speak *is* not the Word God speaks. But by the grace of God – i.e. through God's *act* – our words *become* his Word. The term "analogy," he writes, "*is* not . . . correct in itself . . . It [nevertheless] *becomes* correct" in the context of revelation. So "in *our* thinking and speaking similarity *becomes* similar to the similarity posited in the true revelation of *God*." (255/226; Barth's emphasis). Although we are powerless to restore to our words their original divine authenticity, Barth writes, nevertheless "in our knowing this analogy of truth *becomes* [or *comes to be*],[16] by means of the decision of his grace" (260/230). The very same relationship, and the same contrast between the verbs *to be* and *to become*, is the hallmark of Barth's theology of religion. The climax and turning point of section 17 ("God's Revelation as the *Aufhebung* of Religion") arrives with these words: "No religion *is* true. A religion can only *become* true, i.e. correspond to that which it gives itself out to be and is taken to be." The model for the relationship is the justification of the sinner, which means that the analogy of faith is at bottom an analogy of grace: "The true religion is, like the justified human being, a creature of *grace*."[17] Precisely the same

---

[15] George Hunsinger, *How To Read Karl Barth: The Shape of His Theology* (Oxford: Oxford University Press, 1991), p. 30.

[16] My translation is deliberately more literal than ordinary English usage can bear; the published translation says that the analogy "comes into being," which is better English but obscures Barth's characteristic contrast between *sein* and *werden*. Eberhard Jüngel has captured this distinctive usage in the title of his book *Gottes Sein ist im Werden* (ET: *The Doctrine of the Trinity: God's Being is in Becoming* [Grand Rapids, MI: William B. Eerdmans Publishing Co., 1976]).

[17] Barth, *KD*, vol. I, part 2 (Zurich: Theologischer Verlag Zürich, n.d.), p. 356; cf. *CD*, vol. I, part 2, ed. G. W. Bromiley and T. F. Torrance, trans. G. T. Thomson and Harold Knight (Edinburgh: T. & T. Clark, 1956), pp. 325–6. See Garrett Green,

must be said of the relationship between the divine Word
and human words: although our words *are* not the Word
of God, they can *become* the Word of God – by God's grace.

At this point we can cast a glance back at Derrida. For
he, too, is wont to speak in terms not simply of presence
or absence but of some more complex relationship that is
irreducible to the one or the other. "We must not suppose," notes Bennington, "that because Derrida questions
presence he must therefore be a thinker of absence, empti-
ness, nothing."[18] To explain why this is so, we cannot avoid
Derrida's elusive and exasperating "neographism"[19] *différance* (with an *a*) – much as we might wish that we could!
In fact, so far as I can see, one of the best ways to understand the point of *différance* is to see that Derrida introduces
it as the alternative to *presence*. He proposes to replace the
metaphysics of presence with the economy of *différance*.
And his reasons for doing so are once again related to the
way signs function, to what he calls "the problematic of the
sign."[20] "The sign," he writes, "represents the present in
its absence. It takes the place of the present." Thus the
"sign, in this sense, is deferred presence." But the sign is
therefore not simple absence either, since its very purpose
is to represent (re-present) the signified. It should now be
clear why the goal of every metaphysics of presence,
namely, to discover a "transcendental signified," is illusory,
for "the signified concept is never present in and of itself,
in a sufficient presence that would refer only to itself."[21]
About the closest Derrida ever comes to a formal definition

"Challenging the Religious Studies Canon: Karl Barth's Theory of Religion," *Journal of Religion* 75 (1995): 473–86.

[18] Bennington and Derrida, *Jacques Derrida*, pp. 75–6.

[19] Jacques Derrida, "Différance," in *Margins of Philosophy*, trans. Alan Bass (Chicago: University of Chicago Press, 1982), p. 3. Derrida refers to his coinage as a "neographism" rather than a neologism because part of its point is to stress the priority of writing over speech (since the "difference" between *différence* and *différance* depends entirely on the written words, their pronunciations being identical). That is why, presumably, Bennington defines *différance* first of all as "a witticism of Derrida's" (*Jacques Derrida*, p. 70).

[20] Derrida, "Différance," p. 9.

[21] Ibid., p. 11.

of *différance* is this statement: *"Différance* is the non-full, non-simple, structured and differentiating origin of differences." A sign, then, according to Derrida, is neither a presence nor an absence but what he calls a *trace*. In Bennington's paraphrase, traces are not atoms or elements of a system but rather are "traces of the *absence* of the other 'element,' which is moreover not absent in the sense of 'present elsewhere,' but is itself made up of traces. Every trace is the trace of a trace. No element is anywhere present (nor simply absent), there are only traces."[22]

Now it would appear that despite the evident congruence between what Barth says about the dialectic of presence and absence in revelation and Derrida's account of the trace in the economy of *différance* (which likewise involves a dialectic of presence and absence) – despite this similarity Barth and Derrida are surely talking about quite different subject matters. But such a conclusion, I think, would be premature, for sharing a common subject matter is not the only way in which two thinkers can be significantly related. Ward's claim – to return to the disagreement between him and McCormack – is not that Derrida is writing about the same subject as Barth but rather that he has developed conceptual tools more suitable to Barth's subject matter than the tools Barth had at his disposal. What their projects have in common is their involvement with "the same double nature of language"; and Ward maintains that Barth's theological concern with the Word in the words can be clarified with the help of Derrida's philosophical insights into the way linguistic signs function. "With Derrida's notion of *différance*," Ward claims, "the coherence of Barth's theology of language is clarified."[23]

A general theory of language?
McCormack's challenge to Ward's reading of Barth raises a number of fascinating and important questions, and I for

[22] Bennington and Derrida, *Jacques Derrida*, p. 75.
[23] Ward, *Barth, Derrida and the Language of Theology*, p. 34.

one hope that Ward will respond publicly to the charges. For this debate promises to be uncommonly productive, since the opponents are in fact very close to one another in important ways and are pressing an issue of major importance to theologians in the current cultural situation. Since Ward himself, so far as I am aware, has not responded to McCormack, I want to try my own hand at developing a couple of strategic points in their controversy.

Let me first say what I think Ward has accomplished, even if many of McCormack's criticisms should turn out to be true. By "recontextualizing" Barth's theology of the Word in a postmodern setting (a move that so obviously grates on Professor McCormack's nerves), Ward illumines Barth's theological project from a fresh perspective, and one that turns out to be surprisingly revealing. As I have tried to show by looking at the rubrics of the sign, the dialectic of presence and absence, and the uniquely Derridean logic of *différance*, Barth turns out to have anticipated certain concerns that were picked up by others only much later. The very tones in Barth's theology that were most jarring to the ears of his contemporaries now have an almost familiar sound in an age accustomed to the dissonant tones of deconstruction. Theological attention to postmodern philosophy would be justified on these grounds alone, that is, by its raising of questions that direct our attention to aspects of the theological tradition we may have neglected, and by doing so in a way that puts us into conversation with secular intellectuals of our own day. But I will make the stronger argument that there are convergences not only of question but also of method and even – if properly qualified – significant convergences in matters of substance. I want to make good on these claims by looking first at the point where Barth seems most in agreement with Derrida, and then at a point where he seems to diverge from him most radically.

McCormack's first "observation" about Ward's reading of chapter 5 of the *Church Dogmatics* is a charge of misrepresentation: "Barth's problematic was never, at any point," he maintains, "that of a general theory of language."[24] He accuses Ward of forcing Barth into a philosophical discussion in which he in fact declined to participate; and this error is a major part of Ward's alleged "appropriation" of Barth for illegitimate postmodern purposes. Now McCormack is surely right that Barth was never engaged in the kind of general theoretical enterprise represented by *Redephilosophie* and *Sprachphilosophie*, and he offers compelling evidence that Ward exaggerates the connection of Barth with the Patmos Circle. Nevertheless, in his own way – and that means as a theologian – Barth surely *was* interested in a general theory of language. Buried in a footnote near the end of Ward's book is an important reference to something Barth says in the opening paragraph of chapter 1 of the *Church Dogmatics*: "there is no genuinely profane speech. In the last resort, there is only talk about God."[25] This statement, rendered somewhat freely by the translator, follows Barth's blunt opening assertion that "not all human talk [*Rede*] is talk about God," even though "it really could and should be [*könnte und müßte wohl so sein*]." The reason it should be is simply that everything, all the possible objects of our speech, have their origin and destiny in God (*von ihm her und zu ihm hin sind*). For this reason (now translating the passage cited by Ward more literally), "there should be and ought to be no profane talk but rather, understood in terms of its ultimate subject matter [*in letzter Sachlichkeit*], only talk about God." In a few broad strokes, Barth proceeds to lay out "a general theory of language" – not indeed a *Redephilosophie* but rather a virtual *Redetheologie*. He does so by situating and grounding human language, what we could call the linguistic human

[24] McCormack, "Review," p. 101.
[25] Barth, *KD*, vol. 1, part 1 (Zurich: Theologischer Verlag Zürich, n.d.), p. 47. Ward takes his translation from *CD*, vol. I, part 1, ed. G. W. Bromiley and T. F. Torrance, trans. G. W. Bromiley, rev. edn. (Edinburgh: T. & T. Clark, 1975), p. 47 (cited by Ward, *Barth, Derrida and the Language of Theology*, p. 244, note 8).

condition, in the context of the biblical narrative of salvation. The subjunctive modalities of Barth's opening statements (*könnte, müßte, dürfte*) point to our actual present situation as "fallen, lost, and damned recipients of mercy" living not in the *regnum gloriae* but in the *regnum gratiae*, "the present [age] between the times of creation and redemption." Our speech is understood by contrast with the speech both of original humanity (*Menschen des Urstands*) and eschatological humanity (*Menschen des Reiches der Herrlichkeit*), for whom all talk "as such" can be interpreted as talk about God. We, on the other hand, dwell in a kingdom of unlikeness, whose linguistic "symptom" (Barth's preferred metaphor) is a division, separation, distinction, or divorce (*Scheidung* carries all those connotations) running right through the heart of our speech. Furthermore, this linguistic division is a "provisional" (*vorläufig*) indicator pointing toward "that final division, that event, in which God is the one who acts."[26]

Can we not say that here Barth and Derrida, from their very different perspectives and out of their very different interests, are dealing with the same subject – and even, up to a point, saying similar things about it? They are one in their conviction that human speech is not a transparent window on reality, that in some deep sense using language is a self-contradictory enterprise, one bound to fall short of its mark. As much as we would like to mean what we say, we seem condemned always to mean both more and less. Seeking wholeness, we inevitably speak in fragments; intending univocity, we equivocate in spite of ourselves. (Not only the white man, as they say in the old Hollywood westerns, "speak with forked tongue.") And both Barth and Derrida issue repeated warnings against the temptation to think that we can transcend the inherent ambiguities of human language. At one point, at least, they even agree on a name for the wrong way of thinking about language:

---

[26] Barth, *KD*, vol. I, part 1, p. 48; *CD*, vol. I, part 1, p. 48 (my translation).

metaphysics. If such a convergence exists, limited as it is to a narrow but important range of human experience, a dialogue between them is both possible and potentially fruitful. Viewed from the theological side, Barth's *Redetheologie* allows us to interpret Derrida's economy of *différance* as a philosophical description of what it means to be language-users in the age of grace. It allows us to hear the deconstructionist warning against the metaphysics of presence as a postmodern reminder of the dangers of trying to usurp the role of God in our human speaking and writing. Most important of all, Derrida's account of what it means to be users of signs offers new conceptual tools for restating in our own time what Barth in his day called the dialectic of "veiling and unveiling" in God's self-revelation of his Word in our words.

Barth's Christian semiotics
The more difficult part of a conversation between Barth and Derrida will come at the point where they appear to diverge. I can imagine at least the possibility of convincing a deconstructionist that faith in the God of Jesus Christ does not commit one to the metaphysics of presence and does not presuppose a transcendental signified of any kind. I find it much harder to imagine Derrida accepting Barth's identification of Jesus Christ as the "sign of all signs." If such is the case, what does it tell us about the relationship between Christian faith and postmodern philosophy?

Let us look at the context of Barth's comment about Christ as sign. To begin with, we take note (with a sideways glance at Derrida) of what Barth does *not* say: he does not identify Jesus Christ as a "transcendental signified," as a moment of pure presence that grounds our otherwise shifting system of signs; rather, he identifies him precisely as sign, and thus subject to the vicissitudes of all signs (in Derrida's terms), to the conditions of "secondary objectivity" (in Barth's terms). To do otherwise, we should note, to attempt to exempt Jesus Christ from the linguistic human condition, would amount to semiotic docetism, to an implicit denial of the full humanity of the incarnate one. It might even imply that simply to name Jesus Christ would render him present – a move that would turn every theologian (indeed, every Christian) into a conjurer. At the very least it would turn Jesus into a "transcendental signified" by presupposing that we had extralinguistic access to his presence. Barth contrasts the sign-character of Christ precisely with his essential being: in revelation Jesus Christ becomes *faßbar* "not in his *Wesen* but rather in sign" (223/199). St. Paul, writing of "the gospel of the glory of Christ," says something similar: "We have this treasure in earthen vessels, to show that the transcendent power belongs to God and not to us" (2 Corinthians 4.7). Signs, understood the way Barth – and Derrida – understands them, are thoroughly earthen.

Barth goes so far as to identify revelation itself with signification: "This *is* God's revelation: that God has given to the creature chosen and determined for this purpose the commission and the power to represent and depict him [*ihn zu vertreten und darzustellen*], to bear witness to him." There follows immediately the decisive sentence: "The Word became flesh: that is the first, original, and governing sign of all signs" (233/199). We should note first of all the qualifier "governing" (*regierend*).[27] Barth is saying that in the story of Jesus Christ we have the hermeneutical key that renders God's "secondary objectivity" intelligible to us. Without ceasing to be a sign, this sign nevertheless governs our use and interpretation of all signs. Because it does so as a sign (and not as a "transcendental signified"), it does not escape the economy of *différance*. In attempting to paraphrase Barth's theology of the knowledge of God, Ward comments that "without revelation we occupy a

---

[27] The use of "controlling" to translate *regierend* in the published translation lends a harshly authoritarian tone that is not implied by Barth's diction. It is also theologically imprecise, since the God of Israel and the church *governs* the world in freedom rather than simply "controlling" it.

world of circulating semiotics."[28] But even *with* revelation, on Barth's account, we occupy such a world; for our signs do not somehow become fixed once we attend to revelation. In the final subsection of chapter 5, where Barth examines the veracity or the truth-character (*Wahrhaftigkeit*) of the knowledge of God, his analysis culminates in a discussion of what it means that our knowledge of God is a knowledge in faith. Here he returns to a recurrent motif in his dogmatics, the circular logic of theology,[29] which is represented by the very structure of section 27 ("The Limits of the Knowledge of God"). For that knowledge originates – has its *terminus a quo* or originating limit – in the hiddenness of God; and it eventually returns, as its *terminus ad quem* or ultimate limit, to the same divine hiddenness. In this way our knowledge of God is circular; it runs its course from the divine mystery to the divine mystery. Barth faces up to the problem of circularity with disarming candor, acknowledging that it may be an indication that we have not understood our knowledge of God as *wahrhaftig*. In other words, the circular logic of the knowledge of God could turn out to be a vicious circle. Barth does acknowledge that there are also *circuli veritatis*, circles of truth, but refuses to take refuge in that notion, acknowledging that in our intention to trace the *circulus veritatis Dei* we might be deluding ourselves by means of a mere "word play" or a "systematic *Deus ex machina*" (278–9/246). Even our appeals to faith, revelation, and grace (right as they are) offer no ultimate insurance against the possibility of self-deception. Expressed in the postmodern language of Derrida, Barth is saying that there is an undecidability between the *circulus veritatis Dei* and the *Deus ex machina* that calls for the decision of faith or unfaith. We will return to the necessarily unsecured nature of the knowledge of faith, but first

---

[28] Ward, *Barth, Derrida and the Language of Theology*, p. 29.
[29] See Green, "Challenging the Religious Studies Canon," p. 478, note 11, for further references to the circular logic of theology in Barth.

we must acknowledge another important aspect of Barth's identification of Jesus Christ as "governing sign."

Listen once more to the linchpin of Barth's Christian semiotics: "The Word became flesh: that is the first, original, and governing sign of all signs." Notice that, strictly speaking, Barth does not identify Jesus as sign – or rather, he does so in a particular way. The governing sign is not the man himself, not even the God-man, as a *being* (this is what Barth means when he says "not in *Wesen* but in sign"). Instead Barth names an *event*, the becoming-flesh of the Son of God in Jesus. This event, and not any thing or being, is the "sign of all signs." In keeping with Barth's actualism, we may surely paraphrase here: Jesus Christ *is* not the governing sign; rather, he *becomes* the governing sign – by the grace of God! But what is this event of incarnation but the epitome of the whole story of Jesus – indeed, of the whole story of the world told from the vantage point of God's redeeming love of his lost creation? The sign of Jesus Christ governs our speaking and writing, not by conjuring up a pure presence that secures our use of signs against ambiguity, but rather by directing our attention to the constitutive pattern that renders the whole story of God's gracious intercourse with his creation apprehensible to us. Expressed in somewhat different conceptual terms, the narrative of Jesus Christ is the catalyst by which the paradigm or normative pattern of the Holy Scriptures snaps into imaginative focus. That paradigm becomes in turn the root metaphor (the *analogia fidei*) by which our own lives are brought into analogical relationship with the story of the incarnation of Jesus Christ at the heart of the story of God and the world. "The Word became flesh" functions for Barth as the epitome of that scriptural paradigm and hence as the "governing sign of all signs" because it orders all our signs according to the analogy of faith. In this way God utters the Word in, with, and under our words.

The supplementary logic of grace

Much of the vehemence of McCormack's attack on Ward's reading of Barth appears to derive from his assumption that Ward accuses Barth of inconsistencies and contradictions in his account of how God speaks his Word in our words. To make matters worse in McCormack's view, Ward then suggests that Barth stands in need of a Derridean "supplement." "There is no aporia in Barth's theory of theological language," McCormack declares testily, "needing to be filled by Derrida or anyone else."[30] But surely here it is McCormack who has misread Ward. Granted that Ward's prose could be clearer (a fault that seems endemic to admirers of Derrida), his penultimate chapter on "Barth and the Economy of *Différance*" is not a corrective but rather a highly sympathetic interpretation of Barth's theology in the light of Derrida's "economy of *différance*." Far from accusing Barth of contradiction, Ward (with help from Derrida) seeks to demonstrate the "coherence" of Barth's theology of the Word, which "otherwise *has been seen* as a contradiction which logically flaws his Christology and the soteriological operation of the Trinity."[31] Ward appeals to Derrida in order to defend Barth against charges of inconsistency. Or perhaps it would be more accurate to say that Ward acknowledges inconsistencies in Barth while arguing that he is right to be inconsistent – right for reasons that Derrida has brought to light. Read as an example of Derrida's economy of *différance*, "Barth's theological discourse is understood as a rhetorical strategy presenting both the need to do and the impossibility of doing theology." McCormack claims that "Ward has not grasped Barth's particularism,"[32] but it would be more accurate to say that Ward uses Derrida to explicate the hermeneutical heart of that particularism, namely, Barth's identification of

---

[30] McCormack, "Review," p. 106.
[31] Ward, *Barth, Derrida and the Language of Theology*, p. 247 (my emphasis).
[32] McCormack, "Review," p. 102.

Jesus Christ as "the first, original, and governing sign of all signs." Ward paraphrases Barth's principle as follows: "Jesus Christ is the name of the remembered promise of a future presence, which circulates within the economy of *différance*. He is the promised Word, inaugurating and endlessly promoting the chain of signifiers which defer its final, realized presence."[33] Theologians may surely differ on the question of whether this postmodern setting of Barth's theology is an advance over Barth's own way of making the same points, for example, by stressing the circular character of dogmatics, its continual exposure to both *Anfechtung* and comfort. But the discussion is worth having, if only because so many of our contemporaries appeal to Derrida, frequently using him to discredit or dismiss theology. We have a precedent in Barth's own *ad hoc* use of philosophy in the service of dogmatics. If he can harness even so volatile a notion as Hegelian *Aufhebung* (one of his favorites), surely we can be permitted an occasional theological appeal to *différance* without plunging headlong into the "abyss of deconstruction."

Derrida's notion of *supplément* offers one model for the conversation between Christian theologians and postmodern philosophers – one that I find particularly attractive because it dovetails so well with a Christian understanding of our common life together under grace. In what we can call vulgar postmodernism – the ideology that has so often poisoned our professional societies and polarized our faculties by politically correct but philosophically misguided appeals to Derrida – deconstruction is identified with refutation. This perversion of postmodernism leads to an academic form of "Gotcha!" that works like this: If I can expose the unacknowledged play of opposites lurking in your favorite texts, I win the game! But if I understand the logic of supplementarity correctly, its moral implications are quite different. The fundamental hermeneutical

---

[33] Ward, *Barth, Derrida and the Language of Theology*, p. 248.

situation in which we all find ourselves as users of signs, which Derrida indicates by the word *différance*, entails that no text can ever be complete or self-sufficient, which in turn implies that every text stands in need of a supplement. For a supplement expresses what *cannot* be said in the original text. Note well: not just what *is not* said, but what *cannot be* said without rending the fabric – the "textile" as Derrida calls it – of the text, in other words, what makes the text the text. That is not a failing of the original, but it does represent the inevitable limits to which all texts are subject. (An excursus on Jesus' parable of the wineskins would no doubt be in order here.) The logic of grace in Christian teaching (including surely Karl Barth's dogmatics) is a logic of supplementarity; it shows us why we need each other, since none of us is hermeneutically self-sufficient. As Christians, we attribute this situation not to the unfortunate but unavoidable limitations of finitude but rather to grace: God has so arranged things that we cannot say what needs to be said (ultimately, the Word of God) on our own – and what God has ordained is good! This supplementary logic of grace has an historical dimension as well: we need those who have preceded us in the faith; we need their texts, and they need our interpretations. We can never forget them, for a supplement does not replace the text it supplements. In this way we catch a glimpse of what might be called the hermeneutical communion of saints.

But the supplementary logic of grace, according to the Christian vision, is not confined to the saints. Professor McCormack (who may have been exposed to too much vulgar postmodernism) takes umbrage at Ward's suggestion that "Derrida has provided Barth's theology of language ... with a philosophical supplement." He neglects to note that Ward goes on to say, "Barth provides Derrida's economy of *différance* with a theological supplement."[34] In

[34] Ibid., p. 256.

the long run, I suspect that secular deconstructionists will have greater difficulty accepting this mutual supplementarity than will Christian theologians, but that is a question the secularists will need to settle for themselves. From the theological side of the conversation, however, I see some promising openings, which in conclusion I would like to mention.

I want to return to the point of hermeneutical vulnerability that Barth reaches in the conclusion of his theology of the knowledge of God in chapter 5 of the *Church Dogmatics*, because it goes to the heart of the differences finally separating Barth from Derrida, and Christian theology today from postmodern philosophy. Immediately after acknowledging the impossibility of securing the truthfulness of our knowledge of God against reduction to a vicious circle, Barth makes what is perhaps the most remarkable statement of the entire chapter. If we take seriously the claim that only God's grace distinguishes the *circulus veritatis Dei* from the *Deus ex machina*, Barth writes, "then we can surely wish to have it no other way than that we cannot in fact defend ourselves in the face of that question" (279/246). Not only *are* we defenseless as believers, Barth is saying, we should *want* to be! (Those critics of the "neo-orthodox" Barth, whom McCormack so effectively refutes, should pay closer attention to passages like this one.) Like Derrida, Barth embraces *différance* (though surely for very different reasons) and thus opposes every attempt at theological closure as a refusal to trust oneself wholly to the grace of God.

Finally, some examples from the New Testament can be briefly cited as exegetical support for the Christian refusal to seek security by evading *différance*. There is a remarkable resistance to closure in the final sentence of John's gospel: "But there are also many other things which Jesus did; were every one of them to be written, I suppose that the world itself could not contain the books that would be written" (John 21.25). (If Mark's gospel indeed ends at 16.8, it would be an even more dramatic instance; but I will stay out of that debate for now.) The ending of John's gospel manages to achieve a literary "sense of an ending" while at the same time indicating the supplementary logic of the narrative of Jesus Christ. A quite different sort of example is the recurrent theme of asking for a sign in the gospel narratives. The crowds repeatedly demand a sign from Jesus, and he repeatedly refuses – rather, he gives them a different kind of sign from what they desire. "And he sighed deeply in his spirit, and said, 'Why does this generation seek a sign? Truly I say to you, no sign shall be given to this generation.' And he left them" (Mark 8.12). In the fourth gospel, this withdrawal of Jesus hints at a salvific purpose: ". . . and I, when I am lifted up from the earth, will draw all men to myself" (John 12.32). Jesus withdraws from us to save us. "When Jesus had said this, he departed and hid himself from them" (John 12.36b) – which is followed immediately by the evangelist's comment, "Though he had done so many signs before them, yet they did not believe in him." They did not believe, we may surmise, because Jesus' signs do not deliver the security of complete presence; they are promises yet to be fulfilled. Jesus draws all people to himself by allowing himself to be "lifted up," crucified – "erased" we might even say with Derrida.[35] We know Jesus only "under erasure," because otherwise we might be tempted to hold on to him in the present – to force him to be present, to stay with us. But Jesus, now as then, does not come as fulfilling presence but as summoner: "Follow me!" is not the announcement of the end of the road but an invitation to travel. Presence, as a term of Christian

---

[35] Jean-Luc Marion sounds a similar note when he proposes to "cross out G⊕d" (with the cross of St. Andrew). *God Without Being: Hors-Texte*, trans. Thomas A. Carlson (Chicago: University of Chicago Press, 1991), p. 46. The question I would like to ask Marion, however, is whether this "crossing out" is only a limitation forced upon us by our finitude or a manifestation of God's grace to be affirmed and celebrated. Like so many modern theologians, he sees the great danger to theology and faith in idolatry. For a discussion of the dangers of the iconoclastic bias in modern theology, see Garrett Green, *Imagining God: Theology and the Religious Imagination* (Grand Rapids, MI: William B. Eerdmans Publishing Co., 1998), pp. 91–7.

theology, is always an eschatological term: *parousia*. The logic of grace is a logic of supplementarity. By means of the continually fulfilling but never fulfilled rhythm of our life in Christ, God draws us forward, draws us into the divine life.

It is not just individual New Testament books that have open-ended endings. Can it be mere coincidence that the church's scriptural canon itself ends with this prayer: "Amen. Come, Lord Jesus!"? But wait – there is still one more verse: "The *grace* of the Lord Jesus be with all the saints. Amen."

7

The hermeneutic imperative: interpretation and the theological task

... a good interpretation of a text is one that has "breathing space," that is to say, one in which no hermeneutic finally allows you to resolve the text – there is something that is left to bother, something that is wrong, something that is not yet interpreted.

Frei

And beginning with Moses and all the prophets, he interpreted to them in all the scriptures the things concerning himself.

Luke 24.27

The late modern crisis of interpretation, occasioned by the rise of the hermeneutics of suspicion, is part of a larger pattern of change in the way our culture reads texts, especially its sacred texts, those that nourish and undergird our sense of reality and orient us in the world. Hans Frei has shown how and why realistic narrative reading of the Bible went into "eclipse" in eighteenth- and nineteenth-century hermeneutics. Before the rise of historical criticism, Christians from the earliest times "had envisioned the real world

---

The opening epigraph is taken from Hans W. Frei, "Conflicts in Interpretation: Resolution, Armistice, or Co-existence?" in *Theology and Narrative: Selected Essays*, ed. George Hunsinger and William C. Placher (Oxford: Oxford University Press, 1993), p. 162.

as formed by the sequence told by the biblical stories."[1]
Under the sway of this precritical hermeneutic, the biblical
story was read literally, which meant that people took for
granted that the narratives described actual events; but Frei
points out how different this assumption was from the
modern practice of treating the text as "evidence" that certain historical happenings actually took place. He also
reminds us that earlier Christian interpreters used figural
or typological exegesis both as a way of binding the diverse
components of scripture into one complex narrative and as
a means for extending the biblical world to encompass the
whole of extra-biblical reality, including the lives of those
who read the Bible. Thus, Frei writes, "Biblical interpretation became an imperative need, but its direction was that
of incorporating extra-biblical thought, experience, and
reality into the one real world detailed and made accessible
by the biblical story – not the reverse" (3). For reasons that
Frei demonstrates, the older implicit assumption that literal
meaning and historical reference belong together began to
break down, so that the "logical and reflective distance
between narrative and reality increased steadily . . . provok-
ing a host of endeavors to bridge the gap" (5). Much of the
history of theology in the past two centuries is the chronicle
of those bridge-building projects. The assumption behind
all of them has been that, "whether or not the story is true
history, its *meaning* is detachable from the specific story
that sets it forth" (6).

The most fateful consequence for theology of this
modern hermeneutical sea-change is the reversal of what
Frei calls the "direction of interpretation" (5). Once textual meaning had been detached from the story itself,
the hermeneutical race was on to work out the most
plausible description of that (nonnarrative) meaning and

[1] Hans W. Frei, *The Eclipse of Biblical Narrative: A Study in Eighteenth and Nineteenth Century Hermeneutics* (New Haven, CT: Yale University Press, 1974), p. 1. Subsequent references to this book will be made parenthetically in the text.

thereby to show how the Bible, as its vehicle or medium, continues to be meaningful for modern people. The result has been the long series of what I have called accommodationist theologies: all those attempts, beginning with Kant's own reinterpretation of the Christian religion, to show how the Bible, even though its narratives cannot possibly be true "literally," nevertheless discloses a nonnarrative meaning that is both true and relevant to people living in the modern age. By "literal," of course, the modern interpreter no longer means what was once taken to be the literal sense of scripture but rather its historical plausibility. Because of this "confusion of history-likeness (literal meaning) and history (ostensive reference)" (12), modern theology has thought its most pressing task to be the adaptation of Christian truth – which unfortunately has come to us in the vehicle of implausible biblical narratives – to the critically honed sensibilities of the modern world. Like Rudolf Bultmann, who felt sure that the modern radio listener could not possibly credit stories about a three-storied universe as the word of God, accommodationist theologians have offered us a succession of proposals for "demythologizing" the gospel – or whatever the functional equivalent of demythologizing may be for a particular theologian. As I have also argued, this accommodating move almost always involves at its core a "depositivizing" interpretation of Christian truth – a removal of the embarrassing concreteness and particularity which adheres to the Christian message in its classic form. With the help of Frei and others, we have now begun to see the irony of this quintessentially modern theological project; for the very positivity deemed to constitute the problem is the flesh and bone of realistic narrative, the primary genre in which the Christian gospel is inscribed. The point does not depend, however, on the privileging of narrative, since positivity is likewise integral to other genres, such as poetry, prophecy, or apocalyptic.

Narrative eclipse and hermeneutical suspicion

The decline of realistic reading of the Bible in the eighteenth and nineteenth centuries, represented by Frei in the image of eclipse, might also be conceived as a vacuum, a kind of hermeneutical low pressure system, which other ways of reading rushed in to fill. On the theological side, the new accommodationist approaches affirmed the continued meaningfulness of the Bible, not on the basis of its narrative but in spite of it. These liberal theologians saw themselves as offering a salutary alternative to a discredited orthodoxy, which itself tried to shore up the Bible's plausibility by appealing to external authority of one kind or another (typically confessional for Protestants and ecclesiastical for Catholics). With the benefit of hindsight we can now recognize that the real threat to liberal theology came not from the embattled orthodoxy on its "right" but rather from those explicitly secular and anti-Christian readings of the Bible on its "left" – those interpretations that Ricoeur has taught us to call the hermeneutics of suspicion. As biblical criticism increasingly undermined the plausibility of what all parties now took to be the "literal" meaning of the biblical text (i.e., its ostensive reference to events in the past), those with a stake in the truth claims of Christianity went in the accommodationist direction, while those who thought the truth of the Bible had been disproved by modern criticism sought to explain how human beings could ever have believed such unlikely narratives in the first place. The early Feuerbach found the explanation in the human urge to express our collective identity in the self-alienating projections of religion, while his later theory interpreted religious illusion as the futile defense of helpless human beings against an all-powerful nature. Marx shifted the emphasis of Feuerbach's projectionism by locating the motive of alienation in the historical dialectic of economic exploitation and class struggle. Freud, while retaining the notion of religion as projection, found the motivation for religious alienation in the unconscious desires of adult individuals to regain the lost security of infancy in the face of hostile reality. And Nietzsche, at once the most brilliant and the most passionately anti-Christian of all the masters of suspicion, located the nerve of religious falsification of reality in the poisonous envy directed by the weak and sickly elements of society against the noble vitality of the strong and healthy. Important to us here are not the considerable and often incompatible differences among these classic varieties of suspicion but rather their commonality. For all of them take religious belief to be a form of false consciousness – not a deliberate falsehood but rather a systematic misunderstanding of one's own experience of the world. Anyone who thinks that human beings are liable to this kind of illusory self-deception will read the Bible suspiciously, as a text that must first be decoded – read against its own intentions – before it can be properly interpreted.

The rise of the hermeneutics of suspicion, then, was the complement to the eclipse of biblical narrative, the other side of the coin. The texts that once told the story of the one real world were now unmasked as the distorters of reality, the fantasies of a false consciousness out of which we must be raised before we can discover, and recover, our true humanity. Whatever their differences, the masters of suspicion from Feuerbach to Nietzsche and his postmodern disciples today all tell variations on this common theme, which might be summarized in the claim that religion is "bad imagination." Tracing the roots of suspicion behind Marx, Nietzsche, and Freud to Feuerbach brings out starkly the central role of imagination in the hermeneutics of suspicion. For in Feuerbach, both early and late, the secret of religion – and simultaneously the source of its illusory nature – is imagination. Later thinkers were more subtle, but for Feuerbach religion's primal error is simply its reliance on imagination. All imagination is bad imagination on Feuerbach's account, the "peacock feathers" that disguise the true nature of reality. Freud is probably closest to Feuerbach at this point, for not only does he identify religion specifically with illusion but he contrasts it unfavorably with the "reality principle." While insisting that not all illusions are bad, he leaves no doubt that to continue imagining the world religiously is to choose the fantasies of a lost childhood over the realism of adult rationality.[2] Marx, too, interprets religion as illusion and identifies the progress of the race with the dis-illusioning of mankind. His account of the ways in which religion mis-imagines the world are more nuanced than Feuerbach's and more socially and historically grounded than Freud's, but his insistence that religious imagination is the culprit is just as unwavering.

With Nietzsche the plot thickens. On the one hand, he is the culmination of that line running from Feuerbach through Marx and Freud that accuses religion – and in his case it is explicitly the *biblical* religion of Jews and Christians that is to blame – of falsifying reality by imagining another, fictional world in which the values of the real world have been inverted. But on the other hand, it is also Nietzsche who appears to cut the ground from under the very dichotomy of illusion and reality by reducing the question of truth to the will to power and suggesting that all we have are interpretations, not facts – in other words, that we have no choice but to rely on imagination. If the first Nietzsche is the culmination of the nineteenth-century hermeneutics of suspicion, the second is the inspiration for the postmodern hermeneutic of suspicion. In this twentieth-century incarnation, one could say, imagination returns with a vengeance, threatening to sweep the notion of reality itself into the vortex of hermeneutical relativity.

Of particular significance, especially for the work of

---

[2] Sigmund Freud, *The Future of an Illusion*, especially §VI (*The Standard Edition of the Complete Psychological Works of Sigmund Freud*, ed. James Strachey, vol. XXI [London: Hogarth Press, 1961]), pp. 30–3.

theology, is the fact that in both the nineteenth- and twentieth-century versions imagination is the key to religion as
well as the focus of hermeneutical suspicion. There is one
important difference, however, that has changed the cultural context in which theology does its work. Whereas
nineteenth-century thinkers often talked as though they
wanted to banish imagination altogether in order to have
unmediated access to "reality," in the late twentieth century far more people, secular quite as much as religious, are
prepared to acknowledge the role of imagination in virtually all human endeavors, including the natural sciences.
Such a climate is more hospitable to theology, since its
necessary entanglement with imagination no longer isolates
it from other intellectual enterprises. If Nietzsche's assertion that "facts do not exist, only interpretations," stands
as a kind of motto for the twilight of modernity, it represents a challenge no longer faced by theology alone.

The necessity of interpretation

A favorable cultural climate for theological work is no
doubt encouraging as we attempt to rethink for our age
what it means to read the Bible as scripture; but it does not
alter the obligation of theologians to be guided by their
own proper criteria, regardless of the popularity or
unpopularity of the outcome among their secular colleagues. Fortunately there are sound *theological* reasons for
believing that we can escape the devil's choice between
an authoritarian appeal to a single textual meaning and a
hermeneutical relativism that undermines all scriptural
authority.

The first step toward an alternative is to acknowledge the
open-ended character of biblical interpretation. To borrow
Paul Ricoeur's terminology, biblical language always contains a "surplus of meaning," which implies that the interpretive task is never completed. For Ricoeur, this aspect of
biblical language is rooted in its symbolic nature: "symbols

give rise to an endless exegesis."[3] Without necessarily buying into Ricoeur's entire hermeneutical program, one can acknowledge this important insight into the nature of metaphoric language. A true metaphor is based on an analogy between something known and something to be elucidated; and it is impossible to say in advance where the limit of the analogy will be found. Metaphors are essentially open ended because the interpreter can never preclude the possibility of discovering further analogical insight. Ricoeur maintains accordingly that "real metaphors are not translatable" though they can be paraphrased; "such a paraphrase," however, "is infinite and incapable of exhausting the innovative meaning" (52). I would say more cautiously that the paraphrase of a metaphor is *indefinite*; whether it is infinite is something that cannot be known in advance. But the outcome is what I am calling the hermeneutic imperative: since "no concept can exhaust the requirement of further thinking borne by symbols" (57), every interpretation is incomplete. As we saw in the previous chapter, the same conclusion is reached by a different route, whether we begin with the unavoidable instability of the network of signifiers emphasized by Derrida and other postmodern philosophers, or with Karl Barth's specifically theological account of language in its inescapable relation to the mystery of God. Each of these paths leads us to the realization that in principle no interpretation can ever be complete. Good philosophy, according to one of Wittgenstein's best-known aphorisms, allows us to know when we can stop doing philosophy.[4] Good theology, on the other hand, shows us why it is never possible to stop interpreting, that

---

[3] Paul Ricoeur, *Interpretation Theory: Discourse and the Surplus of Meaning* (Fort Worth, TX: Texas Christian University Press, 1976), p. 57.

[4] "The real discovery is the one that makes me capable of stopping doing philosophy when I want to. – The one that gives philosophy peace, so that it is no longer tormented by questions which bring itself in question." Ludwig Wittgenstein, *Philosophical Investigations*, trans. G. E. M. Anscombe, 2nd edn. (New York: Macmillan Co., 1958), §133 (p. 51e).

is, to stop doing theology. This necessity is what I am calling the hermeneutic imperative.

From the standpoint of scripture – which is to say, theologically – the hermeneutic imperative is not simply a matter of exegetical method but a fundamental insight into the nature of the world and our relation to it. That insight was expressed with characteristic brilliance by that enigmatic Christian critic of the Enlightenment, Johann Georg Hamann. One of the basic motifs of his thought is what one commentator calls the "iconic or linguistic character of history."[5] When one endeavors to view reality through the lenses of scripture, as Hamann consistently sought to do, not only the biblical text but all events become *deutungsbedürftig* – in need of interpretation. For Christians, the world itself demands to be interpreted: that is the sign of its creatureliness, its essential relatedness to God. Nothing more clearly separates the sensibility of secular modernity from that of biblical faith than the latter's commitment to the *Deutungsbedürftigkeit* of the world – not just its interpretability but its pressing *need* for interpretation. From the standpoint of secular modernity the world simply *is*; to the believer it cries out for interpretation. Another way to say it: for the believer the only way to have the world – to apprehend it Christianly – is to imagine it according to the paradigm rendered in its classic shape by the canon of scripture.

If the meaning of the text is always open ended, it follows that there can be no escape from interpretation, and interpretation requires the active engagement of the imagination. The meaning of scripture is never simply given; it is always the fruit of an interpretive act. The inescapability of interpretation implies the hermeneutic imperative. For those who seek to live by the Bible – that is, to read the Bible scripturally – interpretation is not an optional or

---

[5] "Bild- bzw. Sprachcharakter der Geschichte" (Sven-Aage Jørgensen, *Johann Georg Hamann* [Stuttgart: J. B. Metzlersche Verlagsbuchhandlung, 1976], p. 90).

auxiliary activity but rather the very essence of the matter. To read the Bible as scripture *is* to interpret it – and to interpret the world and oneself at the same time. This formal feature of biblical hermeneutics corresponds to what the Bible itself calls the *living* character of the word. Taking the Bible as scripture means taking it as the Word of God; and since the God of the Bible is the Living God, a free agent who cannot be manipulated or treated as a mere object, the act of reading is necessarily a personal – i.e. an *inter*personal – act. Just as I cannot "interpret" you as though you were a finished product or a fixed text, so *a fortiori* I cannot treat the Word of God as simply given, fixed, and available to my understanding. The literal sense of the biblical text tells us (if we are reading scripturally) what God *says*; but it requires an act of interpretation to discern what God *means*. Just as in the case of human agents, God does not necessarily mean the same thing every time he says the same words.[6] Free agents are not the slaves of their words but rather use language as a way of communicating their meaning to other free agents. Such a situation, precisely because both parties are free, always entails the possibility of failure, of *mis*understanding. Interpretive risk is an unavoidable aspect of mere human communication; and it is all the greater when the speaker is the Living God, whose ways are not our ways and who dwells in thick darkness.

---

[6] Note that the distinction between "what God says" and "what God means" is not the same as Krister Stendahl's problematic attempt to distinguish between "what [the Bible] meant and what it means" ("Biblical Theology, Contemporary," in *The Interpreter's Dictionary of the Bible* [New York: Abingdon Press, 1962], vol. I, pp. 419–20). Stendahl's distinction depends on the hermeneutically questionable possibility of establishing a stable "original" meaning for a text (what it meant to the original hearers or readers) that can become the basis for contemporary interpretation of the text – that is, saying what it means in our situation today. My distinction, on the other hand, is not historical but theological. It assumes that a text always "means" in a concrete situation, so that the meaning – better, perhaps, the significance – cannot be permanently fixed, secured against change. This interpretive meaning, always the fruit of hermeneutical labor, presupposes not an original *historical* meaning but simply the text itself, what it literally *says*.

A number of philosophers and theologians have recognized the hermeneutical imperative, calling it by a variety of names. It is implied, for example, not only by Ricoeur's "surplus of meaning" but also by Derrida's insistence on the instability of all signs. What is not so commonly noticed, however, is its specifically theological significance. The main point can be put simply: the never-to-be-completed interpretive task is something *good*. It would be a grave error to treat the hermeneutic imperative as though it were simply a problem to be endured, a perhaps inevitable but nonetheless lamentable consequence of our finitude. On the contrary, it is a sign of God's grace, a source of joy and hope for believers. Because God is a Living God, one who is free to do and to say new things, we can turn to him, to his word in scripture, in anticipation of genuinely new insight. The inevitability of interpretation is the hermeneutical consequence of the mystery of God. Surely it is a cause for celebration that no one has the last word about the meaning of scripture. The Last Word, after all, is reserved to God alone: "I am the Alpha and the Omega, the first and the last, the beginning and the end" (Revelation 22.13, echoing Isaiah 44.6 and 48.12). The last *human* word in the New Testament is therefore a prayer uttered in faithful anticipation: "Come, Lord Jesus!" (Revelation 22.20). The most harmful consequence of biblical objectivism (what is commonly though inaccurately called "literalism") is that it forecloses on the hermeneutical openness of scripture, and thus – ironically – misreads the Bible in its very attempt to be faithful to its words. One of the soundest theological insights of the Protestant Reformers – one that must surely be endorsed by all Christians today – was their confidence that *sola scriptura* implies not a backward-looking traditionalism but rather a hopeful confidence that God will continue to shed new light from scripture. A church whose central activity is the interpretation of scripture is not the guardian of a timeless deposit of faith but rather the *ecclesia semper reformanda*. This insight is not the property of Protestants alone. Nowhere, in fact, in the history of the biblical religions has the hermeneutic imperative been applied with greater devotion than in the Judaism of the Talmudic rabbis. In this tradition *commentary* becomes the ongoing and life-giving response of the faithful to the revealed Word of God. The notion of Oral Torah, which can sound to Christian ears like a dangerous compromise of biblical authority, can be understood instead as a way of insuring that the written word never calcifies into a dead literalism. The doctrine of the dual Torah runs the risk of undermining scriptural authority only if it is used to evade or subvert the written scriptural text. Rightly employed (from a Christian standpoint at any rate), the dual Torah is a reminder that the written words of the Bible are the means by which the Living God addresses us today – and address is essentially oral. The Word of God is meant to be *heard*, that is, to be received as the active communication of one who speaks.

Scripture on interpreting scripture

The Bible itself offers some intriguing hints about interpretation, including the interpretation of the Word of God. Since theology's task is to articulate the grammar of the biblical paradigm, it makes sense to examine what we might call the scriptural hermeneutics of scripture. Since the Bible appeals not to the theoretical faculties directly but to the imagination, we will not, of course, expect to discover in its pages a theory of interpretation. Instead we shall find images of interpretation, often (but not always) in narrative passages that can serve as windows or lenses through which to view our own late modern hermeneutical puzzles, metaphors or analogies for our contemporary situation.

Let us consider first of all a passage in which we can see, as it were, scripture in the making. The books of Ezra and Nehemiah tell the story of the return of the Jews from exile to Jerusalem, a narrative that includes the reestablishment of civic and cultic life in the land after the traumatic rupture of defeat and exile. One important feature of that refounding of institutions is the establishment of what amounts to a scriptural canon, the written text of Torah. When Ezra reads the law to the returned exiles, the narrator tells us, the Levites "helped the people to understand the law, while the people remained in their places. So they read from the book, from the law of God, with interpretation. They gave the sense, so that the people understood the reading" (Nehemiah 8.7–8). Notice that the Levites did not simply read the law, as though its meaning were obvious, but rather *interpreted* the Torah as they read. They not only told the people what God's law *said* ("read from the book") but what it *meant* ("gave the sense"), "so that the people *understood* the reading." The canonizing of the text, far from ending or stabilizing interpretation, positively requires it. The fact that the text is scripture, God's Word, requires that one engage in the work of interpretation. A popular misconception holds that the authority of scripture renders interpretation unnecessary. According to what we might call the fundamentalist hermeneutical principle, the Bible can be read *without interpretation* – indeed, faithful reading precludes interpretation. This principle, which is in fact a heresy, is quite different from the Reformers' principle that *scripture interprets itself*. The former ignores or denies the paradigmatic nature of all reading; the latter assumes what George Lindbeck calls "intratextuality" – that the scripture is to be interpreted in terms of its own implicit paradigm. When Christians gather regularly to hear the Word of God, they do not typically attend simply to the public reading of scripture but rather to preaching, which involves the active interpretation of scripture; and they participate in liturgy, the concrete enactment of scriptural meaning. Like the Levites in the time of Ezra, Christian preachers accompany the reading of the Bible with the endeavor to proclaim its meaning, so that the people will understand. At least one denomination, the United Presbyterian Church USA, requires that preaching always accompanies the celebration of the eucharist. This stipulation, rooted in the Reformers' critique of medieval abuses of the mass, is based on the sound theological principle that word and sacrament are complementary and inseparable. The integrity of liturgical action requires the ongoing interpretation of the Word of God.

Another and more dramatic Old Testament example of biblical hermeneutics is found in the fifth chapter of Daniel, where the prophet interprets the "handwriting on the wall." The context for the message is the royal company's profaning of the temple vessels by drinking from them at the feast (in a kind of anti-eucharist). Daniel prefaces his interpretation with a review of Nebuchadnezzar's prideful fall from grace and Belshazzar's own lack of humility. Thus the prophet prepares his hearer morally for exegesis. The king's response shows that he has heard the message (but it nevertheless does not save him from its consequences) – much like the case of David after hearing Nathan's parable (2 Samuel 12). Daniel's faithfulness to God, even in exile and persecution, contrasts with the king's failure to honor "the God in whose hand is your breath, and whose are all your ways" (Daniel 5.23); their ability (or inability) to interpret the Word of God precisely parallels their faithfulness (or faithlessness). No account of the mechanism or method of interpretation is provided. All we are told is that the faithless reader can make no sense of the Word of God, while the faithful reader understands it at once – as demonstrated by his ability to expound it.

A particularly dramatic New Testament example of the scriptural hermeneutics of scripture casts the risen Christ himself in the role of interpreter. Luke's gospel culminates in the most extensive postresurrection narrative in the New Testament, the story of the anonymous encounter of the resurrected Jesus with two disciples on the road to Emmaus. At the heart of this narrative is a hermeneutical issue, for their conversation revolves around the question of how to interpret the death and reported resurrection of

Jesus. When Jesus joins them on the road, they do not recognize him for reasons the text does not explain, reporting only (in the passive voice) that "their eyes were kept from recognizing him" (verse 16). When he asks them what they have been discussing, they respond sadly (verse 17) with an account of Jesus' life and death "as though it were a matter of past history" (as Karl Barth notes).[7] Jesus, still unrecognized by his traveling companions, responds with a rebuke, accusing them of ignoring "all that the prophets have spoken." Luke then summarizes the remainder of Jesus' discourse in a single comprehensive sentence: "And beginning with Moses and all the prophets, he interpreted to them in all the scriptures the things concerning himself" (verse 27). The climax of the story, of course, comes later, when they recognize Jesus in the breaking of the bread at the evening meal (verses 30–1). The description of the moment of recognition – "And their eyes were opened and they recognized him" – refers back to verse 16, repeating not only the key terms ("eyes," "recognize") but also the passive grammatical structure. While the eucharistic emphasis of this climax is commonly noted, its essential connection to the earlier conversation is often overlooked. Here, as so often in the New Testament, word and sacrament mutually reinforce one another. The intimate relation between the two is explicitly underscored by the disciples' first response: "Did not our hearts burn within us while he talked to us on the road" – and, lest the specific content of the discourse be missed – "while he opened to us the scriptures?" (verse 32).

The remarkable fact about this encounter is that even the resurrected Jesus turns to the interpretation of scripture in order to explain himself to his disciples. Christians today might be excused for supposing that, although we must struggle with scriptural interpretation in order to gain

---

[7] Karl Barth, *Church Dogmatics*, vol. III, part 2, ed. G. W. Bromiley and T. F. Torrance, trans. Harold Knight et al. (Edinburgh: T. & T. Clark, 1960), p. 471.

insight into God's ways, surely such is not the case for Jesus. We, no doubt, must earn our meaning by the sweat of our brows; but surely if Jesus were here, he could simply declare to us the truth! But the experience of the Emmaus disciples tells us otherwise. An old and tenacious principle of rationalist exegesis holds that the Bible accommodates itself to our weakness, teaching us through stories what really ought to be grasped in pure conceptual form. (Even so staunch a critic of Enlightenment rationalism as Hegel retains this prejudice in his fateful distinction between the picture-language of religious *Vorstellung* and the translucent purity of the *Begriff*.) But the rationalist and Hegelian myth of pure transparency must be rejected by theologians who take their cue from scripture. *Vorstellung* is for us the higher mode of knowing, on which *Begriff* must always remain dependent; intellect derives its nourishment from imagination. For God has chosen to reveal himself not in transparent doctrines appealing to pure reason but in opaque symbols and narratives that appeal to the imagination. Hendrik M. Vroom comments on what I have called the myth of pure transparency in the following passage:

> For some important reasons Western culture has developed in such a way that universal truths, expressed as clearly and distinctly (*clare et distincte*) as possible have been given priority. Christian theology has been strongly influenced by that cultural ideal and has often given central place to religious doctrines. But life is not all clear, and the most profound insights in this life and the world are not clear propositions. They are expressed in similes, metaphors and stories. The "pattern of meanings embodied in symbols" that is handed from one generation to another in religious traditions is not a clear or even systematic pattern, but a variegated whole, with a great deal of "hermeneutical space" and possibilities for adaptation to new situations.[8]

---

[8] Hendrik M. Vroom, "Religious Hermeneutics, Culture and Narratives," *Studies in Interreligious Dialogue* 4 (1994): 194.

This "hermeneutical space," I am convinced, is the same one that Hans Frei calls "breathing space," even crediting the insight to those radical deconstructionists who deny any connection between meaning and truth. "In the period of modernity," Frei notes, "interpreters have been so ardent, so hot in pursuit of the truth of the text, that texts were often left little 'breathing space'"; and he goes on to identify "good interpretation" as one that respects this space, "one in which no hermeneutic finally allows you to resolve the text – there is something that is left to bother, something that is wrong, something that is not yet interpreted."[9] As we saw in the previous chapter, not only Karl Barth but also Jacques Derrida would agree with Frei at this point. For Derrida the uninterpreted remainder is a symptom of the indeterminacy to which all texts are subject, the inevitable trace of *différance* in which all use of signs is implicated. Barth, like Frei, would adduce a theological reason for "breathing space," namely, the way in which God's Word surpasses every attempt to articulate it in human words. For Christian theology hermeneutical breathing space is implied by the hermeneutic imperative, which we may thus paraphrase as a commandment: Thou shalt not interpret exhaustively!

In conclusion, I want to try grounding the hermeneutic imperative and its corollary, hermeneutical breathing space, theologically, for I am convinced that they are not peripheral or incidental principles but spring from the very heart of faith itself. The opacity of scriptural images is no doubt due in part to the self-imposed limits of our sinfulness; but I want to argue that sin is not its only or its most important ground. Seeing the world biblically means seeing the world as *deutungsbedürftig*, yearning to be interpreted. It is a sign of its finitude, yes – but better, the sign of its creatureliness, its essential relatedness to God. The Lord God has created a world, so say the biblical witnesses, that is an enigma, a surd, apart from its divine origin and destiny. Seen in its

[9] Frei, "Conflicts in Interpretation," p. 162.

godly relationship, the world does not become comprehensible so much as interpretable. It remains mysterious without being meaningless. Indeed, its meaning depends on the divine mystery at its heart, so that its meaning is not a given but is rather a task, a quest. The world's mystery is thus secondary – rooted in the primary divine mystery. The important point is that mystery (whether of God or the world) is not an unfortunate problem or limitation; rather, it is the chief motivator of creaturely inquiry and meditation. God's elusiveness is an aspect of his freedom, and therefore an aspect of his grace; he is beyond our control (cf. mystery of God's *name*). The same is true to a lesser extent for creatures: human relationships thrive on the elusiveness of persons, who can never be known fully. To know a person exhaustively would be to control the relationship. Because persons are free, they are unfinished and thus always unpredictable, at least potentially. Being *reliable* is not the same as being *predictable*.

Scriptural interpretation so conceived is no mere activity of the intellect but engages the whole person, body and soul. Neither is it an activity to be engaged in by isolated individuals, for the Christian imagination, the organ of scriptural interpretation, is forged in communal experience and practice. Stanley Hauerwas has challenged the guild of biblical exegetes by insisting that right interpretation of the Bible "requires transformation of the self." In fact, he accuses both fundamentalist Christians and their enemies the biblical critics of wishing "to make Christianity available to the person of common sense without moral transformation."[10] He proposes a thoroughly communitarian hermeneutic, while insisting that it does not lead to interpretive subjectivism. Here I worry that Hauerwas, like Frei and Lindbeck, is not sufficiently sanguine about the danger that the Christian community itself will "capture" the

---

[10] Stanley Hauerwas, *Unleashing the Scripture: Freeing the Bible from Captivity to America* (Nashville: Abingdon Press, 1993), pp. 35–6.

Bible, treating it as a resource and a weapon against its enemies, while seeking to exempt itself from scriptural scrutiny. (The subtitle of Hauerwas' book is *Freeing the Bible from Captivity to America*; but what is to prevent its captivity to the church?) Might it not be possible to maintain the objectivity of the text while agreeing that "moral transformation" is required? Here the hermeneutic imperative offers a clue, for if the meaning of the text remains forever open and elusive, resisting attempts at interpretive closure, then right reading of the Bible requires a kind of humility. The message has been "rigged" in such a way that the powerful and the arrogant are bound to miss its point. God has "hidden these things from the wise and understanding and revealed them to babes" (Luke 10.21). This is the point at which liberation hermeneutics is half right: the poor, the oppressed, and the weak do indeed have a hermeneutical advantage, for they, unlike the rich young ruler who encountered Jesus on the road, are unencumbered by the things of this world and are thus open to hear the good news. I say "half right" because so many liberation theologies politicize the gospel at just this point, trying to read the biblical story of liberation from bondage as a metaphor for a partisan political program. The Bible itself, on the other hand, typically employs political events as metaphors or parables for God's transformation of human life in all its aspects. Thus the Lucan version of Jesus' beatitude "Blessed are you poor" (Luke 6.20a) is protected against a narrowly political reading by Matthew's version, "Blessed are the poor in spirit" (Matthew 5.3a).

God gives himself to the world, so Christians believe and confess, by touching the human imagination, which is inherently dependent on the concrete, the specific, the bodily – that is, on "positivity." For Christians the chief point of imaginative contact with God is Holy Scripture, that epic of positivity whose narratives, poetry, and proclamation are able, by means of their metaphoric inspiration, to render God himself to the faithful imagination. This peculiar relationship of creature to Creator implies that the human animal lives by interpretation. One interpreter of Nietzsche has said that he portrays the human being as *"homo hermeneuticus,* as an organism that invariably and necessarily interprets."[11] Whether or not this is a universal anthropological truth, it is surely true that the Christian is *homo hermeneuticus.* To meditate on God's word is the believer's joy. In the words of Psalm 63,

> O God, thou art my God, I seek thee,
> my soul thirsts for thee;
> my flesh faints for thee,
> as in a dry and weary land where no water is.
>
> . . .
>
> My soul is feasted as with marrow and fat,
> and my mouth praises thee with joyful lips,
> when I think of thee upon my bed,
> and meditate on thee in the watches of the night. . . .

And from Psalm 119,

> Oh, how I love thy law!
> It is my meditation all the day.

The hermeneutic imperative is one element of an adequate theological response to the hermeneutics of suspicion, but more needs to be said. In the final chapter I want to pursue the problem of how to live a life of faithful imagination in the face of suspicion and relativity in the twilight of modernity.

---

[11] Karen L. Carr, *The Banalization of Nihilism: Twentieth-Century Responses to Meaninglessness* (Albany, NY: SUNY Press, 1992), p. 28.

8

The faithful imagination: suspicion and trust in a postmodern world

Crux probat omnia.

Luther

Behold, I send you out as sheep in the midst of wolves; so be wise as serpents and innocent as doves.

Matthew 10.1

Throughout the previous chapters I have made use of the historical thesis of Paul Ricoeur, according to which a "hermeneutics of suspicion" – epitomized in the writings of Marx, Freud, and Nietzsche – arose in the nineteenth century and profoundly altered the way in which we read the authoritative texts of our traditions, including the Bible. And in chapter 6 I extended Ricoeur's category to include a postmodern permutation of hermeneutical suspicion, suggesting that Nietzsche can be seen both as the culmination of the modern version and the originator of the postmodern successor. I also indicated briefly in the opening chapter that despite my indebtedness to Ricoeur for his powerful analysis of the modern hermeneutical crisis, I find him a less helpful guide in seeking to respond to it theologically. His own solution could be

The first epigraph was "Luther's hermeneutical axiom," according to Rowan Williams, "The Literal Sense of Scripture," *Modern Theology* 7 (1991): 130–1.

called a semiotic mysticism, an attempt, as he puts it, to "return to a point that is situated prior to the dichotomy between subject and object" in order to apprehend anew "the manifestation of Being as the logos that gathers all things."[1] Like Mircea Eliade, Ricoeur is committed to a position that amounts to a kind of natural theology of symbols, one which presupposes a primordial "sacred" reality that manifests itself symbolically in a variety of religious forms. A Christian theologian, bound to the God of Israel and of Jesus Christ, as witnessed to in the scriptures of the Old and New Testaments, cannot begin from such a presupposition, convincing as some may find it on philosophical or experiential grounds (though I must confess that I do not find it a compelling presupposition on those grounds either). Since Ricoeur is surely right that we cannot simply return to an earlier stage in our cultural history, what we need to discover is a way forward – a theological perspective that can point beyond the dilemma of hermeneutical naiveté or hermeneutical suspicion toward what Ricoeur himself has named a "second naiveté" and Hans Frei once referred to as a "generous orthodoxy."

Living with suspicion

A theologically adequate response to the hermeneutics of suspicion must begin by recognizing that the challenge is not simply an external one but rather has roots within theology itself. Behind Marx, Nietzsche, and Freud stands Feuerbach, the paradigmatic antitheologian of modernity, who deftly, if rather maliciously, turned the implicit logic of accommodationist theology against itself. Hans Frei long ago identified two kinds of modern atheism, which correspond to what Ricoeur calls epistemological and

[1] Paul Ricoeur, "Religion, Atheism, and Faith," in *The Conflict of Interpretations: Essays in Hermeneutics*, ed. Don Ihde (Evanston, IL: Northwestern University Press, 1974), p. 463.

hermeneutical doubt.[2] Frei traces the first kind of atheism to the skepticism of Hume, which denies the validity or meaningfulness of belief in God. Like Laplace in his famous reply to Napoleon, Humean atheists have no need for the theistic hypothesis. The second kind of modern atheism owes its origins to Feuerbach and its most powerful expression to Marx. The two types of atheism could hardly be more different, even though they often appear in hybrid forms. "The first sort of atheism, Hume's heritage, remains an external threat to the theologian," Frei observes; "the second becomes an internal one."[3] The second, "Feuerbachian" variety is a "theological" atheism. Far from rejecting the premises of theology, this kind of critique springs from the very soil of theology. It lurks like a chronic infection in the bloodstream of modern theology, threatening at any moment to erupt into a full-blown disease. Suspicion, in other words, is not simply an external threat to be fended off by means of a more effective apologetic; rather, it is a possibility latent in theology itself. But if that is the case, what we require is not a better apologetic by which to defend the faith against its secular opponents but rather a theological therapy to cure the propensity to suspicion that is imbedded in our own tradition.

But this diagnosis is still inadequate, for it assumes that suspicion is the enemy of theology, albeit an internal rather than an external one. The wisest theologians have always recognized that doubt is a necessary moment within the dialectic of faith itself and that the desire to eradicate it utterly is therefore both ill-advised and futile. The same is true of suspicion, which is doubt in its Feuerbachian guise. In recent years a number of theologians have tried to put the hermeneutics of suspicion to

---

[2] Hans W. Frei, "Feuerbach and Theology," *Journal of the American Academy of Religion* 35 (1967): 250–6.
[3] Ibid., p. 253.

work on behalf of the faith rather than against it. One such attempt has been prominent in liberation theology, where suspicion in its Marxian form has been appropriated on behalf of a campaign to free Christianity from its alleged captivity by reactionary and undemocratic forces. Another familiar example is the feminist adaptation of the hermeneutics of suspicion – here understood in a more Nietzschean mode as the critique of power – in order to expose and discredit the patriarchal captivity of the church. Both these projects, I am convinced, suffer from (ironically enough) too uncritical an application of the critiques they import. At their worst, some liberationist and feminist hermeneutics subject theology and the church to alien criteria derived not from the gospel of Jesus Christ but from modern autonomous humanism. There is indeed a valid, even necessary, Christian suspicion; it will be discovered, though, not by the application of secular hermeneutics but rather theologically – that is, by attending to the sources and norms implicit in Christian faith itself. We need therefore to ask the historical question about the origins of suspicion within the Christian theological tradition (as suggested by both Ricoeur and Frei) as well as the theological question about the legitimate Christian grounds for suspicion.

One of the more powerful and interesting theses about the origin of modern suspicion comes from Nietzsche, who traces it to the very heart of Christianity. The long historical development of suspicion culminates in his famous notion of the death of God. "The greatest recent event," he writes – "that 'God is dead,' that the belief in the Christian god has become unbelievable – is already beginning to cast its first shadows over Europe. For the few at least, whose eyes – the *suspicion* in whose eyes, is strong and subtle enough for this spectacle, some sun seems to have set and some ancient and profound trust has been turned into doubt."[4] The chosen few, he writes in *Die fröhliche Wissenschaft*, are those like Schopenhauer who take "unconditional and honest atheism" as their presupposition, which is "a triumph achieved finally and with great difficulty by the European conscience, being the most fateful act of two thousand years of discipline for truth that in the end forbids itself the *lie* in faith in God." But the surprise is that this dramatic change of consciousness is rooted in Christianity itself: "what it was that really triumphed over the Christian god [was] Christian morality itself, the concept of truthfulness that was understood ever more rigorously ... translated and sublimated into a scientific conscience, into intellectual cleanliness at any price."[5] The discipline of conscientious self-doubt that Christian piety had fostered over the centuries ("the father confessor's refinement of the Christian conscience") Nietzsche believes to be the source of modern atheism itself, a training in systematic suspicion of one's own innermost motives that eventually devoured itself! He is so enamored of this thesis that he later cites this passage in the third essay of *The Genealogy of Morals*, and links it to a universal principle. "All great things," he announces, "bring about their own destruction through an act of self-overcoming [*Selbstaufhebung*]." Thus "Christianity *as a dogma* was devoured by its own morality ... After Christian truthfulness has drawn one inference after another, it must end by drawing its *most striking inference*, its inference *against* itself."[6] In other words, according to Nietzsche, modern suspicion is not

[4] Friedrich Nietzsche, *The Gay Science*, trans. Walter Kaufmann (New York: Random House, 1974), p. 297 (§343), Nietzsche's emphasis; the original can be found in the Kritische Studienausgabe (hereafter KSA), ed. Giorgio Colli and Mazzino Montinari (Berlin and New York: Walter de Gruyter, 1967–77), vol. III, p. 573. The word translated as "suspicion" is *Argwohn*.

[5] Nietzsche, *Gay Science*, p. 307 (§357); KSA, vol. III, p. 600.

[6] Nietzsche, *On the Genealogy of Morals and Ecce Homo*, trans. Walter Kaufmann and R. J. Hollingdale (New York: Random House, 1967), p. 161; KSA, vol. V, pp. 409–10.

only the product of Christianity itself but is in fact a by-product of its greatest value, the will to truth. Nietzsche understands himself to be applying more radically than Christians this underlying motive of the Christian conscience itself.

As so often with Nietzsche, his analysis is at once strikingly insightful about Christian faith and profoundly opposed to it. Stated another way, Nietzsche and the modern Christian share deep character traits, and yet they could hardly be more dramatically opposed to one another in terms of their ultimate commitments. Untangling the strands of Christian and Nietzschean suspicion is one way to bring out those similarities and differences. The same analysis should serve to throw a revealing light on the Christian theology of suspicion and faith, and provide a clue as to how Christians can cope in a relativistic age. Nietzsche is right about the Christian origins of suspicion. Because he does not share the Christian's underlying trust in the gospel message, however, he is able only to imagine that suspicion leading inevitably to the death of God. The irony of Nietzsche's position, viewed from a theological perspective, is that genuine Christian suspicion is in fact grounded in the death of God – that is, in the cross of Christ.

Since Christian hermeneutics is a hermeneutics of the cross, it is there that we must look for the proper criterion of Christian suspicion. At the root of the hermeneutics of suspicion in all its forms is the fear of being deceived, especially by oneself; and it is true of Christian suspicion as well. Nietzsche shares with Freud a sense of the dangerous role of desire in producing illusion, religious and otherwise. In the words of Maudemarie Clark, "Nietzsche claims that a will to knowledge or truth ... requires the internalization of the will to power, the ability to get a sense of power out of denying oneself the satisfaction of interpretations one would like to be true because of what one actually has reason to believe."[7] The Christian, too, fears deception, for the devil is the Father of Lies. The decisive issue is thus how to "discern the spirits," how to distinguish between a "lying spirit" and the Holy Spirit. In 1 Kings 22.22 God says he will be "a lying spirit" in the mouth of the king's prophets. But in Jeremiah 14.14 the Lord says, "The prophets are prophesying lies in my name; I did not send them . . . They are prophesying to you a lying vision." The hermeneutical challenge is to identify and thus to defend against "lying visions" – deceitful appeals to the paradigmatic imagination. But how, after reading the masters of suspicion, are we to identify them? The question is whom to fear. As Jesus warns us, "Do not fear those who kill the body but cannot kill the soul; rather fear him who can destroy both soul and body in hell" (Matthew 10.28). The fear of being deceived is the fear of naiveté; so suspicion and naiveté are correlates. If we take our bearings from the cross, however, our worldly correlations of fear and trust, suspicion and naiveté, are reversed. The gospel redirects our suspicion. In order to see how, we must turn to the positive foundation of Christian suspicion, faith in the gospel of Jesus Christ. But before approaching this task, we need to bring the modern history of suspicion up to the present by considering the uniquely twentieth-century incarnation of the hermeneutics of suspicion, the interpretive relativism that wants to draw Christian faith, along with all other absolutes and "metanarratives," into the vortex of a postmodern perspectivism in which, in Nietzsche's words, "there are no facts, only *interpretations*."

Living with relativism

A great and complex struggle is raging in the world today, on many cultural levels, over relativism. Two seemingly

[7] Maudemarie Clark, *Nietzsche on Truth and Philosophy* (Cambridge: Cambridge University Press, 1990), p. 237. She bases this comment on her reading of *Beyond Good and Evil*, §230 (KSA, vol. V, p. 168).

inexorable developments have been under way for the last four centuries – developments which, until recently, appeared to have opposite effects. One of these historic trends is the continually increasing communication among the world's diverse cultures. From its beginnings in the age of exploration in Europe to the communications explosion in our own lifetime, more groups of human beings have come to know more about other groups – whether they want to or not – than ever before in history. As the last of the truly traditional societies are dragged, however unwillingly, out of the rainforests into the glaring light of the "global village," any vestiges of genuinely isolated tradition that may remain serve only to underscore the inevitability of the trend toward communication. Culturally speaking, there is no place left to hide in the modern world. The other historic development has been the advance of modern science from its beginnings as the "new science" of seventeenth-century Europe to its triumphant dominance of world culture today. So complete has its conquest been that modernity itself is most usefully defined as the age in which science has served as the paradigm for knowledge, truth, and morality.

Throughout most of this period it has seemed that the two forces of modernity, communication and science, were pushing in opposite directions. As each people became aware of the existence of other peoples, it became increasingly difficult to maintain belief in the centrality and supremacy of its own culture. One of the more dramatic effects of the new awareness of diversity has thus been secularization: the progressive loss of authority by traditional, especially religious, institutions and ideas. The very fact of multiple claims to ultimate authority has had the effect of undermining all of them. The other side of the coin has been the advance of science, which seemed to promise an antidote to the diversity and disunity of multiple cultures. The thinkers of the European Enlightenment, wearied and demoralized by a century of confessional strife and wars of religion, discovered in the "new science" the key to a universal rationality based not on the arbitrary and parochial claims of culture but rather on the solid and universal foundation of nature. A major component of the Enlightenment program, as we have seen, was the identification of a natural religion that would isolate and preserve the normative kernel of truth present in all the "positive" religions while discarding the troublesome and useless husks of historical particularity. The authority that science – especially the natural sciences – exerts in world culture today reflects that history: science is the survivor of the culture wars, the guarantor of unity after the demise of all traditional authorities.

Or so it seemed, at least, until recently. A change so fundamental has occurred that many observers now speak of the end of modernity and seize upon the term *postmodern* to characterize the new situation. Whether one adopts this dramatic language or prefers instead to speak of a transformation within modernity makes little difference, so long as one recognizes what has happened: that the relativism of cultures and religions that had long been a part of modern consciousness has now spread to science – or, what really comes to the same thing, is widely *believed* to have spread to science. Given the paradigmatic role that science, and belief in science, has played in the modern era, this change has shaken modernity to its roots. Einstein's two theories of relativity look in retrospect like harbingers, signs of relativism breaking out within the precincts of science itself. In the academic community the change became explicit in "the postempiricist philosophy and history of science"[8] associated with the names of Thomas S. Kuhn and Paul Feyerabend. People in many fields, including theologians, even if they have never read any philosophy of science, now assume that "all data are theory-laden" and

---

[8] Richard J. Bernstein, *Beyond Objectivism and Relativism: Science, Hermeneutics, and Praxis* (Philadelphia: University of Pennsylvania Press, 1985), pp. 79 and *passim*.

take for granted that the principle applies not just to scientific theories but to all theories. This transference is exactly what one would expect if the dominant cultural paradigm is, as I have maintained, science. A paradigm tells us what things are *like*, how the world is, and how we should comport ourselves in it. So if science, once conceived as the reliable source of direct truth about reality, now appears relativistic to influential people, our world itself comes to be relativistic.

The climate of relativism that has engulfed our world in the twilight of modernity also pervades the cultural atmosphere in which Christians live today. It determines the context for our thinking and sets the problems for our living; it is in the very intellectual air that we breathe. The great question confronting theologians, therefore, is how to come to terms with this situation, how to preach the gospel and live in faithfulness to Jesus Christ in a time of rampant relativism. Two primary forms of response are evident in the church today, and both fail in significant ways. Theological liberals seek an accommodation with the cultural "situation" (a technical term in the liberal vocabulary). If the relativity of all religious traditions has now come to light, they reason, we Christians are obliged to give up the exclusivism of our past and acknowledge that our path to truth is but one path, even if we find reasons to prefer it to others. This option is the one epitomized in the writings of John Hick. Conservatives, on the other hand, seek to defend the faith against the challenges of secularism, defiantly manning the barricades of absolute truth against the rising tide of relativism. I hope that you can recognize in these crude caricatures at least a rough picture of the current state of Christian theology. Both liberal and conservative theologies, of course, come in more nuanced and often very powerful forms, and I have no intention of simply dismissing any of them out of hand. My point, rather, is to show that the common failing of both sides is rooted in an implicit agreement: both theological liberals and conservatives commonly assume that Christian faith must either side with the absolutist past or abandon its claim to witness to a unique truth. They differ only in the choices they make between these two alternatives, liberals accepting cultural relativism by sacrificing the positivity of the gospel, and conservatives rejecting relativism in the vain hope of returning to the absolute truth claims of the past.

The way out of this dilemma begins with the recognition that the alternatives usually posed to us by both sides represent a devil's choice. The philosopher Richard J. Bernstein has tried to expose the false alternatives in his book *Beyond Objectivism and Relativism*. The title alone is worth the price of the book, though Bernstein's analysis of the problem turns out to be more useful than his attempts to show us the way forward. Nevertheless, knowing one's true situation is at least half the battle, and Bernstein's categories offer some useable tools of analysis for Christians in an age of relativism. What I have earlier called absolutism corresponds to Bernstein's term *objectivism*, defined as the thesis that "there is or must be some permanent, ahistorical matrix or framework to which we can ultimately appeal in determining the nature of rationality, knowledge, truth, reality, goodness, or rightness."[9] Objectivists, according to Bernstein, think that philosophy has the job of identifying and defending the objective structures of reality. Many conservative Christian theologians are clearly objectivists in this sense, typically identifying biblical revelation with reality itself, and defending orthodox Christian doctrine as the objective description of that reality. Essential to the objectivist case, Bernstein maintains, is an implicit threat: "unless we can ground philosophy, knowledge, or language in a rigorous manner we cannot avoid radical skepticism."[10] In this way objectivists and relativists depend on each other

---

[9] Ibid., p. 8.
[10] Ibid.

to make their respective cases. *Relativism*, as Bernstein defines it, maintains that all our fundamental concepts, including those of "rationality, truth, reality, right, the good, or norms" must finally be "understood as relative to a specific conceptual scheme, theoretical framework, paradigm, form of life, society, or culture." No higher appeal is possible than to one of these schemes, of which there is "a nonreducible plurality."[11] The standoff between these two positions continues, maintained by the threat of each that the only alternative is the opposite position. I would add, as Bernstein does not, that the effect of the ongoing dilemma is to make all of us relativists, whether we want to be or not. I believe there are signs of reluctant relativism all around us today. No sooner do determined objectivists manage to legislate some absolute standard (against abortion, for example) than the inevitable undertow of cultural relativism begins to erode its foundations. As a culture, the Western world – and with it the emerging global culture – has lost its confidence that any overarching framework can be maintained. And the stridency of those who argue otherwise bears eloquent testimony to that fact.

Whatever philosophical reasons there may be for wanting to get "beyond objectivism and relativism," I believe that there are powerful theological reasons why Christians can and should do so. The liberal project of trying to accommodate the gospel to modern relativism, now under way for nearly three centuries, is bankrupt, and its dangers to theology and the church have become impossible to overlook. The conservative reaction, however, which seeks to identify the gospel with a foundationalist objectivism, represents an equally disastrous course for theology by trying to bind Christian truth to specific cultural forms. Ultimately, of course, faith in the God of Israel and of Jesus Christ commits one to an absolute – to the norm by which all other norms are set. Christians are in this sense

---

[11] Ibid., p. 11.

foundationalists, taking their bearings from the foundation laid by God in Zion (Isaiah 28.16). This foundation, however, unlike the foundationalist theories of the philosophers, does not appear in this world as an absolute; and attempts to secure it philosophically are bound to fail. Moreover, the very attempt to create a "Christian foundationalism," as we might call it, constitutes a departure from the gospel. It implies that one has missed the theological point in a very basic way, mistaking grace for nature by trying to appropriate the gift of God as a human project. Christians, in other words, are not committed to what Bernstein calls objectivism, despite their absolute commitment in faith. On the contrary, the object of faith will always appear, from the standpoint of this world, as one more of the relativities of the present age. The Christian believer, like Abraham, the father of faith, "look[s] forward to the city which has foundations, whose builder and maker is God" (Hebrews 11.10).

Living in faithfulness

The modernist hermeneutics of suspicion, in its various forms, relied on a dualism of imagination and reality to cast doubt on religion as a form of imagination. In postmodern relativism, on the other hand, imagination has triumphed, but only at the price of losing its purchase on reality. Suspicion is no longer confined to specific programs of imagination, such as Christian belief, but has become absolute. Absolute suspicion, however, like absolute skepticism, is ultimately an impossible and self-contradictory stance: carried to its logical conclusion, the position undermines the ground on which it stands. Even the most radical suspicion must be relative to a trust that grounds and supports it; and that fiduciary ground is ultimately the key to the suspicion. In a figure like Marx, we need not search far for the grounding trust, for Marx's commitment to the scientific certainty of what he named dialectical materialism is well known. He believed passionately that he had discovered the

mainspring of human history, and that passion is what gal-
vanized his followers into a revolutionary political movement and not simply another school of philosophy. For just
this reason Marxism is frequently identified as a religion –
at least a quasi- or a pseudo- one. The case of Nietzsche is
quite different. Attempts to explain Nietzsche's collapse
into madness have been notoriously questionable and often
tendentious; but what person who takes the man seriously
can resist the temptation to try? My own favorite fantasy –
I won't honor it with the name "theory" – is that Nietzsche
succumbed to absolute suspicion. Like his own imaginary
madman who announces the death of God, I imagine
Nietzsche, having "unchained this earth from its sun,"
sucked into the vortex of his own relentless suspicion.
"Whither are we moving?" asks the madman. "Away from
all suns? Are we not plunging continually? Backward, side-
ward, forward, in all directions? Is there still any up or
down? Are we not straying as through an infinite nothing?"[12] Unable to affirm objectivism, Nietzsche yielded to
the vertigo of utter relativism. Like Zarathustra's "Last
Pope," Nietzsche is led to unbelief by his "overgreat honesty" (*übergroße Redlichkeit*).[13] Whether or not Nietzsche
himself was actually devoured by his own suspicion, my
fantasy can serve to bring out the implicit logic of
Nietzschean suspicion. It shares in the negative dialectic of
all atheism, failing to see (in the words of Karl Barth) "that
absolute negation can make sense only against the background of a relative affirmation."[14] Like every parasite, suspicion ultimately depends on its host, and it can succeed in
destroying the host only at the price of its own demise.

Recent theological appropriations of the hermeneutics of

---

[12] Nietzsche, *Gay Science*, p. 181 (§125); KSA, vol. III, p. 481.

[13] Nietzsche, *Thus Spoke Zarathustra*, part 4, in Walter Kaufmann, trans., *The Portable Nietzsche*, rev. edn. (New York: Viking Press, 1968), p. 374; KSA, vol. IV, p. 325.

[14] Karl Barth, *Die kirchliche Dogmatik* (Zurich: Theologischer Verlag Zürich, 1932–67), vol. I, part 2, p. 351 (my trans.); cf. *Church Dogmatics*, ed. G. W. Bromiley and T. F. Torrance (Edinburgh: T. & T. Clark, 1956–69), vol. I, part 2, p. 321.

suspicion have been naive at just this point. They have wanted to use suspicion to root out bad faith without taking responsibility for the implicit grounds of that suspicion. For example, in their eagerness to use a Marxist hermeneutic to expose the complicity of Christianity in economic and political oppression (a fact, let it be noted, that I by no means wish to deny), liberation theologians have failed to take seriously the roots of that hermeneutic in the pseudoscience of "dialectical materialism," whose presuppositions include the self-sufficiency of human historical endeavor and the concomitant rejection of the God of history. Gustavo Gutiérrez, the most influential of the Latin American liberation theologians, wants "to show how liberation praxis serves as the matrix for a new kind of discourse about the faith and new forms of Christian community." It quickly becomes apparent that this "matrix" contains a thoroughgoing ideological agenda: "In such a reordered society the social takeover of the means of production will be accompanied by a social takeover of the reins of political power that will ensure the people's liberty."[15] Although he is critical of those who try "to 'baptize' revolution," Gutiérrez himself adopts uncritically a broad range of ideological concepts and commitments. "It comes down," he writes, "to taking a socialist and revolutionary stand," which he defends on the basis of "a more scientific grasp of reality" – one that allows us to identify "class enemies" and "entails the creation of new human beings" in part "by eliminating private ownership of the wealth created by human labor."[16] Intending to use Marxist analysis as though it were a neutral tool – as though it were not "theory-laden" – Gutiérrez and others have unwittingly compromised the biblical basis of theology by subjecting it to a suspicion rooted in a very different trust. The

[15] Gustavo Gutiérrez, "Liberation Praxis and Christian Faith," in *Frontiers of Theology in Latin America*, ed. Rosino Gibellini (Maryknoll, NY: Orbis Books, 1979), p. 2.
[16] Ibid., pp. 7, 9, 12, 18.

result has been a politicizing of doctrine and an overemphasis on economic and material aspects of both the human good and the divine purpose. Put in other terms, these theologians have failed to recognize the incompatible competing paradigms of biblical faith and dialectical materialism, thereby encouraging Christians to "mis-imagine" the world in significant respects.

A comparable tendency among feminist theologians has had similar consequences. Much attention by recent feminists has been directed to the doctrine of the Trinity. For example, Sallie McFague's widely influential book *Models of God* uses a theory of metaphorical imagination to urge the replacement of traditional trinitarian language with the alternative models of God as "mother, lover, and friend of the world as God's body."[17] By failing to attend adequately to the "theory-laden" nature of such concepts, McFague actually ends by proposing to reintroduce into Christian theology elements of the very same gnostic paradigm rejected (for good reason) by the ancient church. When Rosemary Radford Ruether asserts that "the critical principle of feminist theology is the promotion of the full humanity of women," and grounds that principle in the "revelatory experience" of individuals,[18] she effectively sets up a methodology by which even the Bible can be judged by the standards of an alien paradigm – namely, the subjective experience of modern liberal secularism. "Received ideas are tested by what 'feels right,'"[19] she announces, without perceiving that ideas "feel right" according to the paradigm in terms of which we receive and organize them. The subjection of the biblical paradigm to a more authoritative context is even more explicit in Elisabeth Schüssler Fiorenza's claim that "the revelatory canon for theological

---

[17] Sallie McFague, *Models of God: Theology for an Ecological, Nuclear Age* (Philadelphia: Fortress Press, 1987), p. 93.
[18] Rosemary Radford Ruether, *Sexism and God-Talk: Toward a Feminist Theology* (Boston: Beacon Press, 1983), pp. 18, 12–13.
[19] Ibid., p. 15.

evaluation of biblical androcentric traditions and their subsequent interpretations cannot be derived from the Bible
itself but can only be formulated in and through women's
struggle for liberation from all patriarchal oppression."[20]
Here a hermeneutics of suspicion is at work theologically
that is obviously not grounded in the biblical paradigm,
since it subjects that paradigm itself to suspicion. If there
are good Christian grounds for a critique of patriarchy – as
there most surely are – they require a hermeneutics whose
suspicion stems from an underlying trust in the crucified
Messiah and the God who raised him from the dead.

That grounding trust – I have called it the faithful imagination – is the foundation on which Christian life and
doctrine rest in this relativistic age, as in all ages. It does
not lead to a philosophical foundationalism, however, since
it claims no basis in an incorrigible truth that might somehow be secured by an adequate apologetic. At this point
theology needs to abandon its modernist scruples and
frankly acknowledge its "otherworldly" character: for the
kingship of our Messiah is not of this world (John 18.36),
and "if for this life only we have hoped in Christ, we are of
all men most to be pitied" (1 Corinthians 15.19). Christians
ought not to object when their religion is relativized,
treated as one more of the multiple options in a pluralistic
world; for in worldly terms that is precisely what it is. The
absolute commitment that faith requires is just that: a commitment of *faith*, a willingness to stake all on the truthfulness of the God who has captured our imagination. To
apprehend the absolute object of our faith in imagination
is to abandon every futile attempt to control it, to acknowledge our utter dependence on the vision. The postmodern condition may show us that others, though they
may dare less, are on no firmer ground in worldly terms;
but it cannot ground or justify the Christian hope. The

[20] Elisabeth Schüssler Fiorenza, *In Memory of Her: A Feminist Theological Reconstruction of Christian Origins* (New York: Crossroad Publishing Co., 1990), p. 32.

temptation to press postmodern relativism into apologetic service is a temptation that theologians should resist. It hardly does justice to the gospel of Jesus Christ to argue that you might as well believe it since no other religious or secular option can claim foundational certainty either!

The hermeneutics of the cross ought to lead us to quite different theological conclusions about living faithfully in the twilight of modernity. For the helplessness of the theologian, unable to secure the truth of his or her teachings by means of apologetic argument, mirrors the helplessness of the crucified Christ – of the God we worship, who, as Dietrich Bonhoeffer reminded us in his own hour of helplessness, "lets himself be pushed out of the world on to the cross."[21] If we attend carefully to the paradigmatic drama of the Bible, we catch a vision of the God who, out of his own freedom and love for his creatures, has created a world that depends wholly on grace. The revelation of this God is thus one that can never be turned into a weapon by which we might subdue our enemies or secure ourselves, for God has revealed himself to our *imagination*, so that only by abandoning ourselves in faith, hope, and love to the vision can we apprehend him and have fellowship with him.

The Christian church has been learning a hard lesson during the age of modernity: how to live in a culture it no longer dominates. It is the job of theologians, both pastoral and academic, to help Christians imagine faithfully how to live in this unaccustomed state. There is a deep irony, of course, in the fact that the church's scriptures have always had much to say about how to live in exile and relatively little about how to dominate culture; but it is a comforting irony, for it implies that exile need not be so unbearable a state. As Jeremiah wrote to the Jewish exiles in Babylon, we ought to build our houses, raise our families, and seek the welfare of our secular neighbors (cf. Jeremiah 29).

---

[21] Dietrich Bonhoeffer, *Letters and Papers from Prison*, enlarged edn., ed. Eberhard Bethge (New York: Macmillan, 1972), p. 360.

There is an echo of the prophet's advice in the exhortation of the apostle: "Beloved, I beseech you as aliens and exiles to abstain from the passions of the flesh that wage war against your soul. Maintain good conduct among the Gentiles," he writes, "so that . . . they may see your good deeds and glorify God on the day of visitation" (1 Peter 2.11–12). We, too, are finding it hard to sing the Lord's song in a strange land, but it is probably best not to spend much energy lamenting over lost Christendom, for we, like the Israelites of old, made quite a mess of things when we were in charge. According to the New Testament, the experience of exile ought to orient us toward the future rather than the past. The letter to the Hebrews reminds us that the saints of old "acknowledged that they were strangers and exiles on the earth" and by "speak[ing] thus make clear that they are seeking a homeland" (Hebrews 11.13–14).

Theologians in the age of modernity, now rapidly approaching its end, have resisted the suggestion that Christian faith is a mode of imagination. Their hesitation was understandable so long as critics of the faith contrasted the world of imagination with the real world, the one assumed to be accessible by means of the sciences, which deal in facts, *not* fantasy. Now that the dualism of imagination and reality, the bedrock of the modernist mind, is crumbling, theologians find themselves in a new situation that calls for a different set of assumptions. It is time to acknowledge unapologetically (in both senses of the word) that religion – all religion, including the Christian – speaks the language of imagination, and that the job of theology is therefore to articulate the grammar of Christian imagination. Theology must become imaginative – again, in both senses of the word – for it must understand itself to speak the language of imagination, and it must pursue its task with imaginative creativity: in short, it must articulate the grammar of the Christian imagination imaginatively! Such a theology (you could call it postmodern if you insist) will sound oddly orthodox to liberal ears, for doctrinal orthodoxy insists on the integrity of the scriptural imagination, testing it continually for conformity to the biblical paradigm. For God has chosen to reveal himself in the world in a manner accessible only to imagination. That is just as it ought to be, for only in this way can divine and human freedom both be assured. Christian theology ought to strive for an "imaginative literalism"; that is, it should adhere tenaciously to the *sensus literalis* of scripture in the faith that only here, in these metaphoric images, does one encounter the Living God. From the perspective of the world, such faith must appear unsecured, a figment of imagination with no more claim to truth than other imaginings. But from the standpoint of the faithful imagination of the Christian believer, the fantasies of God are more real than the realities of men, guaranteed as they are by the power of the Spirit.

Appendix
Hamann's letter to Kraus

Translated and annotated by Garrett Green
Königsberg, 18 December 1784

Clarissime Domine Politice![1]

Because my stiff old bones are hardly capable any longer of peripatetic philosophy, and my moments for labyrinthine strolls do not always occur *before* meals but also occasionally between courses *ab ovis ad poma*,[2] I must now take refuge in a macaronic quill,[3] in order to convey my thanks

---

Some of the footnotes are adapted from other sources, including the explanatory notes in the edition of the letter included in *Was ist Aufklärung? Thesen und Definitionen*, ed. Ehrhard Bahr (Stuttgart: Reclam, 1974). Two articles containing detailed analysis of this letter have also been helpful, and are recommended to readers interested in pursuing the interpretation: Oswald Bayer, "Selbstverschuldete Vormundschaft: Hamanns Kontroverse mit Kant um *wahre* Aufklärung," in *Der Wirklichkeitsanspruch von Theologie und Religion*, ed. Dieter Henke, Günter Kehrer, and Gunda Schneider-Flume (Tübingen: J. C. B. Mohr [Paul Siebeck], 1976), pp. 3–34; and E. Büchsel, "Aufklärung und christliche Freiheit: J. G. Hamann contra I. Kant," *Neue Zeitschrift für systematische Theologie* 4 (1962): 133–57. See also chapter 3 above.

[1] A Latin address: "Most Revered Master Politician (*or* Statesman)!" Christian Jacob Kraus (1753–1807), professor of practical philosophy and political science at the University of Königsberg, was a student and friend of Kant.

[2] Latin aphorism "from eggs to apples" (i.e. from soup to nuts) normally used for long-winded introductions that take forever to get to the point.

[3] A pen for writing in macaronic style. The *Oxford English Dictionary* defines *macaronic* as "a burlesque form of verse in which vernacular words are introduced into a Latin context with Latin terminations and in Latin constructions." The Italian Tifi degli Odasi (d. 1488), author of *Carmen macaronicum*, is credited as its originator. Besides the mixing of languages, the satirical-comical style is typical of macaronic literature.

to you for the enclosed *Berlinsche Christmonath*[4] in the cant-style, which the comic historian of comic literature[5] has rendered as "Kantian style" *per e*,[6] like an *asmus cum puncto*.[7]

To the "Sapere aude!" there belongs also from the very same source the "Noli admirari!"[8] *Clarissime Domine Politice*! You know how much I love our Plato[9] and with what pleasure I read him; I will also gladly yield myself up to his guardianship for the guidance of my own *understanding*,

---

[4] A reference to the December 1784 issue of the *Berlinische Monatsschrift*, in which Kant's essay "An Answer to the Question: 'What Is Enlightenment?' " appeared on the first page. The original German is available in *Kant's Gesammelte Schriften*, ed. Königlich Preussischen Akademie der Wissenschaften, vol. VIII (Berlin: W. de Gruyter, 1910), p. 35 (hereafter cited as AA, followed by volume and page numbers); translated by H. B. Nisbet in *Kant's Political Writings*, ed. Hans Reiss, trans. H. B. Nisbet, 2nd edn. (Cambridge: Cambridge University Press, 1991), p. 54 (hereafter cited as Reiss, followed by the page number).

[5] Carl Friedrich Flögel, in the first volume of his *Geschichte der komischen Litteratur* (1784), characterized the "cant-style" as follows: "The low speech (which in England is sometimes called *the cant style*) was dominant in England at the end of the last century and was introduced by the courtiers of Charles II, who, in order to express their contempt for the ceremony that had characterized the preceding age, succumbed to the opposite extreme and affected a liveliness of manners and conversation as well as a loose, ungrammatical vulgarity of expression . . . *Richard Steele* says that this *Kantischer Styl* is derived from a certain *Andreas Cant*, who was a Presbyterian clergyman in an uneducated part of Scotland, and had obtained through practice the gift of speaking from the pulpit in such a dialect that he was understood only by his own congregation and not even by all of them" (pp. 174 f.; cited in Bahr, *Was ist Aufklärung?*, 60–1). Notice that Flögel renders the English "cant style" as *Kantischer Styl*, which Hamann exploits as a pun on Kant's name.

[6] According to a note in Bahr (p. 61) *per e* means "through (the omission of the terminal letter) 'e.' " In this way English "cant-style" becomes German "Kant-Stil," which Hamann writes as "Kantschen Styl."

[7] According to a note in the Bahr ed. (p. 61, attributing the insight to Arthur Henkel), Latin *asmus* becomes *asinus* ("ass") *cum puncto* ("with a dot") – i.e. when one puts a dot over the first upright of the "m," thus turning it into "in." *Asmus*, a shortened form of "Erasmus," was used as a pen name by Matthias Claudius, with whom Hamann corresponded. The phrase *cum puncto* derives from Hebrew grammar, where it refers to the addition of vowel points. Why one would turn *Asmus* into *asinus* in this way remains unexplained, as does Hamann's reason for referring to it.

[8] Kant's "*Sapere aude!*" ("Dare to know!") – his "motto" of the Enlightenment (AA, vol. VIII, p. 35; Reiss, p. 54) – comes from the *Epistles* of Horace (1.2.40); the phrase "Nil admirari" ("to marvel at nothing"), which Hamann has altered to "Noli admirari!" ("Marvel not!"), is found in *Epistles* 1.6.1.

[9] A reference to Kant (see Bayer, "Selbstverschuldete Vormundschaft," 19). It may also be relevant that Kraus lectured on Plato.

though *cum grano salis,*[10] without incurring any guilt[11] through lack of *heart.*

To remind a professor of logic & critic of pure reason of the rules of explication [*Erklärung*] would be virtual high treason; since, moreover, you have taken your Hutchinson away from me without returning his *Morals,*[12] I possess no other organon in my paltry supply of books. I am just as little able to account for [*mir aufzuklären*] the coincidence of Jewish and Christian agreement[13] in guardianlike [*vormundschaftliche*] freedom of thought, because the royal librarian in a most merciless manner has refused me the second volume;[14] irrespective of how much I have contributed with all my powers to assisting at the birth of the cosmopolitico-platonic chiliasm[15] by means of wishes, reminders, intercession, and thanksgiving.

---

[10] Latin, "with a grain of salt."

[11] "*. . . ohne eine Selbstverschuldung . . . zu besorgen*" – the first of Hamann's many ironical allusions to Kant's definition of enlightenment as "self-incurred [*selbstverschuldet*] immaturity" (AA, vol. VIII, p. 35; Reiss, p. 54). Hamann plays on the root term *Schuld,* which can mean "guilt," "fault," or "debt" – nuances that are lost in translation.

[12] "Hutchinson" is presumably a reference to the Scottish moral philosopher Francis Hutcheson (1694–1746). The book in question may be Hutcheson's *System of Moral Philosophy,* published posthumously in 1755. Hamann frequently complains in his letters about unreturned books he has loaned.

[13] An allusion to the footnote at the end of Kant's essay (AA, vol. VIII, p. 42; Reiss, p. 60). Kant states that while he knew of the publication of Mendelssohn's essay on the same question in the *Berlinische Monatsschrift,* he had been unable to obtain a copy of the journal and so sent his own essay off to Berlin "as a means of finding out by comparison how far the thoughts of two individuals may coincide by chance." Hamann had apparently also been unable to obtain the issue of the *Berlinische Monatsschrift* containing Mendelssohn's essay and knew of Kant's contribution only because Kraus had sent him a copy of the journal.

[14] The "royal librarian" is Johann Erich Biester (1749–1816), editor of the *Berlinische Monatsschrift* and royal librarian in Berlin. The essays of both Mendelssohn and Kant appeared in the second volume of the journal.

[15] Chiliasm (from the Greek word for "thousand") is the doctrine that the millennium, a thousand-year reign of Christ on earth, will be inaugurated at the Second Coming (see Rev. 20.4). Hamann alludes here to Kant's use of the term in "Idea for a Universal History with a Cosmopolitan Purpose," which had appeared in the November 1784 issue of the *Berlinische Monatsschrift.* Kant had commented that "philosophy too may have its *chiliastic* expectations [*ihren Chiliasmus*]" (AA, vol. VIII, p. 27; Reiss, p. 50). Later, in *The Contest of the Faculties,* Kant uses the term to designate one of the three possible futures of historical humanity, namely, the conception that the human race will continually progress, for which his preferred term is "eudaemonism" (AA, vol. VII, p. 81; Reiss, p. 178).

I can therefore tolerate gladly seeing enlightenment, if not explained, at least elucidated and expanded more aesthetically than dialectically, through the analogy of immaturity and guardianship. Except that for me the *proton pseudos*[16] (a very significant coinage that can hardly be translated unclumsily[17] into our German mother tongue) lies in that accursed adjective *self-incurred.*[18]

Inability is really no fault, as our Plato himself recognizes; and it only becomes a fault through the *will* and its lack of *resolution* and *courage* – or as a *consequence* of pretended faults.[19]

But who is the indeterminate *other*,[20] who twice appears anonymously[?] Observe, *Domine Politice*, how the metaphysicians hate to call their persons by their right names, and prowl like cats around the hot broth.[21] I, however, see the enlightenment of our century not with cats' eyes but with pure & healthy human eyes, which to be sure have become somewhat dull through years and lucubrations[22] and sweets, but which I find ten times preferable to the moonlight-enlightened eyes of an *Athene glaukopis.*[23]

I ask therefore yet a second time with catechetical freedom: who is the *other* of whom the cosmopolitical chiliast

---

[16] Greek, "the first lie," i.e. the basic error from which all further errors follow.

[17] Hamann's use of the word *unflegelhaft* may be a pun on Flögel's name and an allusion to his skill as translator (see note 5 above).

[18] A reference to the term *selbstverschuldet* in the opening line of Kant's essay: *"Enlightenment is man's emergence from his self-incurred immaturity."* (See note 11 above.)

[19] The root of Kant's term *selbstverschuldet* (self-incurred) is *Schuld* (fault). In the opening paragraph of his essay, Kant says that immaturity is self-incurred when it results from "lack of resolution and courage" to use one's own reason. (See note 11 above.)

[20] Kant twice uses the phrase "without the guidance of another" in the opening paragraph of his essay.

[21] The German idiom means "to beat around the bush"; the translator has rendered it literally because of Hamann's reference to "cats' eyes" in the next sentence.

[22] *Lucubration* is hard work or study, especially at night (from Latin *lucubrare*, to work by artificial light) – possibly another in Hamann's ongoing series of word plays on en*light*enment.

[23] "Owl-eyed Athena," epithet for the Greek goddess, referring not only to her holiness but also to her flashing eyes, which penetrated the dark of night, and to her gift of vision to human beings. Hamann writes it in Greek characters.

prophesies? Who is the other layabout[24] or guide that the author has in mind but has not the heart to utter[?] Answer: the tiresome guardian who must be implicitly understood as the correlate of those who are immature. This is the man of death.[25] The self-incurred guardianship and not immaturity –

Why does the chiliast deal so fastidiously with this lad Absalom?[26] Because he reckons himself to the class of guardians and wishes thereby to attain a high reputation before immature readers. – The immaturity is thus self-incurred only insofar as it surrenders to the guidance of a blind or *invisible* (as that Pomeranian catechism pupil bellowed at his country pastor)[27] guardian and leader. This is the true man of death –

So wherein lies the *inability* or *fault* of the falsely accused immature one? In his own laziness and cowardice? No, in the blindness of his guardian, who purports to be able to see, and for that very reason must bear the whole responsibility for the fault.

With what kind of conscience can a reasoner [*Raisonneur*] & speculator by the stove and in a nightcap[28] accuse

---

[24] The reference of *Bärenheuter* ("lazybones," "idler") remains obscure. It could conceivably be a pun on the name of Johann Christoph *Berens*, Hamann's friend, who along with Kant had tried to reconvert him to Enlightenment ideals after his London conversion in 1758.

[25] Possibly an allusion to 2 Sam. 12.5, where David, after hearing Nathan's parable of the poor man's ewe lamb, unknowingly passes judgment on himself: "As the Lord lives, the man who has done this deserves to die." The German is closer to Hamann's diction: "So wahr der Herr lebt, der Mann ist ein Kind des Todes, der das getan hat."

[26] A reference to the biblical story of the son of David who rebelled and was killed in battle against his father's army. Here, "Absalom" presumably refers to Frederick the Great, who as a young man also rebelled against his father. The "chiliast" is, of course, Kant, whose deferential stance toward Frederick is criticized by Hamann.

[27] The anecdote referred to here is obscure. Pomeranians were sometimes regarded as country bumpkins, hence Hamann has the Pomeranian catechism pupil, presumably reciting the Nicene Creed, mispronounce the German *"unsichtbar"* by placing emphasis on the wrong syllable. Pronounced this way, *unsichtbar* can mean "blind" and possibly "obscene."

[28] The idiom *hinter dem Ofen hocken* means to be a stay-at-home, never to stir from one's hearth. Besides its literal meaning, *Schlafmütze* also implies a dull or sleepy person.

the immature ones of *cowardice*, when their blind guardian has a large well-disciplined army[29] to guarantee his infallibility and orthodoxy[?] How can one mock the *laziness* of such immature persons, when their enlightened and self-thinking guardian – as the emancipated gaper[30] at the whole spectacle declares him to be – sees them not even as machines but as mere shadows of his grandeur,[31] of which he need have no fear at all, since they are his ministering *spirits* and the only ones in whose existence he believes[?][32]

So doesn't it all come to the same thing? – believe, get on parade, pay,[33] if the d— is not to take you. Is it not *sottise des trois parts*?[34] And which is the greatest and most difficult? An army of priests [*Pfaffen*] or of thugs, henchmen, and purse snatchers? According to the strange, unexpected pattern in human affairs in which on the whole nearly everything is paradoxical,[35] believing seems harder for me than moving mountains,[36] doing tactical exercises[37] – and the

---

Hamann is accusing Kant of being an armchair philosopher, one who sits comfortably at home by the hearth while accusing others of laziness and cowardice.

[29] Cf. the concluding paragraph of "What is Enlightenment?" where Kant's enlightened ruler "has at hand a well-disciplined and numerous army to guarantee public security" (AA, vol. VIII, p. 41; Reiss, p. 59).

[30] "To describe as 'enlightened' and to glorify a man who deals with human beings as this king does – that could be done only by an 'emancipated gaper [*eximirter Maulaffe*],' an existentially uninvolved spectator" (Büchsel, "Aufklärung und christliche Freiheit," p. 151).

[31] In the last paragraph of his essay Kant says that "man . . . is *more than a machine*" (AA, vol. VIII, p. 41; Reiss, p. 60); and his enlightened ruler "has no fear of shadows" (AA, vol. VIII, p. 41; Reiss, p. 59; trans. has "phantoms"). The reference to his "grandeur" (*Riesengröße*) may contain a pun on Frederick the *Great*.

[32] Hamann implies that Frederick believes not in God but only in his subjects as "his ministering spirits."

[33] "The officer says: Don't argue, get on parade! The tax-official: Don't argue, pay! The clergyman: Don't argue, believe!" (AA, vol. VIII, pp. 36–7; Reiss, p. 55).

[34] French, "stupidity on three sides," adapted by Hamann from the title of an article by Voltaire, *Sottise de deux parts* (1728).

[35] Hamann takes this language nearly verbatim from the last paragraph of Kant's essay.

[36] Cf. Matt. 17.20; 1 Cor. 13.2.

[37] Hamann's phrase *Evolutionen u Exercitia machen* is presumably technical terminology derived from French military usage (*évolutions tactiques*, "tactical exercises"). French was the official language of Frederick's Prussian government, including the customs office where Hamann was employed.

financial exploitation of immature persons, *donec reddant novissimum quadrantem*³⁸ –

The enlightenment of our century is therefore a mere northern light, from which can be prophesied no cosmopolitical chiliasm except in a nightcap & by the stove. All prattle and reasoning [*Raisonniren*] of the emancipated immature ones, who set themselves up as guardians of those who are themselves immature, but guardians equipped with *couteaux de chasse*³⁹ and daggers – [all this is] a cold, unfruitful moonlight without enlightenment for the lazy understanding and without warmth for the cowardly will – and the entire response to the question posed [is] a blind illumination for every immature one who walks at *noon*.⁴⁰

Written on the holy evening of the fourth and final Sunday of Advent '84 *entre chien et loup*.⁴¹

By the *Magus in telonio*,⁴²
    bound to *Clarissimi Domini Politici* and Morczinimastix,⁴³
        and *released* from his ex- and esoteric freedom,

³⁸ "... till they have paid the last penny" (cf. Matt. 5.26; Luke 12.59).

³⁹ French, "hunting knives." Frederick the Great hired French tax collectors for service in Prussia.

⁴⁰ Perhaps an allusion to the riddle of the Sphinx: "What is it that walks on four legs in the morning, on two at noon, and on three in the evening?" Oedipus gave the correct answer: "Man, who first crawls on all fours, then walks upright, and in old age needs a stick as a third leg" (Betty Radice, *Who's Who in the Ancient World* [New York: Penguin, 1973], p. 225). Thus the "one who walks at noon" would be the adult, the "mature" one. Büchsel suggests an allusion to Isa. 58.10: "If you pour yourself out for the hungry and satisfy the desire of the afflicted, then shall your light rise in the darkness and your gloom be as the noonday" ("Aufklärung und christliche Freiheit," p. 153, note 52). Another possibility is 1 Thess. 5.12: "For you are all sons of light and sons of the day; we are not of the night or of darkness" – a passage that contains all the right metaphors for Hamann's case against Kant.

⁴¹ The French expression ("between dog and wolf") refers to twilight, when one cannot distinguish dog from wolf.

⁴² "Wise Man of the Customs House" (Latin, *telonium*, "customs house"). Hamann, widely known as "Magus in Norden," worked as a civil servant in the customs office in Königsberg.

⁴³ This term is coined on the analogy of Greek *Homeromastix* ("hostage of Homer"), used of grammarians who searched for errors in Homer. Hamann calls Kraus "Morczinimastix" because in 1784 he had published an exposé of the confidence man Johann Gottlieb Hermann, alias Friedrich Joseph Freiherr von Mortczinni.

misunderstood by poets and statisticians.
Even in the darkness there are divinely beautiful duties
And doing them unnoticed – –[44]
    Matt. 11.11[45]

P.S.

My transfiguration [*Verklärung*] of the Kantian explanation [*Erklärung*], therefore, comes to this: *true enlightenment* [*Aufklärung*] consists in an emergence of the immature person from a supremely *self-incurred guardianship*. The fear of the Lord is the beginning of wisdom[46] – and this wisdom makes us *cowardly* at lying and *lazy* at inventing – but all the more courageous against guardians who at most can kill the body and suck the purse empty – all the more merciful to our immature brethren and more fruitful in good works of immortality. The distinction between the public and private service of reason is as comical as Flögel's[47] being worthy of laughing at and laughing about. It is a matter, to be sure, of unifying the two natures of an *immature person & guardian*, but making both into self-contradictory hypocrites is no *arcanum* that needs first to be preached; rather, here lies precisely the nub of the whole political problem. What good to me is the *festive garment* of freedom when I am in a slave's smock at home?[48] Does Plato too belong to

---

[44] These two lines are cited from a source that Hamann had long ago forgotten. He had quoted them more than two decades earlier in a letter to Moses Mendelssohn (Johann Georg Hamann, *Briefwechsel*, ed. Walther Ziesemer and Arthur Henkel [Wiesbaden: Insel-Verlag, 1956], vol. II, p. 129). There, too, Hamann identifies himself as one who prefers darkness: "I avoid the light, my dear Moses, perhaps more out of fear than maliciousness . . ."

[45] "Truly, I say to you, among those born of women there has risen no one greater than John the Baptist; yet he who is least in the kingdom of heaven is greater than he."

[46] Prov. 9.10.

[47] Hamann refers here to Kant's distinction between the "public" and "private" uses of reason (AA, vol. VIII, p. 37; Reiss, p. 55). For Flögel, see note 5 above.

[48] Possibly an allusion to the parable of the king's wedding feast (Matt. 22.1–14). Hamann is questioning Kant's argument that while the "public" use of reason to write and criticize must remain free, the "private" use of reason may be limited by the terms of the contracts into which one enters (e.g., the clergyman may write critical articles about church doctrine, but his sermons must conform to the teachings of his church).

the *fair sex*[?] – which he slanders like an old bachelor.[49] Women should *keep silent in the congregation*[50] – and *si tacuissent, philosophi mansissent.*[51] At home (i.e. at the lectern and on the stage and in the pulpit) they may chatter to their hearts' content. There they speak as guardians and must forget everything & contradict everything as soon as, in their own self-incurred immaturity, they are to do indentured labor for the state. Thus the public use of reason & freedom is nothing but a dessert, a sumptuous dessert. The private use is the *daily bread* that we should give up for its sake. The *self-incurred immaturity* is just such a sneer as he makes at the whole fair sex, and which my three daughters will not put up with. *Anch' io sono tutore!*[52] and no lip- or wage-servant [*Maul- noch Lohndiener*] of an overseer – but prefer immature innocence. Amen!

49 Presumably an allusion to Kant's comment: "The guardians who have kindly taken upon themselves the work of supervision will soon see to it that by far the largest part of mankind (including the entire fair sex) should consider the step forward to maturity not only as difficult but also as highly dangerous" (AA, vol. VIII, p. 35; Reiss, p. 54).

50 Hamann is citing Paul's dictum that "women should keep silence in the churches" (1 Cor. 14.35). In the following verse the apostle continues, "If there is anything they desire to know, let them ask their husbands at home." Hamann takes up this contrast between silence "in the congregation" and speaking "at home."

51 The Latin phrase ("if they had kept silent, they would have remained philosophers") is presumably adapted by Hamann from the story told by Boethius in book VII of *The Consolation of Philosophy.* A "certain fellow who had falsely taken upon him the name of a philosopher, not for the use of virtue but for vainglory" was put to the test by another, who berated him in order to determine "whether he were a philosopher or no by his gentle and patient bearing of injuries." The would-be philosopher "took all patiently for a while, and having borne his contumely, as it were, triumphing, said: 'Dost thou now at length think me a philosopher?' To which he bitingly replied; 'I would have thought thee one if thou hadst holden thy peace [*si tacuisses*].'" Boethius, *The Theological Tractates* (Cambridge, MA: Harvard University Press, 1936), pp. 216–17.

52 Italian, "I, too, am a guardian!" – an ironic variation of the exclamation "Anch' io sono pittore!" ("I, too, am a painter!"), allegedly uttered by Correggio before a picture of Raphael.

Bibliography

Alexander, W. M. *Johann Georg Hamann: Philosophy and Faith*. The Hague: Martinus Nijhoff, 1966.

Arndt, William F. and Gingrich, F. Wilbur. *A Greek-English Lexicon of the New Testament and Other Early Christian Literature*. Chicago: University of Chicago Press, 1957.

Barth, Karl. "An Introductory Essay." In Ludwig Feuerbach, *The Essence of Christianity*, pp. xx–xxi. New York: Harper & Row, 1957.

———. *Die kirchliche Dogmatik*. Zurich: Theologischer Verlag Zürich, 1932–67. *Church Dogmatics*, ed. G. W. Bromiley and T. F. Torrance. Edinburgh: T. & T. Clark, 1956–69.

———. *Der Römerbrief, 1922*. Zurich: TVZ, 1989.

Bayer, Oswald. "Selbstverschuldete Vormundschaft: Hamanns Kontroverse mit Kant um *wahre* Aufklärung." In *Der Wirklichkeitsanspruch von Theologie und Religion: Die sozialethische Herausforderung: Ernst Steinbach zum 70. Geburtstag*, ed. Dieter Henke, Günter Kehrer, and Gunda Schneider-Flume, pp. 3–34. Tübingen: J. C. B. Mohr (Paul Siebeck), 1976.

———. *Zeitgenosse im Widerspruch: Johann Georg Hamann als radikaler Aufklärer*. Munich: Piper, 1988.

Beiser, Frederick C. *The Fate of Reason: German Philosophy from Kant to Fichte*. Cambridge, MA: Harvard University Press, 1987.

Bennington, Geoffrey and Derrida, Jacques. *Jacques Derrida*. Chicago: University of Chicago Press, 1993.

Berlin, Isaiah. *The Magus of the North: J. G. Hamann and the*

Origins of Modern Irrationalism, ed. Henry Hardy. London: J. Murray, 1993.

Bernstein, Richard J. *Beyond Objectivism and Relativism: Science, Hermeneutics, and Praxis.* Philadelphia: University of Pennsylvania Press, 1985.

Biser, Eugen. *"Gott ist tot": Nietzsches Destruktion des christlichen Bewußtseins.* Munich: Kösel-Verlag, 1962.

———. *Gottsucher oder Antichrist? Nietzsches provokative Kritik des Christentums.* Salzburg: Otto Müller Verlag, 1982.

———. "Nietzsches Kritik des christlichen Gottesbegriffs und ihre theologischen Konsequenzen," *Philosophisches Jahrbuch* 78 (1971): 34–65, 295–305.

Bonhoeffer, Dietrich. *Letters and Papers from Prison*, ed. Eberhard Bethge (enlarged edn.). New York: Macmillan, 1972.

Büchsel, Elfriede. "Aufklärung und christliche Freiheit: J. G. Hamann contra I. Kant," *Neue Zeitschrift für systematische Theologie* 4 (1962): 133–57.

Carr, Karen L. *The Banalization of Nihilism: Twentieth-Century Responses to Meaninglessness.* Albany, NY: SUNY Press, 1992.

Clark, Maudemarie. *Nietzsche on Truth and Philosophy.* Cambridge: Cambridge University Press, 1990.

Crites, Stephen D. "The Gospel According to Hegel," *Journal of Religion* 46 (1966): 246–63.

———. "The Problem of the 'Positivity' of the Gospel in the Hegelian Dialectic of Alienation and Reconciliation," Ph.D. dissertation, Yale University, 1961.

Danto, Arthur C. *Nietzsche as Philosopher.* New York: Macmillan, 1965; New York: Columbia University Press, 1980.

Davidson, Donald. *Inquiries into Truth and Interpretation.* Oxford: Clarendon Press, 1984.

Derrida, Jacques. *Margins of Philosophy*, trans. Alan Bass. Chicago: University of Chicago Press, 1982.

———. *Writing and Difference*, trans. Alan Bass. Chicago: University of Chicago Press, 1978.

Dibelius, Martin. "Der 'psychologische Typ des Erlösers' bei Friedrich Nietzsche," *Deutsche Vierteljahresschrift für Literaturwissenschaft und Geistesgeschichte* 22 (1944): 61–91.

Dickson, Gwen Griffith. *Johann Georg Hamann's Relational Metacriticism.* Theologische Bibliothek Töpelmann, ed. O. Bayer et al., vol. 67. New York: Walter de Gruyter, 1995.

Feuerbach, Ludwig. *The Essence of Christianity*, trans. George Eliot. New York: Harper & Row, 1957.

Gesammelte Werke, ed. Werner Schuffenhauer. Berlin: Akademie-Verlag, 1981.

Lectures on the Essence of Religion. Trans. Ralph Manheim. New York: Harper & Row, 1967.

Frei, Hans W. "The Academic Tradition in Nineteenth-Century Protestant Theology." In *Faith and Ethics: The Theology of H. Richard Niebuhr*, ed. Paul Ramsey, pp. 16–40. New York: Harper & Row, 1965.

The Eclipse of Biblical Narrative: A Study in Eighteenth and Nineteenth Century Hermeneutics. New Haven, CT: Yale University Press, 1974.

"Feuerbach and Theology," *Journal of the American Academy of Religion* 35 (1967): 250–6.

Theology and Narrative: Selected Essays, ed. George Hunsinger and William C. Placher. Oxford: Oxford University Press, 1993.

Types of Christian Theology, ed. George Hunsinger and William C. Placher. New Haven, CT and London: Yale University Press, 1992, p. 16.

Freud, Sigmund. *The Standard Edition of the Complete Psychological Works of Sigmund Freud*, ed. James Strachey. London: Hogarth Press, 1961.

Galling, Kurt (ed.). *Die Religion in Geschichte und Gegenwart: Handwörterbuch für Theologie und Religionswissenschaft* (3rd rev. edn.), 7 vols. Tübingen: J. C. B. Mohr (Paul Siebeck), 1957–62.

Gibellini, Rosino (ed.). *Frontiers of Theology in Latin America*. Maryknoll, NY: Orbis Books, 1979.

Glasse, John. "Barth on Feuerbach," *Harvard Theological Review* 57 (1964): 69–96.

Green, Garrett. "Challenging the Religious Studies Canon: Karl Barth's Theory of Religion," *Journal of Religion* 75 (1995): 473–86.

Imagining God: Theology and the Religious Imagination. San Francisco: Harper & Row, 1989; Grand Rapids, MI: William B. Eerdmans Publishing Co., 1998.

"Positive Religion in the Early Philosophy of the German Idealists," Ph.D. dissertation, Yale University, 1971.

Hamann, Johann Georg. *Briefwechsel*, ed. Arthur Henkel. Frankfurt: Insel-Verlag, 1965.

Sämtliche Werke, ed. Josef Nadler. Vienna: Herder, 1949–57.

Hart, Kevin. *The Trespass of the Sign: Deconstruction, Theology and Philosophy*. Cambridge: Cambridge University Press, 1989.

Harvey, Van A. *Feuerbach and the Interpretation of Religion*. Cambridge: Cambridge University Press, 1995.

Hauerwas, Stanley. *Unleashing the Scripture: Freeing the Bible from Captivity to America*. Nashville: Abingdon Press, 1993.

Hays, Richard B. "Salvation by Trust? Reading the Bible Faithfully," *Christian Century*, 26 February 1997, pp. 218–23.

Hegel, Georg Wilhelm Friedrich. *Hegels theologische Jugendschriften, nach den Handschriften der Kgl. Bibliothek in Berlin.* Reprint of 1907 edn. Frankfurt am Main: Minerva, 1966. *On Christianity: Early Theological Writings*, trans. T. M. Knox and Richard Kroner. New York: Harper & Brothers, 1961.

Vorlesungen über Rechtsphilosophie 1818–1831, ed. Karl-Heinz Ilting. Stuttgart-Bad Cannstatt: Friedrich Frommann Verlag (Günther Holzboog), 1974.

Hertel, Friedrich. *Das theologische Denken Schleiermachers: Untersucht an der ersten Auflage seiner Reden "Ueber die Religion".* Zurich: Zwingli Verlag, 1965.

Hunsinger, George. *How To Read Karl Barth: The Shape of His Theology*. Oxford: Oxford University Press, 1991.

Jaspers, Karl. *Nietzsche und das Christentum*. Hameln: F. Seifert, 1946.

Jeanrond, Werner G. *Theological Hermeneutics: Development and Significance*. London: Macmillan, 1991.

Jørgensen, Sven-Aage. *Johann Georg Hamann*. Stuttgart: J. B. Metzlersche Verlagsbuchhandlung, 1976.

Jüngel, Eberhard. *The Doctrine of the Trinity: God's Being is in Becoming*. Grand Rapids, MI: William B. Eerdmans Publishing Co., 1976.

Justin Martyr. *Writings of Saint Justin Martyr*, trans. Thomas B. Falls in *The Fathers of the Church* vol. VI, ed. Ludwig Schopp et al. Washington, DC: The Catholic University of America Press, 1948.

Kant, Immanuel. *Immanuel Kant's Critique of Pure Reason*, trans. Norman Kemp Smith. New York: St. Martin's Press, 1965.

Kant's Gesammelte Schriften, ed. Königlich preussischen Akademie der Wissenschaften. Berlin: Walter de Gruyter, 1910.

Kant's Political Writings, ed. Hans Reiss, trans. H. B. Nisbet (2nd edn.). Cambridge: Cambridge University Press, 1991.

Die Religion innerhalb der Grenzen der blossen Vernunft, ed. Karl Vorländer. Philosophische Bibliothek, vol. XLV. Hamburg: Felix Meiner, 1956.

Religion within the Limits of Reason Alone, trans. Theodore M. Greene and Hoyt H. Hudson. New York: Harper & Brothers, 1960.

Katz, Jacob. "Orthodoxy in Historical Perspective." In Peter Y. Medding (ed.), *Studies in Contemporary Jewry*, vol. II, pp. 3–17. Bloomington: Indiana University Press, 1986.

Kaufmann, Walter. *Nietzsche: Philosopher, Psychologist, Antichrist* (4th edn.). Princeton, NJ: Princeton University Press, 1974.

Kearney, Richard. *The Wake of Imagination: Toward a Post Modern Culture*. Minneapolis: University of Minnesota Press, 1988.

Kent, John. "Religion & Science." In *Nineteenth Century Religious Thought in the West*, ed. Ninian Smart, John Clayton, Steven Katz and Patrick Sherry, vol. III, pp. 1–36. Cambridge: Cambridge University Press, 1985.

Kierkegaard, Søren. *Philosophical Fragments*. Princeton, NJ: Princeton University Press, 1985.

Köster, Peter. "Nietzsche-Kritik und Nietzsche-Rezeption in der Theologie des 20. Jahrhunderts," *Nietzsche-Studien* 10/11 (1981/2): 615–85.

Kuhn, Thomas S. *The Structure of Scientific Revolutions* (2nd enlarged edn.). Chicago: University of Chicago Press, 1970.

Leff, Gordon. *Medieval Thought: St. Augustine to Ockham*. London: Merlin Press, 1958.

Livingston, James C. *Modern Christian Thought* (2nd edn.). Upper Saddle River, NJ: Prentice-Hall, 1997.

Loughlin, Gerard. *Telling God's Story: Bible, Church and Narrative Theology*. Cambridge: Cambridge University Press, 1996.

Lowe, Walter. *Theology and Difference: The Wound of Reason*. Bloomington and Indianapolis: Indiana University Press, 1993.

Lyotard, Jean-François. *The Postmodern Condition: A Report on Knowledge*, trans. Geoff Bennington and Brian Massumi. Theory and History of Literature, vol. X. Manchester: Manchester University Press, 1984.

McCool, Gerald A. *Catholic Theology in the Nineteenth Century:*

The Quest for a Unitary Method. New York: Seabury Press, 1977.

McCormack, Bruce L. *Karl Barth's Critically Realistic Dialectical Theology: Its Genesis and Development, 1909-1936.* Oxford: Clarendon Press, 1995.

"Article Review: Graham Ward's *Barth, Derrida and the Language of Theology,*" *Scottish Journal of Theology* 49 (1996): 97–109.

McFague, Sallie. *Models of God: Theology for an Ecological, Nuclear Age.* Philadelphia: Fortress Press, 1987.

Marion, Jean-Luc. *God Without Being: Hors-Texte,* trans. Thomas A. Carlson. Chicago: University of Chicago Press, 1991.

Michalson, Gordon E., Jr. *Fallen Freedom: Kant on Radical Evil and Moral Regeneration.* Cambridge: Cambridge University Press, 1990.

Milbank, John. *Theology and Social Theory: Beyond Secular Reason.* Oxford: Blackwell, 1990.

Nielsen, Kai. "Wittgensteinian Fideism," *Philosophy: The Journal of the Royal Institute of Philosophy* 42 (1967): 191–209.

Nietzsche, Friedrich. *Kritische Studienausgabe,* ed. Giorgio Colli and Mazzino Montinari. Berlin and New York: Walter de Gruyter, 1967–77.

The Gay Science. Trans. Walter Kaufmann. New York: Random House, 1974.

On the Genealogy of Morals and Ecce Homo. Trans. Walter Kaufmann and R. J. Hollingdale. New York: Random House, 1967.

The Portable Nietzsche, rev. edn. Trans. Walter Kaufmann. New York: Viking Press, 1968.

Truth and Philosophy: Selections from Nietzsche's Notebooks of the 1870s, ed. and trans. Daniel Breazeale. Atlantic Highlands, NJ: Humanities Press, 1979.

The Will to Power, ed. Walter Kaufmann, trans. Walter Kaufmann and R. J. Hollingdale. New York: Random House, 1967.

Nisbet, H. B. (ed.). *German Aesthetic and Literary Criticism: Winckelmann, Lessing, Hamann, Herder, Schiller, Goethe.* Cambridge: Cambridge University Press, 1985.

O'Flaherty, James C. *Johann Georg Hamann.* Boston: Twayne Publishers, 1979.

222

O'Flaherty, James C., Sellner, Timothy F., and Helm, Robert M. (eds.). *Studies in Nietzsche and the Judaeo-Christian Tradition*. University of North Carolina Studies in the Germanic Languages and Literatures, no. 103. Chapel Hill, NC: University of North Carolina Press, 1985.

Paden, William E. *Religious Worlds: The Comparative Study of Religion* (2nd edn.). Boston: Beacon Press, 1994.

Picht, Georg, and Rudolph, Enno (eds.). *Theologie – was ist das?* Stuttgart: Kreuz-Verlag, 1977.

Proudfoot, Wayne. *Religious Experience*. Berkeley and Los Angeles: University of California Press, 1985.

Ricoeur, Paul. "The Critique of Religion," *Union Seminary Quarterly Review* 28 (1973): 205–12.

Freud and Philosophy: An Essay on Interpretation. New Haven, CT and London: Yale University Press, 1970.

Interpretation Theory: Discourse and the Surplus of Meaning. Fort Worth, TX: Texas Christian University Press, 1976.

"Religion, Atheism, and Faith." In *The Conflict of Interpretations: Essays in Hermeneutics*, ed. Don Ihde, pp. 440–67. Evanston, IL: Northwestern University Press, 1974.

Ruether, Rosemary Radford. *Sexism and God-Talk: Toward a Feminist Theology*. Boston: Beacon Press, 1983.

Sauter, Gerhard. "Nietzsches Jesusbild als Frage an eine 'Theologie nach dem Tode Gottes'." In *Neues Testament und christliche Existenz: Festschrift für Herbert Braun zum 70. Geburtstag am 4. Mai 1973*, ed. Hans Dieter Betz and Luise Schottroff, pp. 401–19. Tübingen: J. C. B. Mohr (Paul Siebeck), 1973.

Schäfer, Klaus. "Zur theologischen Relevanz der Jesus-Deutung Friedrich Nietzsches." In *Wort Gottes in der Zeit: Festschrift Karl Hermann Schelkle zum 65. Geburtstag*, ed. Helmut Feld and Josef Nolte, pp. 319–29. Düsseldorf: Patmos-Verlag, 1973.

Schaff, Philip. *Creeds of Christendom* (6th revised and enlarged edn.), 3 vols. Grand Rapids, MI: Baker Book House, 1977.

Schleiermacher, F. D. E. *The Christian Faith*, ed. H. R. Mackintosh and J. S. Stewart. Edinburgh: T. & T. Clark, 1928; reprinted New York: Harper & Row, 1963.

Hermeneutics: The Handwritten Manuscripts, ed. Heinz Kimmerle, trans. James Duke and Jack Forstman. American

Academy of Religion Texts and Translation Series, ed. Robert Ellwood, Jr., No. 1. Missoula, MT: Scholars Press, 1977.

On Religion: Speeches to its Cultured Despisers, trans. John Oman. New York: Harper & Row, 1958.

Schmidt, James (ed.). *What Is Enlightenment? Eighteenth-Century Answers and Twentieth-Century Questions.* Berkeley and Los Angeles: University of California Press, 1996.

Schüssler Fiorenza, Elisabeth. *In Memory of Her: A Feminist Theological Reconstruction of Christian Origins.* New York: Crossroad Publishing Co., 1990.

Smith, Ronald Gregor. *J. G. Hamann, 1730–1788: A Study in Christian Existence.* New York: Harper & Brothers, 1960.

Stendahl, Krister. "Biblical Theology, Contemporary." In *The Interpreter's Dictionary of the Bible*, vol. I, pp. 419–20. New York: Abingdon Press, 1962.

Tillich, Paul. *Dynamics of Faith.* New York: Harper & Brothers, 1957.

Tindal, Matthew. *Christianity as Old as the Creation*, London, 1730. Facsimile reprint, ed. Günter Gawlick. Stuttgart-Bad Canstatt: Friedrich Frommann Verlag (Günther Holzboog), 1967.

Turner, Denys. *Marxism and Christianity.* Oxford: Blackwell, 1983.

"Mysticism or Mystification? How To Tell the Difference," unpublished paper, March 1997.

Unger, Rudolf. *Hamann und die Aufklärung: Studien zur Vorgeschichte des romantischen Geistes im 18. Jahrhundert.* Jena: Eugen Diederichs, 1911.

Van Huyssteen, J. Wentzel. *Essays in Postfoundationalist Theology.* Grand Rapids, MI: William B. Eerdmans Publishing Co., 1997.

Vroom, Hendrik M. "Religious Hermeneutics, Culture and Narratives," *Studies in Interreligious Dialogue* 4 (1994): 189–213.

Ward, Graham. *Barth, Derrida and the Language of Theology.* Cambridge: Cambridge University Press, 1995.

Westphal, Merold. "Nietzsche and the Phenomenological Ideal," *The Monist* 60 (1977): 280.

Suspicion and Faith: The Religious Uses of Modern Atheism. Grand Rapids, MI: William B. Eerdmans Publishing Co., 1993.

Williams, Rowan. *Arius: Heresy and Tradition*. London: Darton,
    Longman & Todd, 1987. See especially "Postscript
    (Theological)," pp. 233–4.
    "The Literal Sense of Scripture," *Modern Theology* 7 (1991):
    130–1.
Winch, Peter. *The Idea of a Social Science and its Relation to Philo-
    sophy*. New York: Humanities Press, 1958.
    "Understanding a Primitive Society," *American Philosophical
    Quarterly* 1 (1964): 307–25.
Wittgenstein, Ludwig. *Philosophical Investigations*, trans. G. E. M.
    Anscombe (2nd edn.). New York: Macmillan Co., 1958.

Index